Praise for *Aspire High*

The authors of *Aspire High* absolutely live up to the name of their imagined school, as they build a challenging picture of a modern educational establishment. The sweep is bold, revolutionary and demanding, with students placed firmly in their rightful place at the center. Tokenism and buzzword bingo are ruthlessly skewered as we discover what real student voice and parental engagement look like when correctly implemented. However these are not just theories—an accessible approach, packed with real-life exemplars, guidance tables and a helpful Listen, Learn and Lead structure make this excellent book as practical as it is challenging. Read this book and you will not only see how we could all Aspire High, but also how to get there.

—*Tony Parkin*
Disruptive Nostalgist and Educational
Technologist. Former Head of ICT Development at SSAT

Student voice and student leadership are often overlooked in schools. *Aspire High* provides invaluable resources for engaging students to help each school become "the best it can be"! I keep a copy of *Aspire High* on my desk for consultation and . . . inspiration!

—*Tom Edwards*
Assistant Professor, Educational Leadership,
University of Southern Maine
Former Superintendent and Principal

I LOVE this book. Quaglia and his team have done it again! This book is like a volcano being dropped into old school traditions. BOOM! Disruption rocks.

—*Dr. Lizzy Asbury*
Chief Innovative Officer
Asbury Consulting, LLC

Several decades ago, Ted Sizer published *Horace's Compromise*, a book that sent shock waves through the high school teaching and leadership world. Sizer's book had a significant impact on me, my teaching, not to mention our profession. *Aspire High* is this generation's wake-up call. The authors articulate a vision for high schools that is compelling and clear. They remind us that students' aspirations should drive the entire high school experience. This book is full of great ideas that will transform high schools around the world.

—*Douglas Fisher*
San Diego State University

Aspire High is a call to action for all who recognize the urgent need to re-think the way we "do" school. Quaglia et al. takes an honest look at the current reality of the teaching and learning environment and challenges us to do things differently. Every leader, teacher, or student who feels powerless to impact and change the reality of their school should read *Aspire High*, share its philosophy with their colleagues, look for short term wins, but plan for total transformation.

—*Melissa P. Morse*
Director, Instruction and Innovative Practice
Cobb County, GA

The book is great. *Aspire High* pulls together decades of school-based experiences and is comprehensive in weaving aspirations into the instructional process. The Listen, Learn, and Lead concept sits well in my thought process and I love the Step-Stride-Sprint challenges at the end of each chapter. The charts are useful summaries that draw the whole chapter together. Great work!

—*Steve York*
Former Deputy Superintendent of
Montana's Office of Public Instruction, principal, and teacher.

This book is long overdue. Any educator who believes that education is about preparing every young person for success in this ever changing global society will find this book hard to put down. Rest assured that at the end of this book you will want to take action to ensure you are doing everything you can to create a truly authentic education fit for the world today.

—*Steve Kenning*
CEO The Aspirations Academies Trust

The appeal of Dr. Quaglia's research and writing is its relevance to the education desperately needed by our young people today. As an advocate of his aspirations framework for over 15 years I have been constantly impressed with the fact that he and his team never stand still. This book provides a great deal of food for thought for educationalists with the desire to provide an education truly fit for the world today.

—*Paula Kenning*
Chief Learning Officer, the Aspirations Academies Trust
Executive Principal, Rivers Academy England

Based on solid research, countless interactions with hundreds of educators and thousands of students, *Aspire High* provides a developed and organized blueprint for the actualization of the QISA student aspiration framework. *Aspire High* is a noteworthy addition to the field which can function, in my opinion, as a driving force for change in education with an intentional focus on improved student learning and achievement. *Aspire*

High is a significant improvement on previous works promoting student engagement and collaborative culture in schools because it provides easy to use, well organized and detailed plans for universal application as an improvement process for schools and school districts.

—Tony Pierantozzi
Former Superintendent of Schools in four districts

As a teacher of 25 years, I found *Aspire High* to be that rare mix of inspiration, affirmation, and justification that reminded me why I joined the profession in the first place. The researched-based attention to pedagogy illustrated in concrete narrative had me reimagining my course, my classroom, and my professional interactions with students, colleagues, and administrators. As I strive to balance the art of teaching with today's educational environment to effect a productive and memorable experience of growth and learning for my students, *Aspire High* will be an invaluable resource for me.

—Dan Kirk
High School English Teacher
Pittsburgh, PA

As a high school student, this book appeals to me as it asks teachers and learners to share information and listen to one another. *Aspire High* encourages teachers to reach out to all learners and foster their growth using varied practices. The integration of teacher and student explorations into diverse forms of research and learning allow the student to use the strategies that best suits him or her.

—Autumn
High School Sophomore
Tampa, FL

My passion and belief that all schools CAN be places that effectively meet the needs of ALL students, allowing them to thrive and reach their fullest potential has been revived! Quaglia and his colleagues paint a picture of the school that every teacher wants to teach in, and that every parent wants their children to learn in. This beautifully articulated narrative infused with powerful data and realistic strategies has inspired me to sprint towards the Aspire High vision for schools. Without doubt, readers will be challenged to measure their own choices and actions against the author's quest for "amazingness" and the dream for all schools to Aspire High!

—Dr. Lisa Lande
Executive Director
Teacher Voice & Aspirations International Center

Aspire High

Imagining Tomorrow's School Today

Russell J. Quaglia

Michael J. Corso

Kristine Fox

Gavin Dykes

CORWIN
A SAGE Publishing Company

FOR INFORMATION:

Corwin

A SAGE Company

2455 Teller Road

Thousand Oaks, California 91320

(800) 233-9936

www.corwin.com

SAGE Publications Ltd.

1 Oliver's Yard

55 City Road

London EC1Y 1SP

United Kingdom

SAGE Publications India Pvt. Ltd.

B 1/I 1 Mohan Cooperative Industrial Area

Mathura Road, New Delhi 110 044

India

SAGE Publications Asia-Pacific Pte. Ltd.

3 Church Street

#10-04 Samsung Hub

Singapore 049483

Executive Editor: Arnis Burvikovs

Senior Associate Editor: Desirée Bartlett

Senior Editorial Assistant: Andrew Olson

Production Editor: Amy Schroller

Copy Editor: Amy Harris

Typesetter: C&M Digitals (P) Ltd.

Proofreader: Rae-Ann Goodwin

Indexer: Robie Grant

Cover Designer: Candice Harman

Marketing Manager: Lisa Lysne

Printed in the United States of America

ISBN 978-1-5063-1137-1

This book is printed on acid-free paper.

SFI Certified Sourcing
www.sfiprogram.org
SFI-00453

16 17 18 19 20 10 9 8 7 6 5 4 3 2 1

Contents

Foreword

Several years ago, as the superintendent of an urban district, we were faced with the challenge of transforming our comprehensive high school into five small learning communities. During a particularly heated discourse on how to organize these small schools, I learned a valuable lesson: allow students to have a voice in decisions that impact their daily lives. As Marcus jumped up and shouted an idea that proved to be far more innovative than those of the adults, we were immediately silenced and we all looked like we had been slapped. In hindsight, we should have been. You see, we had fallen prey to the error that so many educators make routinely—deciding what kids want without even asking them. Allowing kids to share what it is they need to be more engaged in their own learning seems like common sense; however, we rarely do that and, when we do, we usually override their ideas because we know better. No wonder so many kids question our motives and commitment to them.

Since that critical lesson from a disillusioned but determined teen, I came to recognize, but not accept, that student voice is a missing ingredient in far too many school-reform agendas and, even more importantly, is neither sought nor valued. Soon after that fateful day, I met someone who transformed my thinking and my work—Russell Quaglia. Meeting Russ is akin to traveling back in time to the 1960s (for those who have experienced Russ in person, you get my reference), and his steadfast belief in the value of engaging students has had a profound, almost mystical, influence on me. His collaboration with Mickey Corso (a tireless advocate for kids), Kristine Fox (an amazing innovative thinker), and Gavin Dykes (the ultimate global leader) on *Aspire High* is a symphony of thoughts, ideas, experiences, and practices framed by their intentional work on engaging students to dream and hope and find their purpose. It is a true gift to the field of education.

Aspire High places readers into a space of possibilities. Most of education research and the multitude of books written on school reform focus on the expected "hows": how to lead, how how to train teachers, how to assess educators, and how to measure learning. The missing ingredient in this "how to" list is how to purposefully design learning environments that are responsive to students' needs and their quest for meaningful engagement in their learning. *Aspire High* lifts us to this higher vision. By focusing on a mission of providing " each and every student with the ability to dream and set goals for the future while inspiring them in the present to reach those goals," the authors challenge us to return to our core mission as educators: to ensure every student realizes success and to offer them hope for their future and not merely orchestrate schools so that they fit into our present.

Each of the chapters in *Aspire High* incorporates Listen, Learn, and Lead strategies. This design allowed me to stitch the chapters together in a way that brought relevance as well as a personal recommitment to action. This book, while promoting a concept that the authors readily admit does not exist in total anywhere, poses essential questions for us to ponder and fortifies its tenets by highlighting relevant researchers and proven practices. This blending of both pushes readers to question the philosophies by which we lead and the practices we support. What we as readers can easily discern is that the voices of students are predominant and necessary in the land of *Aspire High*.

Recognizing that leading school change is a marathon, the authors differentiate various possibilities by orchestrating them into three starting points: Step, Stride, and Sprint. This approach, vastly different from almost every other book, respects that educators and students are at various points of development—whether in their own learning or in their quest to lead effectively. How fortunate for the field that Russ, Mickey, Kristine, and Gavin respect our collective differences.

Throughout my own career, I have lived by the belief that what we offer to our students tells them what it is that we value. *Aspire High* breathes life into this core belief. It challenges all of us to cajole students from the sidelines of the education playing field and to join us as partners on the expansive field of life—inviting them to call the plays, to help plan their next move, to forecast what they need, and to be coached on the most important journey of their lives—becoming. Russ made a significant difference in my life and his collaboration with Mickey, Kristine, and Gavin will have a profound impact on how we view our roles and those of our students. This inspiring book ends with a call to action—to act boldly and to be intentional. For me, *Aspire High* opens up a world of possibilities and allows our kids—every kid—to dream, to hope, to become. If *Aspire High* is realized, our mission is realized.

—Deb Delisle
Executive Director/CEO ASCD
Former Assistant Secretary of Elementary and
Secondary Education; former Ohio State Superintendent;
former superintendent, principal, and teacher.

Preface

While the actual process of writing this book took us about one year from first keystroke to publication, the ideas began formulating long before that. Mickey, Kristine, and I travel frequently (immense understatement)—sometimes together, sometimes solo, and sometimes as duos. When together, whether on a long drive to a school site or sipping coffee (tea for Kristine, double-decaf espresso for Mickey), we would dream in detail about what the "best school ever" would look like. What would the most important components of that school be? How would teachers and students work together? What would the role of the administration be? What would a school need to do to ensure that everyone's voices are being heard? Where could a place exist that would guarantee that each and every person in the school achieves his or her aspirations? Recently, while he was the Quaglia Institute's Visiting Scholar, we added the incredibly insightful and internationally informed voice of Gavin Dykes to those conversations.

I cannot even begin to count the multitude of various ideas put forth for the ultimate "Aspirations School." Some ideas intrigued me, while others only convinced me that we were in the car together way too long! Over time, the dream of what the school could be turned into discussions about reality. Our thoughts became more concrete, more grounded. The possibilities for success became more real, and we realized that the need for a new kind of school had become more critical.

This book represents a vast collection of knowledge. While it took 12 months to pull together, it has been 30 years in the making (yes, we all wish we had written this a bit earlier in our careers!). We now share our collective vision for the aspirations school—Aspire High—with you, not necessarily to adopt, but to adapt. Our goal is to light a fuse for change, to allow you as the reader to dream about the possibilities and then turn those dreams into action in a way that makes a difference in your school.

When you do take action, keep in mind that the essential underpinning of this work is the importance of *voice*. We believe with every ounce of our professional beings that we must be willing to learn from those around us: students, teachers, support staff, administrators, parents, and the community at large. To think we have the answers and know better than anyone else is naïve. As this book will demonstrate, throughout our journey we took the time to listen to the various stakeholders in schools, and we were committed to learning from and understanding their beliefs, ideas, reflections, and suggestions. We have listened to and we have learned from the very individuals who know best what it is like to be in school and what it will take to make the very best school. Armed with the knowledge from this process, we dare to lead the way, sharing what we believe is essential for any school to Aspire High!

I started this preface by referencing how the people you surround yourself with reflect who you are (and I believe, shape who you become). This also applies more broadly to the environments we spend time in, as they likewise influence who we are. I have been fortunate enough to be surrounded by some amazing people, and I have learned a tremendous amount as an educator by working in amazing school environments. Our hope is that this book will challenge you to develop a school environment that is a positive influence for students and teachers alike—an environment where *everyone* is encouraged to achieve his or her aspirations, where *everyone* contributes her or his voice, and where *everyone* is given the support needed to succeed.

While we do not have control over all of the events in our lives, we can control the environment within which we want young people and teachers to learn and grow. In spite of endless rules and regulations, we also have control over the choices that we make every day in education. We can *choose* to place ourselves in school environments that are positive. We can *choose* to surround ourselves with people who are dedicated to a similar journey. If your current school and the educators you work with are not on the same path, how can you continue your essential growth toward progress and innovation? Your voice, your values, and your passion are important to move forward. The sound of negativity in schools can be deafening—your goal is to ensure that your voice and related actions for positive change are louder!

THE JOURNEY

As you will see, the book *Aspire High* is about the school Aspire High—a school that exists in its entirety only in our imaginations, but whose parts are very much grounded in reality, based on our collective experiences and learning. We have assembled Aspire High from research, best practices collected in our travels around the world, and countless conversations, focus groups, and interviews with educators and students. We have been in very few schools that are across-the-board amazing, but we have been in *amazing* classrooms, observed *amazing* teaching and learning, and witnessed *amazing* school leadership. This book gathers all these pockets of "*amazingness*" into one dream: Aspire High.

As you "walk" through Aspire High and meet the learners and leaders, you will encounter a great deal of research that supports the vision of the school. Aspire High was not just conjured up over coffee/tea and long road trips. It was consciously created from the best of what we have learned in over 100 years of combined experience in education. The research will include frequent references to the *Quaglia School Voice* surveys. Over the years, we have collected data on millions of students and tens of thousands of educators. The unfortunate fact is that the aggregate results have not changed that much from year to year over the past decade. If anything, they have gradually declined in important areas.

By way of rationale for why schools and classrooms must change, we have included results from the most recent student and teacher aggregates (2016). Between fall 2015 and spring 2016, the *Quaglia School Voice Student Survey* was completed by 48,185 students in Grades 6–12, representing 249 schools from across the United States. When a school administers the survey, every student is a respondent. There is no sampling. The schools represented used the survey "off the shelf," so to speak, to measure their school climate and culture; the schools were not selected by us. The gender breakdown is roughly even, and the grade levels are also fairly even and range from a low of 12% (Grade 12) to a high of 18% (Grade 9). The results are both racially and socioeconomically diverse—including urban, suburban, and rural schools, as well as reservation schools and charter schools.

The most recent aggregate of the *Quaglia School Voice Teacher Survey* comprises a total of 4,021 staff members who took the survey during the 2015–2016 school year. Of those, 75% were classroom teachers, 15% were certified support staff, and 10% were support staff; males made up 26% of respondents, and 74% were female. A majority of respondents (55%) indicated that they had worked in schools for 11 years or more and that 49% had a master's degree or more, 41% held a bachelor's, 3% an associate's, 6% a high school diploma or equivalent, and 1% a doctorate.

The surveys themselves are based on the Aspirations Framework, developed and supported by the Quaglia Institute for Student Aspirations (QISA) and its partner, the Teacher Voice and Aspirations International Center (TVAIC). A full articulation of this framework is available in *Student Voice: The Instrument of Change* (2014). Our core belief is that schools should inspire *all* students to dream about the future and inspire them in the present to work toward those dreams. These efforts are fostered through the 3 Guiding Principles—Self-Worth, Engagement, and Purpose—and the 8 Conditions that support a school in living out these Principles: Belonging, Heroes, Sense of Accomplishment, Fun & Excitement, Curiosity &

Creativity, Spirit of Adventure, Leadership & Responsibility, and Confidence to Take Action. These aspects of the teaching and learning environment are essential if schools are to Aspire High.

Goal	Guiding Principles	Conditions
Aspirations	Self-Worth	**Belonging**: Feeling as if you are a part of a group, while knowing you are special for who you are
		Heroes: Having people who believe in you and are there for you when you need them
		Sense of Accomplishment: Being recognized for different types of success, including effort
	Engagement	**Fun & Excitement**: Enjoying what you are doing, whether at school, work, or play
		Curiosity & Creativity: Asking "Why?" and "Why not?" about the world around you
		Spirit of Adventure: Being excited to try new things, even if you don't know that you will excel
	Purpose	**Leadership & Responsibility**: Making decisions and taking responsibility for your choices
		Confidence to Take Action: Setting goals and taking the steps you need to reach them

Aspire High is not only possible today, but it is necessary, as you will see in the Introduction. The time for schools to focus on all students' aspirations—*their* dreams, hopes, goals, and their present efforts to reach those goals—is now. And that effort must be particular and personalized, not a vague, generic goal of getting into college or being "career-ready" (whatever that means in a world with nearly limitless, continuously emerging career opportunities). The process begins by reimagining the roles of four main participants within the life of a school: students, teachers, principals, and parents.

Chapter 1 and Chapter 2 turn the traditional classroom around and make students the teachers and the teachers the learners. In a world of instant access to information, learning should be embedded in interdisciplinary, real-world, relevant projects, and the learning should be a continual process for students *and* teachers. Students often learn best by teaching, and teachers can learn a great deal from students; they should be partners in the learning process. At Aspire High, teachers see themselves as Lead Learners—being primarily responsible for overseeing the learning process rather than directing instruction.

Chapter 3 takes the increasingly demanding job of a principal and invites an approach that not only distributes leadership (spreading responsibility for the far-too-numerous administrative tasks) but also inspires and amplifies the voice of all members of the school community. A vital component is having the principal engage as the school's primary connection with the surrounding community. This is essential at Aspire High, where learning is not limited by a school's walls, but is intertwined with the community.

Chapter 4 takes on the persistent issue of parental participation. Particularly at the secondary level, it is far too easy to excuse the disconnect between home and school as "developmental" and "inevitable." The fact is that nearly all students believe their parents care about their education. The challenge for schools is to create systems of involvement that are suited *to the parents* and capitalize on what the students already know—that their parents do care about their education.

In Chapter 5, we articulate the principles for designing policies we believe advance the mission of inspiring students in the present to reach their dreams. First and foremost is the inclusion of Student Voice. Additionally, policies must be grounded in current research, rather than functioning in the default mode of "We have always done it this way." In particular, Aspire High's policies ensure that the Self-Worth, Engagement, and Purpose of each student, staff member, parent, and community member are fostered. By way of example, these principles will be applied in five scenarios.

Chapter 6 is about pedagogical strategies and the ability to maximize student learning. This chapter examines four strategies: interdisciplinary learning, metacognition, self-assessment, and mastery learning. Used with a high degree of intention, each of these can play an important role in a school where students are the teachers and teachers are Lead Learners.

Chapter 7 extends the critical importance of being intentional with the use of technology at Aspire High. Given the rapid rate of change and creative application in this area, an exhaustive discussion on this topic is unachievable! Attention is paid to the way in which technology can create "anytime, anywhere, anyone" learning and support students as creators and innovators.

In Chapter 8, a tour of Aspire High makes it clear that it is not a building, but an approach—a way of viewing education that consciously considers the learning spaces, the outdoor environment, the community, and the world. Aspire High aims to be fully integrated into the community, with community members as partners who contribute to Aspire High and with students contributing to the community through internships and learning experiences that only the real world can provide. Finally, in Chapter 9, we will present a challenge and invite you to Aspire High.

Throughout the book, each chapter contains three main components: a Listen section that describes Aspire High, a Learn section that reviews research in support of Aspire High's approach, and a Lead section designed to inspire you to take action. After a brief introduction, the Lead section presents concrete applications for teachers, principals, and students and invites you to Step, Stride, or Sprint, depending upon your current starting point.

As you read, you are likely to agree with much of what we have written, and hopefully you will pause for deeper consideration of all aspects of Aspire High. However, our goal is not to merely influence your thinking. We aim to influence your *actions*. *We are writing to disrupt the current system*, for which there is a great deal of evidence suggesting it is simply not working for far too many students.

Our hope is that this book inspires you to aspire higher and that you invite your students to be partners on the journey. Student Voice is at the heart of this book, and Student Voice should serve as a seed of inspiration in schools. We recognize that educational nonfiction is not the most sought-after genre for students, and while this book may not be the next page-turner for teenagers, we do know they care about their experiences in school. *We are expecting—indeed, counting on—you to share what you have learned with your students and involve them in the transformation of your school.* Students are "the instrument of change." Take action together—and do not wait for the start of the next school year or term. In schools, we generally change for one of two reasons: mandates from policy makers (who rarely step foot in a school) or a desire to make a difference. Do not be driven by mandates—you and your students deserve much more than that. Be the change you want to see in your school—today!

—Russell J. Quaglia (on behalf of the team)

Acknowledgments

You may have heard the saying "Show me who you spend time with and I will tell you who you are." I used to hear this from my mom throughout high school, but too casually shrugged it off as an adolescent. It is, however, etched in my memory, and I now can only hope her words are true, as I have the good fortune of working and spending time with the most extraordinary and talented people on the planet. Michael Corso, Kristine Fox, and Gavin Dykes, with whom I worked on this book, are three such people. They possess such incredible insight and passion—personally and professionally—that it is impossible not to become inspired by them.

Dr. Michael Corso is one of the most engaging and inspirational thought leaders of our time. Of all the decisions I have made in my professional life, the one that stands out as the smartest is hiring Mickey, more than 15 years ago. He is not only a gift to the Quaglia Institute team, but a gift to education. As a person and professional, Mickey is brilliant, innovative, passionate, trustworthy, and caring. Mickey's inquisitiveness about life is matched only by his insatiable desire to make schools better for both teachers and students. He is the most unselfish and generous person I know, putting others before himself on all occasions. It is a blessing to call Mickey my friend and colleague.

Dr. Kristine Fox has been working with me for over 25 years. We collaborated on our first book, *Believing in Achieving*, over two decades years ago. We often look back at that book and ask each other, "What were we thinking?" Not because the book is not good, but because we can now recognize that it was just the starting point of our work, and the amount we have learned since then has surpassed our expectations! To say Kristine is a doer would be the ultimate understatement. There is no other person I know who can transform an idea into an actionable item more efficiently and effectively, with impeccable quality, than Kristine. While she is comfortable working in the background, her innovative thinking most assuredly leads the way and is at the forefront of all that the Quaglia Institute does. In addition to being the most productive human I have ever met, Kristine is part of the foundation upon which the School Voice and Aspirations work continues to grow.

Gavin Dykes is an international educational leader and one of the most genuinely kind and insightful people I know. He can transition seamlessly from leading the Education World Forum to having a hot beverage and conversation in a local coffee house. Without exception, when you meet with Gavin, he is wholeheartedly engaged in the exchange of ideas; he makes you feel as if you are the center of the universe. He is one of the greatest facilitators of our time. Gavin's listening skills enhance his own incredible insights and abilities as a facilitator; he is a true synthesizer of ideas who readily transforms them into action. His vast array of global travels and experiences in education, including conversing with renowned educational leaders, informed Gavin's own vision for the very best school, which he graciously brought to this book.

It is people like Mickey, Kristine, and Gavin who inspire me. I listen to them (although they may dispute that at times!), I always learn from them, and I lead more effectively having spent time with them.

As you will learn, this book gives witness to a combined century of observations, conversation, insights, wonderments, judgments, deliberations, decisions, passions, and actions. The four of us have dedicated our professional lives to making schools better for all students and teachers. For each of us, that journey began at the front of a classroom, and we have had the privilege of spending the last several years trotting the globe. By either invitation to enter or barging in, we have visited your classrooms, your schools, and your districts, and we have been watching, collecting, and dreaming.

As you will also learn, this book is a compilation of those visits and dreams. We have taken the best of what we have seen and heard and spun it all up into one school: Aspire High. So we must acknowledge, first and foremost, you! Students, teachers, administrators, parents, and community members who more and more recognize that the inherited industrial model of schools is less and less effective at ensuring the success of every student—unwilling to accept the status quo, you have been exceptional in your willingness to challenge and change. Despite rules and regulations, policies and procedures, systems and structures that have been in place since the 1930s, you have found a way to be resourceful, innovative, and creative. Despite a top-down hierarchical organizational chart that pressurizes schools with high-stakes testing, you have found a way to listen to one another, to learn from one another, and to lead with one another. In this book, we have tried to amplify and synthesize your efforts. Several of you have actually contributed your story to this volume. To those who have found their way into these pages either implicitly or explicitly, thank you!

Closer to home, we work with an amazing team of educators at the Quaglia Institute. Dr. Brian Connelly's restless desire and relentless effort to improve the schools he works with are an inspiration. Dr. Susan Inman's tireless work with administrators, teachers, and students—most especially in schools in Ohio and South Carolina—prove that "when the going gets tough, the tough get going." Dr. Lisa Lande, our newest addition to the leadership team as director of the Teacher Voice and International Center, continues to make her mark in the field with her professionalism, insights, and uncompromising desire to make sure all the voices in school are heard and valued. Frequent road trips and daily conversations with these Quaglia Institute leaders and outstanding educators are woven throughout this book. We are so very grateful.

We couldn't zip around the world without a team that stays home to mind the office, answer the phones, crunch the numbers, manage the social-media side of our lives, review our work, make us smarter, and see to the nitty-gritty of running a nonprofit that has dozens of partnerships. Director of Operations Deborah Young and Sue Harper, administrative assistant and Director of Everything Else, keep us all sane and grounded. We are appreciative beyond words.

We would also like to acknowledge the unwavering support of Deb Delisle, Executive Director/CEO of ASCD. Whether working at the local, state, or national level, she always puts students first. We continue to listen and learn from Deb and look forward to a future of leading together! We are grateful for her kind words in the Foreword.

Without question, our most vibrant partnership is with Corwin. The entire team at Corwin is unwavering in support of our writing, our surveys, and our professional services. Special thanks to Monique Corridori (aka ATQ . . . All Things Quaglia). Monique is not only an amazing colleague, but a dear friend whom we admire, respect, and, quite frankly, love! We also want to pay tribute to our editor, Arnis Burvikovs. Arnie believed in us and our work from the very beginning. He is demanding, direct, honest, and holds us to the highest standards possible (we would not want him any other way). We trust that you and your incredible team renew our self-worth as professionals, our engagement in this field, and our sense of purpose as thought leaders by your commitment to this work. Even as we seek to amplify Student and Teacher Voice, we thank the Corwin family for amplifying ours.

—Russell J. Quaglia (on behalf of the team)

PUBLISHER'S ACKNOWLEDGMENTS

Corwin gratefully acknowledges the contributions of the following reviewers:

Beth Havens
Educational Consultant
Learning Havens LLC and Charleston County School District
N. Myrtle Beach, SC

Cheryl Hunt
Educator
Education Service Center Region 11
White Settlement, TX

B. R. Jones
Supervising Principal
South Jones High School
Ellisville, MS

About the Authors

Russell J. Quaglia is a globally recognized pioneer in the field of education, known for his unwavering dedication to Student Voice and aspirations. Dr. Quaglia has been described by news media as "America's foremost authority on the development and achievement of student voice and aspirations." His innovative work is evidenced by an extensive library of research-based publications, prominent international speaking appearances, and a successfully growing list of aspirations ventures.

Among these ventures, Dr. Quaglia authored the *School Voice* suite of surveys, including *Student Voice, Teacher Voice, Parent Voice*, and *iKnow My Class*. His books, *Student Voice: The Instrument of Change, Principal Voice: Listen, Learn, and Lead*, and (together with Lisa L. Lande) *Teacher Voice: Amplifying Success* have received international acclaim.

In addition to founding and leading the Quaglia Institute for Student Aspirations, Dr. Quaglia also founded and currently chairs the Aspirations Academies Trust, a sponsor of primary and secondary academies in England built on his aspirations research. Most recently, he has founded the Teacher Voice and Aspirations International Center, dedicated to amplifying the voice of teachers for them to realize their aspirations and reach their fullest potential.

Dr. Quaglia earned his bachelor's degree at Assumption College, a master's degree in economics from Boston College, and master of education and doctorate degrees from Columbia University, specializing in the area of organizational theory and behavior. He has been awarded numerous honorary doctorates in humanitarian services for his dedication to students. Dr. Quaglia's work has also led him to serve on several national and international committees, reflecting his passion for ensuring that Student and Teacher Voice are always heard, honored, and acted upon.

Michael J. Corso is the former chief academic officer for the Quaglia Institute for Student Aspirations and remains affiliated with QISA. He has returned to the high school classroom and is currently chair of the theology department at Catholic Memorial High School in Boston, Massachusetts. He has a doctorate in education from Boston College, has been an educator for more than 30 years, and has taught at every grade level, kindergarten through graduate school. He is deeply committed to the belief that students are the agents of their own learning. This passion makes him a natural fit for work in the area of student aspirations and Student Voice. Dr. Corso has worked throughout his career to improve teaching and learning through teacher training and education. In his role with QISA, Dr. Corso combines research on student perceptions of their schools with educational theory and the living, breathing practice of students, teachers, and administrators. He is the coauthor of *Student Voice: The Instrument of Change* (2014) and numerous articles and papers on Student Voice, student aspirations, and school change.

Kristine Fox is a senior field specialist and research associate for the Quaglia Institute for Student Aspirations. Dr. Fox received her doctorate from the University of Maine in Educational Leadership, her EdM from Harvard University, and her BA from the University of Michigan. She coauthored with Dr. Quaglia *8 Conditions That Make a Difference* and has been published in *Educational Leadership, American School Board Journal, ASCD Express, Education Week,* and *Principal Magazine.* Throughout her career, Kristine has partnered with students, teachers, administrators, and communities to ensure that Student Voice drives teaching and learning in schools. As a qualitative researcher, she conducts focus groups with students and teachers to better understand the current status of Voice in schools. Dr. Fox has experience as a K–8 administrator and 6–12 teacher.

Gavin Dykes began his working life as a civil engineer before changing his focus and transitioning to teach in colleges and universities, then working to develop education with governments, international agencies, and commercial companies. From the early stages, he focused on innovation in policy and practice, the development of the use of technology to support learning, and the parts that students and teachers can play in codesigning their work.

He gained his international experience and reputation through working with education's stakeholders, from students and teachers to ministers and policy makers. Gavin now holds a range of long-term roles, including as the program director for the Education World Forum, which began in 2004 and each year brings senior education leaders together to debate policy challenges, to practice, and to learn from each other. In the January 2016 event, 97 countries were represented. As program director, Gavin negotiates and sets the agenda. He is also program director for the Asian Summit on Education and Skills, which takes place annually in India.

He is cofounder and Chair of Education of Fast Forward, a charity focused on sharing and improving the understanding of key education issues. Education Fast Forward convenes global discussions and debates using an innovative blend of new technologies and social media to bring participation within the reach of the widest possible range of stakeholders.

Gavin also supports teaching, learning, and innovation in education through a range of consulting roles. He has worked with the OECD, the World Bank, UNESCO, governments, and commercial corporations conducting research, moderating discussion, and writing reports on a range of education issues.

Introduction

Imagining Tomorrow's School Today

Nothing will work unless you do.

—Maya Angelou

TIME FOR A REVOLUTION

By now, it has become commonplace to point out the relative obsolescence of the inherited model of school. Designed for a time when information was hard to get and student populations were soaring due to immigration and new laws requiring compulsory schooling, a model inspired by the punctual efficiency and quality control of the industrial factory made sense. And so empty-headed students, who were "batched by date of manufacture" (Robinson, 2009) sat in neat rows in front of experts in various, distinct subjects such as reading, writing, arithmetic, science, and social studies to have content installed, reviewed, and tested. With hallways as conveyer belts, bells rang to signal classroom shifts, cafeteria lunches, and the conclusion of the day. At the end, diplomas were issued to certify that our "product" was sound and ready for college, work, or a career in a stable world of known jobs.

But just as manufacturing ran into difficulties when overseas competition entered the market, so too has schooling run into trouble in a world where virtually all information, whether reliable or not, is available on the Internet. Once, we relied on authors and publishers to exercise judgment about the veracity and value of information, and the fact that something appeared in print was itself a filter. Now, when we can search and find sometimes thousands of articles on any subject, readers and learners must more urgently learn to apply their critical skills and their own judgment (Rheingold, 2015). The raw materials for producing learning and knowledge are accessible beyond bound books and the confines of a classroom.

Anyone, anywhere, at any time can access nearly anything he or she wants to know. Try it. Want to know how to repair your dryer or hack your smartphone? There are numerous DIY videos on these subjects and thousands of others. Want to read the only surviving manuscript of the Old English text *Beowulf*? Head over to the British Library archive on the web. Always wanted to see the Sistine Chapel? You can stand virtually in the middle of it, turn in any direction with a flick of your wrist, and see each fresco even closer-up than you could in person with just a right click or two.

Many will say none of these experiences are the same as being there, and they would be correct. As *experiences*, they are not equivalent. But all are adequate to the task of learning about dryers or literature or art—maybe even better for learning, if not experiencing, as we can pause the video without the repair person charging extra, hover over an Anglo-Saxon word we don't know to have it translated, and study a fresco without feeling hurried by the tour group behind us that wants to see it too.

We are convinced we are living through the fading days of the inherited model of school—even as it seeks to reinforce itself with more standards and insanely frequent measurement of important metrics such as standardized reading and math test scores. Signs of its decay can be seen in cheating scandals, the opt-out-of-testing movement, the rate of turnover in principalships and superintendencies, the growing number of teachers protesting working conditions by taking all their sick days, declining SAT scores, and the inability of the teaching profession to retain talented new educators. Add this to stagnant graduation rates, student apathy, college remediation and first-year dropout rate, and the school-to-prison pipeline and you have all the signs of a system that is not in need of fixing because it is broken, but in need of scrapping because it is obsolete. It's not about lazy teachers or administrators who are opposed to being accountable. You can't fly a bicycle to the moon no matter how expensive your bike is, how hard you pedal, or how often you measure your heart rate or speed. It is the wrong system of transportation for the job, not the price of the bicycle or people on the bikes that is the problem.

At one time, the challenge effectively answered by the old educational system was that information was bound, and the world was relatively stable. At this time, the challenge that must be answered by any new system of education is that information is boundless, and the world we are graduating students into is far less stable. Technology, globalization, and a host of other patterns and trends have reshaped our social, economic, and civic landscapes, yet the building within which we educate our children has remained, for the most part, unaffected by these shifts. When our children come home from school, the question "What did you learn today?" is now quaint and confining. We should ask, "What did you discuss or deconstruct or disagree with or dream about or design or dare or decide to do in school today?"

In addition to these shifts to the very ground on which education has stood, "the emerging science of learning underscores the importance of rethinking what is taught, how it is taught, and how learning is assessed" (Bransford, Brown, & Cocking, 2000, p. 13). There recently has been a tremendous amount of learning in the fields of brain research, adolescent psychology, family systems, and various related fields that have yet to make their impact on schools fully felt. We know, for example, that cognitive development does not progress through a fixed sequence of age-related stages, but that the mastery of new concepts happens in fits and starts (Flynn, O'Malley, & Wood, 2004). Neuroscience has produced evidence of the fundamental role of emotion in learning, settling long-standing ideological debates about whether educators should be responsible for emotional development (Hinton, Miyamoto, & Della-Chiesa, 2008). We know that the adolescent circadian rhythm undergoes a dramatic shift, yet many high schools begin the day with their students still biologically half asleep. We know that in adolescence a proclivity for risk-taking increases, opening the door for dangerous behaviors, but also potentially healthy, experimental learning experiences. We have known since Erikson (1950) that these years are a time of identity upheaval, confusion, and budding achievement, making it an ideal time to focus on each student's newly emergent hopes, dreams, aspirations, and his or her attendant passion for pursuing these. The growing importance of the peer group at this age makes horizontal, peer-to-peer learning approaches much more effective than adult-to-student approaches, and yet most schools spend most of their time in the latter, not the former, strategies. Thus, the need for a new approach to secondary schooling is called for not only by a changing world but also by the developing human brain, body, affect, and psyche as it transitions from childhood to adulthood.

In addition, *we can no longer conceive of meaningful education without Student Voice.* Student Voice occurs "when students are meaningfully engaged in decision making and improvement-related processes in their schools" (Quaglia & Corso, 2014, p. xiv). This requires adults and students to work in partnership with one another through a process of Listening, Learning, and Leading. Where Student Voice is concerned, *Listening* is an active experience. Student Voice may begin with surveys or focus groups, but it must not end there. Adults and students alike must actively seek out one another's perspective and opinions on matters that affect them. Listening is one part in an ongoing dialogue. Thus, listening, paradoxically, is a part of Student Voice.

Having listened, the Student Voice process continues to learning. *Learning* occurs when we are genuinely open to the other's points of view—when we see the differences in how we experience this or that aspect of school life—not as competing ideas, but as completing ideas. We have a fuller picture of what our school, its policies, its norms, and its customs are like if we see them from multiple angles. Learning is the fruitful outcome of respectful listening and trust.

Learning in this way, in partnership, results in leading *together*. *Leading* in a school context is deciding on the courses of action that will improve the teaching and learning as well as strategically taking action based on what has been learned by listening. Student Voice in this sense is not about students telling their teachers and administrators what they think about their classes and school so that the teachers and administrators go off and fix it *for* the students. Nor is Student Voice student "leadership" as traditionally practiced—student council/government, team captains, club presidents, and the like (which have the added downside of being typically exclusive). Both strategies have adults and students operating independently of one another. Leadership-given Student Voice, rather, is a dialogue of action between educators and students. Student Voice means students having a seat at the table where meaningful decisions are made.

Such a partnership is available (and needed!) at all levels of the educational system, from the youngest preschoolers making choices about what learning center to work at to the university student coteaching with her professor. The aforementioned psychological and social developmental realities make adolescence a particularly potent time to encourage and develop Student Voice. These years are accompanied by significant growth to an adolescent's intellectual capacity. This cognitive development includes an increased ability to think formally and abstractly. As a result, self-determination, questioning of authority, self-efficacy, and a growing independence are all critical factors to leverage in the service of teaching and learning at this age. Every parent of a teenager is aware that his or her child closes off under a top-down approach but is open to influence in an approach that involves trust, listening, and dialogue. Schools should be no less aware of this in their curriculum, assessment strategies, and student management policies. Engaging Student Voice creates a significant learning advantage over approaches that dismiss student input as immature, irrelevant, or simply "icing." Promoting Student Voice is also connected to numerous other educational outcomes: elevated achievement in marginalized student populations, increased classroom participation, improved school reform efforts, better self-reflection and preparation for improvement in struggling students, and decreased behavior problems (Toshalis & Nakkula, 2012). *Learning from our students—who they are, who they want to be, what engages them—is essential if we are going to effectively prepare them for a world in which how they think is as important as what they know.*

To be clear: We are not saying we no longer need schools. We are saying that the traditional purpose of school—to get students ready for college or career—is no longer tenable as the primary aim. In truth, school and college and career are themselves means to greater ends. We are, after all, educating human *beings*, not human doings. The goal is to help each student become! The purpose of Aspire High is simply to get ready!

THE MISSION AND PLAN OF ASPIRE HIGH

The mission of Aspire High is straightforward: to provide each and every student with the ability to dream and set goals for the future while inspiring him or her in the present to reach those goals. Toward that end, each chapter of this book about Aspire High will follow a simple plan. The plan is designed to move you toward action. First, we invite you to *Listen* and look in on a school made possible by the world we live in, not the world as it once was. Each Listen section begins with a short vignette—a scene we imagine as visitors to Aspire High. In these vignettes, you will meet teachers, students, and Principal Harper. They will be guides throughout, and the characters have been inspired by actual educators and students it has been our privilege to know. The Listen section continues with an explanation of how Aspire High approaches the educational theme under consideration in the chapter. Many versions of the future are imaginable. Our own speculation is into the near future to a school that is not only possible, but within reach—as a healthy stretch from where we are now. While plans for new, high-tech buildings and fully modern, blended curricula are no doubt somewhere on the horizon, they are not practically visible from where we currently stand. We want to hold out a vision of Aspire High that is achievable tomorrow, as well as at the end of a five-year plan.

Then, we will ask you to *Learn*. This section will encourage you to deepen your thinking about and understanding of why Aspire High operates as it does. We will share the latest research on the current state of schools and what practices best achieve what you encounter in Listen. In addition to the high-altitude lay of the land provided by research, the school you are in is our concrete starting place. We will ask you to consider deeply *your* building, your students, your classroom, your leadership, your parents, your staff meetings, your policies, your curricula, your assessments, your technology. Is what you are doing working? Are you using the right methods? The right systems? The right policies? Are you achieving the goals you set for yourselves? Are your students having success—not only academically, but also personally, socially, and emotionally? Are your students becoming not just readers and calculators, but themselves? Thus, each Learn section concludes with a set of reflection questions.

Finally, we will call on you to *Lead*. The final section of the chapter asks you to be disruptive—to bring about and lead a genuine rethink and redesign of your classrooms and schools. We are not writing to influence state education agencies or those who make laws for our schools having not been in one since their own college graduation. Frankly, we are tired of waiting for reform at that level. We are writing so that you will take whatever steps are necessary to be the catalyst for local change.

The type of change we are advocating in schools is much more like a marathon than a 100-meter dash. Those who lead such change, as with any good marathoners, require practice (which implies mistakes) and hard work (which implies continuous improvement) in order to be successful. Leading such change has no age requirement, no need for prior experience leading change, and no limits in terms of personal best. What is required is an attitude that will carry you through the good times and bad. And just as no one goes from being even an average fit person (never mind sedentary) to running 26.2 miles, those leading change must train. Your training involves a constant state of listening and learning.

Assuming not everyone runs at the same pace when the starting pistol is fired, the Lead section addresses the small *Steps* that need to be taken to get things moving in the right direction, *Strides* for those that are already moving and want to challenge themselves to the next level of leadership, and a full-on *Sprint* for the elite who are prepared to kick it into high gear to reach goals more quickly for themselves and the school. These challenges are provided for principals, teachers, and students. No matter what your role in school, we encourage you to begin with the reflection at the end of this introduction. This will help you discover your learning starting line and focus you on the tasks ahead that will help *you* advance.

The chapter concludes with a table that outlines typical practices, the invitation to Aspire High, and the practices we believe would encourage you to Aspire Higher! Recall that Aspire High is our vision for the near future—reachable for today's learners, literally, tomorrow. Aspire Higher is our vision for future generations of learners—reachable only if we undertake serious reform systemwide.

THE CHALLENGE

Having sparked your thinking with a vision for our near-term future, added fuel to the fire with research, and stoked the flames with local conversations, we will challenge you not just to tweak your current classroom/school/policy, but to transform it. *We need not an evolution, but a revolution, a genuine breakthrough.* We want to spur you to no longer settle—to leave behind explanations and excuses about uninvolved parents and apathetic children, inconsistently applied codes of conduct, and an incoherent plethora of programs, the "us-versus-them" mentality in all its forms (especially administrators vs. teachers), and the "our-hands-are-tied" insanity of the current testing regime. If we hope to move toward a new way of being learners together, if we

Anthony Bryk is the current president of the Carnegie Foundation for the Advancement of Teaching. In his most recent work, *Learning to Improve* (2015), Bryk argues that improvement science combined with the power of networks offers the field a new approach to reach ever-increasing educational aspirations.

want to be part of Aspire High, we must unbind ourselves from old ways of thinking and interacting that serve neither our students nor us. We must stop following and start leading.

Interspersed throughout the book are stories from around the world, written by students, teachers, administrators, policy makers, and thought leaders. They are part of the movement toward a different way of "being school" together. They represent pockets of thinking and practice that show what is possible right now. While Aspire High may not exist currently in any one place, the ideas and practices that make up Aspire High are out there, waiting to be assembled by those willing to lead the way. As Bryk and his colleagues (2015) write, "Individual educators and institutions are learning much every day, yet as a field we fail to organize, refine, and build on these lessons" (p. 11). We have witnessed that much of what individual educators and schools are learning works to support students' aspirations and want to encourage you to build on it. Aspire High is a work of imagination, but it is not fantasy. The stories exist to inspire you as they have us—to expand your view and to instigate you to gather the pieces that will help make learning meaningful and relevant to all your students and colleagues.

Each of these examples is followed by questions. Reading is typically a solo venture, but revolutionary change is not. We are all for the kind of personal change to classroom practice we have seen throughout our travels and that are articulated in these stories. These educators are our heroes and inspiration. But the kind of transformation we are calling for requires what Parker Palmer refers to as "a pedagogical discourse" (Palmer, 1998). This call for collegial conversation that goes back four decades to Lortie's insistence that the teaching profession needs to move away from a "culture of isolationism" (1975). More recently and more positively, Michael Fullan and Andy Hargreaves have invited us toward an ethos of "professional capital" (2012). These seminal thinkers and others insist that we need to come out of privatized classrooms to dialogue and discuss with one another a new way of being school. We want this book to be part of that conversation at your school.

> **Andy Hargreaves** is the Thomas More Brennan Chair in the Lynch School of Education at Boston College. With Fullan, he is the author of *Professional Capital* (2012), which "is about enacting more equal, higher-attaining, more healthy countries in just about every way that counts. This is why successful countries treat their teachers as nation builders, and how they come to yield high returns in prosperity, social cohesion, and social justice" (p. 185).

STUDENTS AS KEY STAKEHOLDERS IN THE CONVERSATION

We do have a bias that the community of discourse should include your students (see Quaglia & Corso, 2014). Students are neither your customers nor your clients; they are your partners. As we have stated, their points of view on your classrooms, school, and district provide vital information if you are to improve their education. When you assemble the stakeholders, you must make certain that those who have the most at stake—your students—are part of the dialogue. Transformation will emerge not from the monologue of the policy makers droning on about test scores, but from the grass-roots cacophony of the voices of the students and teachers and parents and principal of your school. We expect that you will use these questions to begin a conversation about how you might best implement the ideas found in each chapter.

NOW IS THE TIME

The final step is yours. Having invited you to listen, learn, and lead, only you can act. Truly make a change. Do whatever it takes to make sure every student and colleague you encounter has a voice, has a dream, and has the inspiration necessary to achieve that dream. You may not be part of the problem, but you must become part of the solution. *Together, we can make a difference.* Together, we *will* make a difference. Your school is the place, and now is the time.

- What is your personal educational mission statement? What do you most deeply believe are the goals of education/schooling?
- What is your school's mission and vision statement? Are there any disconnects between what you believe about education and what is articulated as the common cause of your school? If they exist, how do you negotiate these differences?
- How are your actual experiences in school different from these professed missions? Are the lived reality and your core beliefs coherent? How do they diverge and why?
- To what degree are students currently full-fledged partners of your classroom/school? How involved are they in the various levels of decision making? Do they have a voice? Are adults—are you—willing and prepared to listen?

1

Students as Teachers

If we teach today's students as we taught yesterday's,
we rob them of tomorrow.

—John Dewey

LISTEN

Upon entering the classroom, we hear a variety of voices. We are looking for a newly minted teacher and are unable to pick him or her out of the room. The room has about 20 young adults in it. We know (because we have been directed here) that all but one of them are Aspire High students—teenagers, albeit upper-level students. But somewhere in this sea of fresh faces is someone in his or her 20s. So far, this might not be an uncommon scene. Many of us once new to the teaching profession, straight from our undergraduate degrees, have been asked by a parent to be directed to a teacher. Those who have the good fortune of a youthful appearance may still be camouflaged, happily or not, in a room full of older students.

So we look for clues in intonation, behavior, and activity. Surely, a teacher would be teaching. Those in the room are clumped mostly in threes and fours. They are working in groups. Some are gathered around a laptop or other device, some are deep in discussion. One group near the front is somewhat larger. Six people in a jagged semicircle face a whiteboard. A young, neatly dressed woman at the board is explaining a timeline. We approach her, introduce ourselves, and ask if she is the teacher.

A scruffy young man in the semicircle, dressed in khakis and a buttoned-down collar shirt, says, "That would be me. How can I help you?" He tells the student at the whiteboard that she should continue and invites us to the side. We are not entirely surprised, despite the unexpected turn. This is, after all, Aspire High.

Aspire High has, among its core tenets, a belief that young people have something to teach us. This means at least five things:

1. Students can teach us about their future hopes.

2. Students can teach us how they learn best.

3. Students can teach us about the conditions that support their learning.

4. Students can teach us about their interests and areas of expertise as well as the personal experiences of race or otherness that shape their worldview.

5. Students learn by teaching.

First, Aspire High's mission is *to provide all students with the ability to dream and set goals for the future, while inspiring them in the present to reach those dreams.* It is necessary, therefore, for students to teach adults about their hopes and dreams. Genuine aspirations may be influenced by outside factors—the hopes of one's family, role models, economic concerns, and so on. They may also include various broad and intermediate aspirations and goals along the way—postsecondary degrees or certificates, internships, and the like. All of these may be outwardly discernible, and many are evidently common to all students.

But ultimately, each person's particular aspiration arises from within. It is no one's job to dream another's dreams for him or her. Nor is it practical to set out for every student some vague, one-size-fits-all goal to go to college. That's like saying the goal of school is more school! If schools and the adults who staff them are to first and foremost support students in the achievement of the dreams they have for themselves, then first and foremost, the students must teach us who and what they want to be.

This will be an ongoing, emergent experience. Students may change their aspirations as they grow and are exposed to an ever-widening world and its possibilities. Some students will need help to find their passion and path. Adults must take seriously the kindergartener who wants to be a firefighter like his father, as well as the high schooler who wants to be a genetic scientist even though no one in her family has previously gone to college. Teachers must support the student who is struggling to find an identity, as well as those who have "known since they were five" that they wanted to enter a certain field. As students dream bigger and more broadly, their teachers must keep learning from them what they see as their future if they are continuously to inspire them in the present to reach and succeed.

Second, given that same mission, teachers must *learn from each student how he or she learns best*. Most schools have done an excellent job of giving students insights into their learning styles and tendencies. Students know if they are tactile, auditory, or visual learners. They know if they prefer hands-on activities or like to learn from a text. The many learning-style inventories they have been exposed to have developed a degree of meta-cognition that can be extremely helpful to their learning. Students are the foremost experts on how they best learn. This self-awareness accumulates over time, but ironically, the further along in school students progress, the less this is considered important to their learning. Students have this to teach us so that teachers can better support their learning throughout their school experience.

Third, if students have something to teach us about the optimal intrinsic conditions of their learning, they also have something to teach us about *the optimal environmental conditions* of their learning. Consider that eighth graders may have nine to 10 years of familiarity with being schooled. Their point of view on their classroom and school is *expert* (the root of which means "known from experience") and different from our own. They have opinions about when group work is engaging and when it is a distraction. They can teach us when it might be best to read quietly and when they would prefer to be instructed. Students have strong thoughts about peers who disrupt the learning of others, and they know when adults are being condescending. They are good judges of when learning is fun and when having fun is a waste of time. They can teach us about the conditions that affect and improve their learning and what impedes their understanding.

Fourth, students are not tabulae rasae. They enter school with experiences, questions, insights, interests, passions, preferences, likes, dislikes, beliefs, and hobbies. These will continue to develop and change over time. Some know all about dinosaurs; others are adept crafters; still others have a passion for the Revolutionary War. There are elementary school students who can choreograph dances, middle school students who can write code, and high school students who are inventors. There are young and expert mechanics and musicians and moviemakers. *Students have much to teach as experts in their own right about the many things that interest them.*

Furthermore, there is no "color-blindness" at Aspire High. That is to say, race is a factor in students' experiences of the world, as are other physical attributes such as gender or being differently abled. As a result, *students can teach their teachers a great deal about how their backgrounds, thoughts, feelings, and worldviews are shaped by race, particularly if student and teacher come from different racial backgrounds.* Singleton (2013) writes, "When teachers render meaningless any of their students' visible characteristics (including race, sex, age, or physical disability), they give themselves permission not to notice how student characteristics affect student engagement and learning" (p. 105). Since Aspire High seeks student engagement and learning, race as a part of who each student is must be considered.

Fifth and finally, as teachers are well aware, *there is no better way to learn and master something than to teach it.* Students are most effectively learners when they investigate, research, organize, prepare, and then teach their classmates and us what they have learned. As students actively develop lessons, plays, learning experiences, slide decks, and other means of conveying what they have discovered, they move more deeply into the material and understand it in a way they could not have if they had learned it passively from a lecture.

Students at Aspire High teach in all these senses. They teach who they want to be and who they are. They teach what works for their learning and about things they know and want to know. The purpose of their teaching in these first four ways is to set the foundation for their teaching in the fifth way about things all at Aspire High discover through them. At Aspire High, the lines between teaching and learning and between teacher and learner are blurred, nearly beyond recognition.

"Nearly" because adults—those with more experience in learning—have an important role to play. In addition to obvious safety issues, adults must still facilitate, encourage, inspire, guide, probe, and assess the work of younger teacher learners. Far from a laissez-faire approach, when students are teachers, teachers must be highly intentional and expert in the learning process itself. Many of us can admit to teaching on autopilot; but it is impossible to guide the learning of eager, young teacher learners in an unconscious way. Some may think that at Aspire High, where students do most of the teaching, teachers can sit back. On the contrary, teachers at Aspire High must lean forward so that they are fully, mindfully engaged, voraciously learning everything their students are teaching them. Think of how highly focused and attentive driving instructors need to be. Even though they are not in the driver's seat, they must be fully alert and aware precisely because they are not driving. When students are teachers, teachers must have that same kind of expanded, attentive, intentional approach to their students and the environment in which they are learning.

TEACHING TO LEARN

Dashwood Banbury Academy is an Aspirations Academy school located in the Oxfordshire region of England.

Students at Dashwood are routinely asked to teach. Students Natalie, Rabiya, and Daniel were invited to share their thoughts about their experience of teaching at Dashwood Academy.

What does it mean to you when you have the opportunity to teach others?

It means I have the opportunity to pass on information to others and help them to gain useful skills. Also, it can help me learn more about what I'm teaching and to remember the subject. —*Natalie*

It means to me that I have the opportunity to pass on the knowledge that I have gained over the years. It can help others, and sometimes they help me too. —*Rabiya*

It means a lot because it helps other people, and sometimes it helps me as well. It also helps because other people get to learn a lot. —*Daniel*

How does it make you feel?

I feel proud because whoever told me to teach must believe that I have enough knowledge to give it to others. Additionally, I feel nervous and excited. —*Natalie*

I feel confident toward other children—younger and older—and I feel like I can express my feelings with them. I feel grateful and proud of being given this opportunity. —*Rabiya*

It makes me very proud of doing it. It also makes me very grateful for the opportunity. —*Daniel*

What are the benefits to you as a pupil/teacher?

I can learn from my pupils to widen my knowledge. In addition, you can see others progress and you know you have helped them. Your confidence in speaking to a group of people improves, assisting you for the future. —*Natalie*

I think the benefits to me are that sometimes I learn from others, and I can become more confident. My confidence and speaking skill improves. When you teach others, and later on see their progress, you feel proud knowing that you helped them reached their goal and become better. —*Rabiya*

It benefits me by working with little children because I enjoy it, and I don't normally get the opportunity. —*Daniel*

- All three students refer to how having an opportunity to teach helps them learn. In your experience, why does this happen?
- What is the educational benefit of students developing confidence and pride when they teach? Is developing such emotional capacity part of a teacher's responsibility? Why or why not?
- How can you give your students more opportunities to teach?

LEARN

The idea or practice of students as teachers has its roots in myriad educational theories and philosophies. Trends toward student-centered classrooms, active learning, and whole-child learning all provide various levels of teacher-like autonomy and responsibility for students. Student-centered learning by definition is an active experience in which students are responsible for their learning. In schools where students assume active teaching roles, they take on increased levels of responsibility and ownership for their learning and for learning design. Active learning and students as teachers are historically connected to the belief that the primary purpose of school is *for students*, rather than for the transmission of academic content, for supplying workers to an economy (whether industrial, service, knowledge-worker, global, etc.), or for ensuring all citizens have a common body of knowledge. If the purpose of school is for the students—for the development of each student's full potential, what we call their Aspirations—then students must be actively participating in developing and delivering their schooling. They should be engaged in what is traditionally thought of as teaching.

Progressive educators have long asserted the importance of students learning through coconstructing their experiences. Although there are many definitions of a progressive education, it is widely agreed that it involves active participation by all students in decisions that will affect their lives. Likewise, constructivist educators have cautioned that "sage on the stage" teaching simply does not work. Constructivism calls for a much more active role in learning on the part of the students. As early as 1938, Dewey wrote the following:

> There is, I think, no point in the philosophy of progressive education which is sounder than its emphasis upon the importance of the participation of the learner in the formation of the purposes which direct his activities in the learning process, just as there is no defect in traditional education greater than its failure to secure the active cooperation of the pupil in construction of the purposes involved in his studying. (p. 77)

Theorists such as Dewey (1938), Piaget (1957), and Vygotsky (1978) and educators such as Montessori (1964), Perrone (1991), and Noddings

(2003) are among dozens of professionals who have all contributed to and advocated for student-centered learning. Likewise, Goodlad's introduction of nongraded schools, Sizer's essential school movement, Wiggington's Foxfire project, Meier's student-centered schools, and Quaglia's Aspiration Academies in England all encourage learning environments supportive of students as central, active participants in their teaching and learning environments. In such schools, students are involved in what they learn, how they learn, when they learn, and where they learn, as well as having voice and choice about the teaching that leads to their learning. Accordingly, at Aspire High students teach.

Despite this decades-long call to put students at the center of their learning where they construct meaning, make connections, and work toward goals they set for themselves, many schools continue with a traditional "sit and 'git'" approach to education. The challenge with many progressive models, theories, and philosophies is that all too often they remain simply abstractions. Well-intentioned educators may dip into these ideas to use bits and pieces that work for them, but these approaches pervade neither classroom nor school. Nor are they the organizing principles of the underlying systems and structures—from teaching and learning to assessment to district committees to cocurricular activities—within which most teachers operate. Those systems are still dominated by a teacher-as-expert approach and an industrial mindset that sees the acquisition of knowledge divided into specialized disciplines as a model of efficiency. Add the agricultural calendar that schools cannot seem to shake, and we have a fundamentally outmoded approach to teaching and learning that rewards with advancement those students who successfully negotiate the system and fails those who most challenge it. It is a system designed to sort potential white-collar leaders and managers from blue-collar workers that still, more or less, effectively does what it was designed to do. The tail that keeps vigorously wagging this dog is high-stakes standardized testing.

Even many student-centered theories do not include students in the full implementation of student-centered schooling. Ironically, adults research, adults design, adults develop, and adults teach roomfuls of adults how to be more student centered. As Fullan (1991) so pointedly stated, "We hardly know anything about what students think about educational change because no one ever asks them" (p. 182). At Aspire High, Student Voice guides and drives all decisions. Student Voice is not paid lip service; rather, it is a way of being (Quaglia & Corso, 2014). Student Voice does not negate or supplant the role of adults but with Teacher Voice is considered a necessary dialogue partner for *effective* teaching and learning.

> **Michael Fullan** is a worldwide authority on educational reform with a mandate of helping to achieve the moral purpose of all children learning. He has authored numerous books on school change at the structural and systemic level.

At Aspire High, learning emerges from interchange and partnership, not from lecture and power-over.

The students-as-teachers model subverts the top-down model still prevalent in many schools in which the teacher leads instruction and students are expected to follow attentively. In such a model, teachers are thought of as classroom "managers" and deliver instruction. While new pedagogical approaches (i.e., hands-on learning, problem-based learning, team learning, integrating technology, having students collaborate, etc.) may make the experience more student-friendly, the underlying paradigm remains the same: The classroom is the teacher's world, and the students are just living in it. However, when students teach, learning shifts from being something transmitted from teacher to student to something *internalized* by the student with the support of the teacher. At Aspire High, the goal of this internalization is to sponsor and inspire students as they strive toward their dreams. An Aspire High classroom is a laboratory for learning in which students and teacher together experiment with experiences, ideas, content, opinions, and real-world activities to hypothesize, test, and prove to one another that what they are learning best promotes their stated goals, hopes, and dreams.

To effect this "upside-down" approach, we need to ask with Fullan (1991), "What would happen if we treated the student as someone whose opinion mattered?" (p. 170). This is a no-cost, achievable-tomorrow starting place. Prior to actually having students teach, Aspire High begins with the belief that students have something to teach us. Kozol (1991) wrote, "The voices of children . . . have been missing from the whole discussion" of education and educational reform (p. 5). According to Cook-Sather (2006), "Student voice, in its most profound and radical form, calls for a cultural shift that opens up spaces and minds not only to the sound but also to the presence and power of students" (p. 5). At Aspire High, adults are asking for, listening to, and learning from Student Voice. Hattie's (2012) meta-analysis shows that teachers' openness to feedback from students on their learning has a .72 effect size on their achievement—among the highest.

Once the adult population is open to taking seriously the opinions, ideas, and voices of students, the school can grow toward the

Jonathan Kozol is best known for his 50 years of work among our nation's poorest and most vulnerable children. He has since devoted nearly his entire life to the challenge of providing equal opportunity to every child in our public schools. *Savage Inequalities* (1991) is his seminal work related to education in poor areas.

John Hattie is an internationally renowned educational researcher most noted for his advocacy of knowing the effect size of the educational strategies one employs. Professor Hattie has been Director of the Melbourne Educational Research Institute at the University of Melbourne, Australia, since March 2011.

fivefold approach to students teaching (as outlined previously). Students then teach about their future hopes, their present inspiration, the conditions that support their learning, their experiences, and what they are discovering and learning. These five elements of students-as-teachers divide into two broad categories. The first four are grounded in what students already know—though none of these is static and all are in constant development. The fifth approach is entirely emergent and is grounded not in what students know, but in what they are coming to know. The first four lay the groundwork for the primary work of schooling, which is the latter.

Students as Teachers of What They Already Know

The first teaching role students must be afforded is to tutor adults about who they are and who they want to be. According to the *Quaglia School Voice National Report* (*QSVNR*), only 52% of students agree with the statement "Teachers make an effort to get to know me," and just 36% agreed that "My teacher knows my hopes and dreams." Knowing students is fundamental to the teaching and learning environment at Aspire High. All students share their hopes, dreams, and talents with the adults and their peers. Adults, in turn, offer autonomy support, which is the interpersonal behavior teachers provide to identify, nurture, and build students' inner motivational resources (Deci & Ryan, 1985; Reeve & Jang, 2006). After this first student teaching practice is established, the learning environment becomes a place that incubates students' personal hopes and dreams. The mission of Aspire High can only be fulfilled if all of the adults have been taught by their students what and who each aspires to be:

> Education, by its very nature, should help people to develop their best selves—to become people with pleasing talents, useful and satisfying occupations, self-understanding, sound character, a host of appreciations, and a commitment to continuous learning. (Noddings, 2003, p. 23)

Knowing students' hopes and dreams seems like a simple idea. Yet this is more than merely asking students *what* they want to do after high school, since many of the opportunities and careers our students will pursue do not even exist today. *Knowing a young person's hopes and dreams encompasses knowing who our students want to be.* Do you want to work outside? Work with people? Contribute to your community? Work in the sciences? Are you

Nel Noddings is well known for her writing related to the ethics of care and education. *The Challenge to Care in Schools* (1992), *Educating Moral People* (2002), and *Happiness and Education* (2003) are among her best-known works.

an artist? Do you imagine yourself doing the same thing for decades? Do you see yourself in an office? Do you want to travel? The adult's role as "learner" here is to not settle for simple one-term responses: "professional athlete" or "store owner" or "veterinarian." Rather, the adult's role is to inquire about how being a veterinarian interests and expresses who the student wants to be. What personal attributes drive you toward wanting to own your own business? To want to direct movies? To want to be a teacher?

The adult role is also to provide context and lend longer experience to the conversation about goals. As we have seen, the definition of aspirations includes not just the future—dreams, goals—but also inspiration and action in the present. Teachers can provide grounding, not in order to deflate a student's dreams—on the contrary, to encourage and promote movement toward those dreams. For example, according to a survey of close to 5,000 students, 72% of high school students want to start a business someday (Schawbel, 2014). Yet typically just over half of all ventures survive into a fourth year (Statistic Brain, 2016). Another example lies with the many young boys who want to be professional athletes. The NCAA publishes statistics on what percentage of high school athletes become professionals (http://ncaa.org). How does this type of information affect a teaching-and-learning environment that begins with students teaching adults about their aspirations? What role does it play in sponsoring students toward their dreams?

In addition to teaching the adults they work with in school who they want to be, students can teach adults about who they are now. Just over half (53%) of students agree with the statement "Teachers care about me as an individual" (QSVNR, 2016). Fundamental to any reciprocal learning experience is knowing the learner. While a traditional approach to teaching and learning may consider personal exchange irrelevant, at Aspire High it is key to the mutuality that leads to the coaching and guidance that inspires students in the present to reach for the goals they have set for their futures.

A conventional route for knowing students in this way comes in the form of an inventory or treasure hunt. While such activities help teachers to know their students, the typical worksheet is used once, filed away, and rarely referred to. However, when students are given the ongoing responsibility of teaching adults about themselves, it is no longer up to the adult to ask, "What did you do this weekend?" It becomes the responsibility of the student to let adults know she recently earned a new belt in karate or that he is becoming interested in pursuing a career in farming. When student interests drive learning, learning cannot occur until interests are known. Without the input of the learners, it becomes impossible to build curriculum and plan lessons or to set objectives and assess whether goals have been met. Educated in an understanding of who is in the classroom *particularly* (not just a general understanding that there are students in the classroom), students and adults can then partner in personalizing lessons and assignments.

The second approach that helps define and build a culture supportive of students as teachers is understanding what inspires them to learn. According to the *QSVNR* (2016), 57% of high school seniors agree with the statement "School inspires me to learn." Inspiration arises from within, whereas motivation is typically externally generated. An example of motivation would be a coach's pep talk. Teachers sometimes try to motivate students to achieve something the *teacher* wants them to achieve—high test scores, better behavior—and may use a carrot-and-stick, pep-talk-like approach that may or may not work. Motivation is about one person trying to move another.

However, inspiration is about moving oneself. School, classes, and teachers spark inspiration when there are trusting, caring, and mentoring relationships and when they tap into individuals' own interests. One way to do this in a school setting is with the right combination of skills, challenges, and support (Quaglia & Corso, 2014). Teachers need students to educate them about what inspires them—that is, what challenges their current skill level and what support they need to succeed. Is it adult role models? Is it a particular field or subject? Is it another person's energy, enthusiasm, and drive? Or all of these and more?

According to Csikszentmihalyi, "Enjoyment appears at the boundary between boredom and anxiety, when the challenges are just balanced with a person's capacity to act" (1990, p. 50). To understand one's own levels of boredom and capabilities requires self-assessment and reflection. This reflection can be encouraged and supported by adult educators and lead in turn to students teaching the adults what they have learned about what inspires them. The narrow assessment of student capacity provided by tests scores does not provide the feedback necessary to judge the inspiration that leads to future success. And whereas academic assessments can be breathtakingly costly, asking what students are inspired by is priced at about half a breath.

> **Mihaly Csikszentmihalyi** is one of the pioneers of the scientific study of happiness and is considered the father of positive psychology. The main thesis of Csikszentmihalyi's most popular book, *Flow: The Psychology of Optimal Experience* (1990), is that happiness is not a fixed state, but can be developed as we learn to achieve flow in our lives.

Inspiration is necessary for both present-moment and lifelong learning. According to research by Thrash and Elliot (2003), mastery of work, absorption, creativity, perceived competence, self-esteem, and optimism were all *consequences* of inspiration. Inspiration fosters these important psychological resources. Another recent study by Milyavskaya and colleagues (2012) showed the connection between inspiration and goal progress with college students. Those who scored higher in the trait *inspiration* reported increased goal progress, and their progress was a result of setting more inspired goals. Therefore, people who were generally more inspired in their daily lives also tended to set inspired goals, which were then more likely to be successfully attained. Inspiration is a kind of perpetual-motion mechanism. Sadly, school can dispirit, instead of inspirit, far too many students. At Aspire High, where there is a mission to support all students in achieving the goals they set for themselves, much time is spent on cultivating inspiration.

Even given a desire to improve students' test scores—a goal Aspire High considers important, but not central—inspiration is a critical factor. A recent study by William Hiss (2014) showed no significant difference in the success rates of students who submit their standardized test scores to colleges and those who don't. A report in the *Eastern Economic Journal* (French et al., 2015) stated results consistently show that high school GPA is a positive and statistically significant predictor of educational attainment and earnings in adulthood. Given the fact that a high GPA often results from inspiration and effort, it makes logical sense for schools to focus on inspiration as a factor in success over a body-of-content knowledge measured by test scores. In fact, tests such as the SAT are now becoming optional for many college admissions since there is little correlation between these scores and collegiate success.

A third approach wherein students are teachers at Aspire High stems from the fact that students and adults see the world differently. Actually, each person sees the world differently than others, and the same is true of each person's view of school. Students possess unique knowledge about their school that adults cannot fully replicate (Mitra, 2009). How often has a teacher taught a lesson she thought was close to perfect only to find out her students were bored or really didn't understand the lesson? In nearly every learning situation, point of view matters. One student may count the paragraphs in eager anticipation of his turn to read aloud, whereas another may dread the very thought of speaking in front of others.

In considering how students experience school, a study from the Quaglia Institute for Student Aspirations (QISA) indicates that six out of 10 (62%) students enjoy working on projects with other students, and nearly eight out of 10 (78%) enjoy learning new things (*QSCVR*, 2016). What does this student viewpoint teach about the best learning environment and experiences? The finding that most students like project-based and collaborative learning is not new; however, far too many classrooms still rely on solo worksheets and one-to-30 lectures and slide decks. If students are communicating how they like to learn and how they learn best, then those who educate them need to listen. As schools continue to move toward more project-based learning, students must be involved in lesson development—or at least be brought into discussions about their learning. Efforts by teachers to change practice can be resisted, subverted, or rejected by students if students do not support or understand them (Erickson & Schultz, 1992; Levin, 2000).

A fourth important piece of information students need to teach adults is about their life experiences. "Youth have the best understanding of the realities of their own lives (whether it is education, health, or the challenges associated with finding a decent job) and as such have much to offer policy-makers" (Youth Employment Network, 2007, p. 11). Aspire High affirms a constructive approach in which knowledge is dependent on the meaning attributed to experiences by a learner or community of learners. A learner's experiences allow him or her to interpret what he or she is learning. An awareness of and the need for culturally responsive pedagogy (CRP) also support this understanding of the importance of student experiences. Gloria Ladson-Billings (1994) created the term *culturally relevant pedagogy* to describe "a pedagogy that empowers students intellectually, socially, emotionally, and politically by using cultural referents to impart knowledge, skills, and attitudes" (p. 17). Teachers who use CRP strategies use the backgrounds, knowledge, and experiences of students to inform their lessons and methodology.

Not only are student experiences an important source and destination for their learning (and so critical for them to teach), but if teachers truly listen to students share their experiences and invite them to actively construct the learning process, then Student Voice can be closely linked to school improvement (Cook-Sather, 2002, 2006; Robinson & Taylor, 2007; Rudduck & Flutter, 2004; Rudduck & McIntyre, 2007). Beyond the classroom itself as a learning environment, Aspire High solicits student experiences and opinions to shape everything from the choice of cafeteria food to curricula.

> **Gloria Ladson-Billings** is a professor at the University of Wisconsin–Madison. For further insights into her work, see "Toward a Theory of Culturally Relevant Pedagogy," *American Educational Research Journal*, Fall 1995, *32*(3), 465–499.

Students as Teachers of What They Are Coming to Know

Because of the commitments to have students teach adults who they are and want to be, what inspires them, and what they are presently engaged in, the culture of Aspire High is conducive for students to teach and learn in partnership with adults. With a foundation firmly set in an experience of adults knowing about and caring who they are, young people can risk the ignorance that leads to new learning and discovery. That project of emerging knowledge is most effectively pursued in teaching what one is discovering to others. It has long been known that to truly learn something you must teach it.

At Aspire High, teachers are called to share the responsibility for teaching with students. Sometimes sharing responsibility seems like too great a risk. Yet it may be easier to see the logic of this idea from its converse: The more we take responsibility away from students, the greater their lack of responsibility and possibly their lack of engagement. This in turn may lead to challenging and unwanted behavior. By increasing student responsibility for all parts of the classroom experience through sharing in what are traditionally teacher tasks, students become fully invested in the learning experience.

Nowhere is this on more prominent display at Aspire High than in the many habits that have students working with other students to support each other's learning. One such practice is a peer-mediated support strategy in which students support peers who struggle academically due to cognitive or other learning disabilities. This set of alternative teaching and learning strategies employs the use of students as instructors for others students in their classes. The positive effects of peer-mediated instruction and intervention (PMII), in particular with students with mild disabilities, are well documented in the literature (Maheady, Harper, & Mallette, 2001). While Aspire High engages in peer-to-peer learning with all students and as a matter of course, it also makes possible a much greater degree of inclusion than if adults solely are responsible for providing such support.

THE POWER OF STUDENT AGENCY

Daniel Kyne, fifth-year student, Scoil Dara, Ireland

Daniel is a member of the International Advisory Board of Excited.ie, Ireland.

In school in Ireland, everyone is learning the same thing. There are so many things that people haven't tried.

For example, youth entrepreneurship—18 months ago, I became involved in entrepreneurship. I knew no one of my age who was similarly involved. Teachers were inexperienced in entrepreneurship, and I soon became a supporter and sometimes teacher for my friends. There was a certain amount of pressure because friends expected me to know everything about entrepreneurship, even though my experience was limited.

Students react differently and well when they are given agency, and power is put into their hands to do things. Once you have any kind of experience as an agent rather than an object of learning, it is very hard to go back. It's like you realize the way things are currently done isn't the best way. You realize that some people's words carry more weight. When a teacher tells you, you take their word for it. It seems as if teachers' knowledge is valued more. (This may be unfair to teachers as well as students.) Lack of trust can come between students and teachers when there is imbalance. They say that student opinions are important, but they are not received in that way.

It is only in this last year that it feels as if my opinions have begun to be valued by teachers. Yet students can be teachers. In these circumstances, perhaps teachers can mediate how well the students teach.

Technology allows students to learn information before they spend school time discussing it. That way, time when at school can be used best.

Everyone becomes a teacher; it's not just the textbook but everyone's opinion that matters. There's a big difference between a teacher and trainer. Education is about having a voice and being able to share.

- Daniel notes that at his school "teachers were inexperienced in entrepreneurship." What are some subjects or topics that students at your school may know more about than teachers? How could their expertise be part of the teaching and learning experience?
- In your experience, how do students react differently when they are given agency? What are some of the challenges of sharing power with students? How is this different from having power over students? How is it different from turning power over to students?
- Do you believe the imbalance in power—that teachers' words "carry more weight"—contributes to a lack of trust between students and teachers? Explain. How could this imbalance be corrected?
- Daniel says that when students teach "perhaps teachers can mediate how well the students teach." Discuss his proposal of shifting roles. In your classroom/school, what steps would need to be taken so that students could teach and teachers mediate how well they teach?

For Reflection

- ◇ What have you learned from students about teaching and learning? What have students taught you, either directly or indirectly, about best educational practices?
- ◇ Describe a time that a student's or a group of students' different perspective made you think differently. What was your starting point of view? How did it change as a result of the student point of view?
- ◇ Discuss with colleagues the challenges of taking a student-as-teachers approach to education. What are the biggest obstacles? What is the greatest promise?
- ◇ Ask a group of students how you could support them in taking more ownership of their learning. What greater responsibility would they like to take on individually? Collectively?

LEAD

By now it should be clear that *the best way to become engaged in learning is to take ownership of what is being taught.* There is no better way to engage students than by having them accept greater responsibility for their own learning and giving them the opportunity and responsibility to teach others. At Aspire High, this peer-to-peer teaching approach also supports inclusion and the accommodations necessary to help all kinds of learners. Teachers need not be overstretched if students are able to work with one other in a teaching capacity. Accepting such responsibility is the key to engaged, meaningful, and lifelong learning. We increasingly see the ineffectiveness and futility of "sit and 'git'" methods of instruction. A class in which a student is merely the passive recipient of the well-meaning activity of some adult instructor is not only increasingly obsolete, but inevitably unproductive.

By definition, ultimate leadership for student-centered learning resides with the student. Only he or she can accept responsibility for putting in the attention and effort necessary to study, learn, understand, and know more than he or she currently does. *Each student is the agent—that is, the leader—of his or her own learning.* However, as in all things presented in this book, improving your school is a team effort. That inherent belief has us identifying the leadership challenges for all the key stakeholders in the education community that have a responsibility to promote the notion of students as teachers.

Schools are systems, and effective leadership attends to the functional relationships among all parts of the system. Thus, in order to lead students as teachers, there must be a leadership role for principals, teachers, and students. Remember, leading school change is a marathon—depending on your starting place, be prepared to *Step*, *Stride*, or *Sprint*.

On your mark. Get set! Go!!

PRINCIPAL

Step ⟹

- *Intentionally spend time in the hallways and classrooms getting to know students and teachers.* A leader who expects to work closely with students and teachers must ensure she or he knows who they are and what issues they believe are important.
- *Involve students and teachers in shaping the school's discipline/student management system.* Giving students more ownership of their learning in the classroom leads to greater engagement and personal responsibility. The same is true for school rules. Allowing students greater autonomy over their behavior is a simple and effective strategy.

Stride ⟹

- *Conduct regular focus groups to gain deeper insight into student and teacher issues.* This takes time and planning but allows administrators to have a deeper understanding of what students and staff are thinking about themselves and the school.
- *Invite students to be part of some staff meetings.* Students should have an opportunity to share with others what they are doing and what they believe will lead to better outcomes for themselves. Active student participation in faculty and staff meetings must be encouraged and fostered by administration.

Sprint ⟹

- *Include students in all meetings when appropriate.* Ensuring that students be included at a faculty meeting is one thing; however, having students participate in curriculum meetings, staff search committees, building leadership teams, teacher-based teams, budget meetings, and the like is really giving students responsibility for their school. Make sure they are a part of decision making in every available way.
- *Require all classrooms to use both formative student feedback as well as student self-assessment.* Of all the things that can be done to ensure the notion of *students as teachers*, nothing is more powerful than consistent and purposeful feedback from students about themselves and the teaching and learning environment. For some principals, this would be a bold thing to enforce, but for others, it is only natural if they expect classrooms to be student centered.

TEACHERS

Step ⟹

- *Begin lessons by connecting to student experiences.* Without a doubt, one of the easiest and most powerful things teachers can do is to know the interests of their students. If teachers do not understand the interests of their students, getting them engaged is merely happenstance. By dumb luck, some examples and lessons will connect meaningfully with the students, but many others will not. Making these connections more intentional begins with learning about students' interests.
- *Develop classroom rules and expectations with your students.* Classroom rules apply to everyone equally. They are not just rules to be followed only by the students and enforced only by a teacher. Everyone is mutually accountable to one another for following and enforcing the rules. Therefore, students should be responsible for both developing the classroom behavior expectations and being accountable to the rules they create. Teachers need to be accountable as well.

Stride ⟹

- *Flip the learning in the classroom.* Let students work together and share their knowledge/expertise during class time. Flipping learning includes realizing that students can learn more working and learning together than listening to a lecture.
- *Know all your students' hopes and dreams.* When teachers know their students' hopes and dreams, students are 18 times more likely to be academically motivated to learn—need we say more?!

Sprint ⟹

- *Coteach with your students.* Have no doubt that this will take more time than presenting the lesson alone, but it will be well worth it—not only for the student who is teaching, but for the other students in the classroom as well.
- *Create opportunities for students to self-assess their work.* Having students assess themselves—provided there is a rubric for assessment—rarely disappoints. In many cases, students are harder on themselves than a teacher would be. Self-assessment teaches students responsibility, self-awareness, and, in some cases, humility.

STUDENTS

Step ===>

- *Share your aspirations with teachers.* It is impossible for teachers to relate to students if they do not know anything about you. Spend a few minutes with teachers and let them know your hopes and dreams for the future. The responsibility for teachers getting to know you is not theirs alone.
- *Attend voluntary after-school meetings and clubs to provide your opinions and ideas.* Traditional schools rarely track down students to elicit their thoughts. Therefore, it is up to students to ensure their voice is being heard. The only way that is going to happen is if students ask to be a part of school decisions and show up to meetings that involve their concerns.

Stride ===>

- *Actively and productively engage in social media that promotes Student Voice.* Students, typically, are more social-media savvy than the adults in their school. Use that advantage to engage social media to promote Student Voice and to learn from the voices of others.
- *Teach someone outside of school what you are learning.* There is no better way to master learning than to be able to teach what you know to others. It is a rewarding experience to share your knowledge and excitement of learning to others, whether formally or informally. Do this as often as possible, especially when people ask, "How is school?" Instead of answering with a generic, "Fine," tell them what you have learned recently.

Sprint ===>

- *Run for a position at your school, local council, or community government.* It is never too early or too late to run for any kind of office. Students who are serious about making school a better place need to put themselves in positions that can influence positive changes. Holding a leadership position is one way to do exactly that. Consider how you will stand up for what you believe in as a leader.
- *Attend and speak at school board meetings.* One of the greatest fears of many people is public speaking. However, students who want to be leaders of change must overcome that fear and be prepared to share their voices in a meaningful and purposeful way with others. If you are going to present or speak, be sure you have done your research and have collected the evidence you need to have your position taken seriously.

Is Your School . . . ?		
TYPICAL HIGH	ASPIRE HIGH	ASPIRING HIGHER
Adults sporadically listen to students.	Adults listen to and learn from students.	Adults colearn with students.
Teachers give some responsibility to students for their learning.	Teachers encourage students to take full responsibility for their learning.	Teachers expect students to be responsible for their own and other students' learning.
There are opportunities for students to share their thoughts and ideas on topics that teachers or administrators decide.	Students are allowed to suggest opportunities and to share their thoughts and ideas.	Students consistently influence the curriculum, as well as teachers and school leaders, with their thoughts and ideas.
Some teachers know some of the hopes and dreams of some students.	Teachers know all of the students' aspirations and infuse them into lessons.	Teachers and students design the curriculum around the hopes and dreams of students.
Students do presentations on lessons the teachers determine.	Students lead the teaching.	Students and teachers cocreate lessons and develop curriculum.
Staff invite students to important meetings.	Students invite staff to important meetings.	Students and staff regularly meet together.
Student government/council is a popularity contest and club.	Student government has fluid participation and a meaningful role in school governance.	Student government includes voting positions on school board.
Students self-assess according to rubrics with little impact on grades.	Student self-assessment is part of the grading process.	Students determine their own course grades in conversation with teachers.
The discipline code is determined and enforced by adults with opportunity for students to share "their side."	The code of conduct includes restorative justice practices and peer adjudication.	The code of conduct is created, adhered to, and administered by joint teams of students and teachers.
The grade portal posts grades reported by the teacher.	The grade portal includes short narratives written by students.	Students enter their own grades and narratives into the grade portal.
Students participate in parent-teacher conferences once or twice a year on set days.	Students lead regular parent-teacher conferences as scheduled by students.	In addition to in-person meetings, a variety of means are used to communicate with parents, both synchronously and asynchronously, with methods that work best for the parents, not just the ones that are convenient for the school.

Is Your School . . . ?		
TYPICAL HIGH	**ASPIRE HIGH**	**ASPIRING HIGHER**
Teachers know students superficially as a student (among many) in their class.	Teachers and students know one another as learners.	Teacher and student relationships are the basis for learning.
The principal mostly knows students who are "frequent flyers."	The principal regularly invites students to meetings and conversations.	All principal decisions are made with student input.
Individual learning plans are for students with special needs and accommodations.	All students have a personalized learning plan.	The entire high school experience is personalized.
Ratios of guidance counselors to students make "guidance" about scheduling and academic emergencies.	All teachers take on a guidance role in supporting students academically and aspirationally.	There is a structured plan to involve community members in a guidance role.
There is little to no connection to the middle school—the transition occurs all in one day.	There are regular visits to and from middle schools.	Middle school students can take classes at the high school; high school students teach and mentor upcoming middle school students.
First-year orientation is brief and led by adults.	First-year orientation is planned and led by students.	Student-led orientation is followed by ongoing student mentoring in the first year.
The connection to the outside community is tenuous and frequently characterized by negative interactions.	Student learning includes community internships.	The community is regularly involved in student learning through in-school and in-community experiences.

2

Teachers as Learners

Learning is a result of listening, which in turn leads to even better listening and attentiveness to the other person. In other words, to learn from the child, we must have empathy, and empathy grows as we learn.

—Alice Miller

LISTEN

The scruffy young man who introduced himself as the teacher invites us to an unoccupied table along the side of the room. All of the activity in the room continues without interruption. As we glance around, we notice that there is nothing that distinguishes this table from any of the others in the room. It is not a typical "teacher's desk" (larger than the others, a kind of office on four legs); it's just a working space. In fact, there is an assortment of working spaces in the room: a few carrels that invite solo work along the edges, computer stations with rolling chairs, two high-top tables with some students standing and others on stools. There are regular tables with chairs around them and a few that have fitness balls as seats.

He pushes aside a laptop to make room, and we sit down in reasonably comfortable chairs. Before we begin, a student approaches and says, "Hey, Steve, can I interrupt for a second?" Steve nods. "Did you say that we should plan for a quiz on Friday or Monday?"

Steve responds, "Can you do a quick poll and see what works best for most people? I'll have you do an announcement before we wrap up."

"OK."

We can't help but begin our conversation with "*Steve*?"

He explains: "At Aspire High, each adult in the building decides how he or she wants to be addressed. The only rule is that we address students as we ask to be addressed. I have colleagues of all ages, not just the younger ones, who go by their first name with the students and address the students by their first names. There are others who go with a more traditional 'Mr.' or 'Ms.' and likewise address the students formally by their last names. It works. The students seem to get it. Everyone feels respected. No one seems to have issues with the variation."

We quip, "To each his own."

"It's more than that, I think," Steve replies. "It's about a personalized approach to teaching and learning. It's what the adult decides best suits his or her personality and way of being with young people. For some, the informality of first names creates a more conducive atmosphere for learning, given their style; for others, using titles does that. Two of my colleagues have PhDs. The students call one of them 'Doc' and the other 'Professor Kate.' In Doc's class, he uses first names for the students. In Kate's class, she goes with Mr. Tom, Ms. Juanita—so a combination of formal and first names just as she is addressed. Since we leave this choice up to all adults, custodians and support staff feel respected because they—not their role—determine how to be addressed by students and the professional staff."

We respond, "I suppose if it helps teachers build a positive learning relationship with their students, . . . that's what matters most."

"It helps us, too," Steve adds. "We learn as much about ourselves when we make that decision as we do about our subject. It's Job One of being a Lead Learner."

"Lead Learner?" we inquire.

"Oh, that's how we refer to the job. We're not 'teachers,' we're 'Lead Learners.'"

A professor of education once remarked that the most profound thing she had ever heard about education was that it was like dog food: Those who research it, who develop it, who package it, who market it, and who lovingly open it and serve it do not have to eat it (attribution unknown). While the comparison may be overdrawn, there is truth in it. Teaching is trending toward an approach in which prepackaged, heavily marketed curricula and assessments based on "industry standards" are dished out by adults to young consumers of education. In far too many schools, teachers are expected to follow a script, to not deviate from normed guidelines, and to stay on pace. The cumulative effect of this trend is that teaching is increasingly about "canned" instruction and decreasingly about learning—either for students or for teachers.

At Aspire High, this tendency is reversed. Teachers not only learn, but they are expected to lead the learning. They don't simply initiate teaching that is instruction; they instigate their own and their students' learning. They ask and pursue genuine questions they do not have answers to. They frequently admit they don't know. They engage in research. They read. They take classes. They study.

Teachers at Aspire High are learners in at least three senses. First, *they learn when students teach* in the ways discussed in the previous chapter. As students share who they are, who they want to be, and what they want to do, as they share what they know and are learning, adults learn from them. This learning must be active. In all the ways young people teach, adults need to listen attentively, question helpfully, add insights, offer their own judgments and experiences, suggest alternatives, and push toward further learning. No one is served if schools simply replace adults-as-lecturers delivering information into empty-headed young people with young-people-as-lecturers delivering information into full-headed adults.

Second, *adults are the school's "leading learners."* They are learning role models, continually curious, constantly questioning, wondering, probing, failing, and pushing themselves and the young people in their classes to go further, deeper, and broader. Both teaching and learning are skills. As such, they both require apprenticeship, ongoing practice, mentoring, and mastery. To become a lifelong learner requires coaching and guidance for as long as possible. School is an ideal time for young people to apprentice themselves to the lifelong learning of professional learners. Apprenticeship has been an effective means of educating the next generation in the economies of the past and can be just as effective as a means of educating students in a time when the most important skill is to learn and adapt.

This role of Lead Learner carries with it the responsibility to be a *guardian* of the learning for the school. There are so many competing interests, goals, and required outcomes in the current school system. These include everything from making a certain grade on a district report card to improving test scores to creating good citizens. Teachers at Aspire High constantly focus their own and everyone's attention on how any new proposal the school undertakes contributes to *learning*. This effort to emphasize and prioritize learning is at the core of what it means to teach at Aspire High.

Third, *professional educators must themselves continually hone their craft.* This includes reading professionally, conducting research, taking classes, observing colleagues, having professional conversations, writing, and experimenting. Alongside the learning done from and with students, educators need to be learning from and with each other. This ongoing update is no different than in other professions where new research, discoveries, ideas, techniques, and tools require continuing study and scholarship.

In the field of education, recent developments in brain research, game-based learning, and improvement science are just a few of the cutting-edge areas teachers must learn about.

This third aspect of teachers' learning from each other takes on a special form during the first two years of a teacher's experience at Aspire High. Aspire High recognizes that these are critical and formative years of the teaching profession and so invests up front in developing long-term professional capacity. Newly hired Lead Learners are paired with a veteran mentor from the outset. Mentor and mentee work beside each other for half of every school day during the first year and closely during the second year. While Aspire High seeks to employ teachers who "look good on paper," the school and its leaders are fully aware that, as a *practice*, becoming an effective professional Lead Learner involves on-the-job training. Having a good transcript from a reputable college of education is no guarantee of effective teaching and does not substitute for the sharp learning curve of the first few years of being in the classroom. Aspire High ensures that new teachers have time to discuss, question, and reflect on their teaching practices with those who have longer experience.

The professional development of all Lead Learners at Aspire High is directly connected to students as teachers and teachers as colleagues. Learning sessions, book studies, observation, and the other tools of professional learning include students. Typically, the traditional purpose of teacher evaluation is for teachers to learn and be held accountable—and currently leans heavily toward the latter of the two purposes. As a result, even the current observe-three-times model (an improvement over the observe-once model) tends to be more of a "gotcha" as evaluators sandwich a needed area of improvement between two positive strokes about a job well done. At the end of the day (i.e., at the end of the year), this type of evaluation is part of a fire-or-rehire process.

At Aspire High, the focus is not on evaluation in this sense, but rather on teacher growth and formation based on what the teacher is consistently, constantly learning and applying. Teacher learning, in turn, is directed by the teacher and is informed by the school's goals. Teachers are not just learning for learning's sake but for their students' sakes—more to the point, for their students' aspirations' sakes. Obviously, students are integral to this growth process. Teachers are held accountable for their learning as it applies to student learning and outcomes. *Inevitably, this learning must make a contribution to their effectiveness as a pedagogue, classroom manager, caring adult role model, and so on.*

LEARN

Aspire High expects teachers to be *learning all the time*. Note how this is different from the prevailing focus on "instructional time." If we were to adopt the language of that model, at Aspire High teachers are not expected to "teach from bell to bell"; they are expected to guarantee the learning from bell to bell. In an era when knowledge is not only ubiquitous but also changing at a rapid and uncertain pace, teacher and student learning—not mere instructional time—is crucial for successful student outcomes. If you ask a teacher at Aspire High what his or her job is, the reply will be, "I am a Lead Learner."

Centrality of Learning for All

Being a Lead Learner at Aspire High requires teachers to assume primary responsibility for ensuring learning is a central and continuous topic of conversation and decision making. No doubt in many instances discussions and decisions are based on financial concerns, efficiency, inflexible state or district policies, confusion over what is equitable, what is expedient for adults, and time constraints, to name just a few. However, Lead Learners at Aspire High assume primary responsibility for ensuring that conversations about all topics are professional and robust and include an emphasis on learning. Accordingly, when staff and students discuss student management, school budgets, or any school policy or practice, questions around learning always surface and are actively pursued. Here are some examples:

- If a consequence for poor student choices is an in-school or out-of-school suspension, teachers first reflect and learn about the impact of that decision on that particular student and discuss how this will affect the student's learning.
- If the state requires more tests and professional development related to testing, the teachers question the school board and write to the state commissioner to ask him or her to articulate how this requirement is a path to more learning.
- When teachers are absent from school, conversations about the impact on student and teacher learning arise.
- When candidates are interviewed to join the staff, they are asked what they have learned recently.
- When the school calendar is being developed, adequate time is set aside for teacher learning to be ample, applicable, and meaningful.

The concern for learning is relentless, and every effort is made for learning to trump all other decision-making factors.

When teachers' teaching is displaced as the central activity in the classroom in favor of everyone (including teachers') learning, those in education whose identity is tied to traditional teaching can become disoriented. But when invited to refocus their attention and efforts on their own and their students' learning, the adults at Aspire High find not just better balance, but a renewed sense of purpose in the educational vocation. According to Sykes (1996), "Teacher learning must be at the heart of any effort to improve education in our society. While other reforms may be needed, better learning for more children ultimately relies on teachers" (p. 465). Nearly all teachers we talk with became educators to make a difference—in the lives of their students, in their communities, and in the world. When that noble purpose becomes sidetracked by high-stakes efforts to teach to tests, the whole enterprise becomes dangerously warped. Inviting teachers to place their own learning alongside their students' is one helpful corrective.

Gary Sykes was a professor of education administration and teacher education who specialized in educational policy related to teaching and teacher education. His research interests centered on policy issues associated with the improvement of teaching and teacher education, on the development of leadership preparation programs, and on education choice as an emerging policy issue.

Roland S. Barth is a well-known author who has experience as a public school teacher and principal. He is the founder of the Harvard Graduate School of Education and the Harvard Principals' Center and the International Network of Principals' Centers. He is an advocate for distributive leadership, which allows both the principal and the teacher to play key roles in the transformation of a school.

Meaningful Teacher Learning

Lead Learners also must be learning continually about their craft. Bateson (1972) pointed out that the word *learning* denotes a change. Vaill (1996), too, defines learning as "changes a person makes in himself or herself that increase the know-why and/or the know-what and/or the know-how the person possesses with respect to a given subject" (p. 21). While traditionally this has been true of students in an obvious way, at Aspire High it is true of Lead Learners as well. Lead Learners are always changing because they are always learning. Teaching the same (i.e., unchanged) subject in the same way at the same pace using the same curriculum from one year to the next is practically unthinkable.

"Practically unthinkable" not in the sense of "almost unthinkable," but in the sense of unthinkable for practical reasons: It doesn't work. That kind of constancy might work for efficient (though perhaps not effective) teaching, but it does not work for learning. As a learning environment, Aspire High creates space and opportunities for Lead Learners to learn and not simply teach what they have already learned. Barth (1990) asserts, "Probably nothing within a school has more impact on students in terms of skills development, self-confidence, or classroom behavior than the personal and professional growth of teachers" (p. 49).

The fact that traditional professional development (PD), which should be about teacher learning, rarely meets teachers' current and ongoing learning needs has been well documented (Borko, 2004; Garet, Porter, Desimone, Birman, & Yoon, 2001). Bransford, Brown, and Cocking (1999) note that "much of what constitutes the typical approaches to formal teacher professional development are antithetical to what research findings indicate as promoting effective learning" (p. 192). Data from the *Quaglia School Voice National Report* (*QSVNR*) indicates this remains true today; while 80% of teachers consider professional development an important part of their educational growth, just 57% report that meaningful PD opportunities exist in their district (2016). This gap between the considered importance and the reported meaningfulness of professional development is as much about the present, tired *process* of teacher learning as it is about much of the current, exhausted content. Aspire High ensures that teachers have autonomy over their learning and the time to pursue the learning goals that are important and relevant to them (rather than the often pro forma, mandated learning which is often perceived as "meaningless"). Teacher learning, however, also must be practiced in relationship to student learning. While learning a new language might be fun and useful for an upcoming vacation, unless there is a connection to student learning and growth, this would not be considered professional learning at Aspire High.

In support of this approach, Aspire High has several traditional learning venues, such as professional learning communities, teacher conferences, and department meetings; however, each of these learning opportunities uses and supports adult learning needs. As adult *learning* needs are independent of the need to accumulate PD hours or graduate credits, the learning effort for teachers is competency based. This means teacher recognition, leadership opportunities, and increases to salary unfold based on demonstrated abilities and application of new knowledge, rather than from the traditional approach of accumulated time—hours in the case of classes or seniority in the case of careers. For example, a teacher who learns about a new approach to Student Voice can invite peers into her or his classroom to assess the effectiveness of the new approach on student learning. In pre- and postconferences with colleagues, students, and/or principal, the teams together discuss how the new learning represents a growth in the teacher's competency.

CREATING COMPETENT TEACHERS

Ray McNulty, Dean of College of Education, Southern New Hampshire University

At the School of Education at Southern New Hampshire University (SNHU), learning from actual classroom experience, coupled with practice demonstrating

(Continued)

(Continued)

how knowledge and skills are used in a classroom, is how educators are evaluated and judged as competent. We work at creating several powerful pathways for preservice and veteran educators to learn and experience the power of competency-based learning. The desire for new and better forms of assessment of learning is at the heart of this shift to a competency-based approach in teacher education.

We invest in this approach because we know there are many preservice and practicing teachers that can pass a written exam about content knowledge needed to teach a topic, but does this mean they can teach it to others? They can even explain in writing the teaching process they should use, but can they really do it? Simply put, education is a contact sport, and only when you have actual contact with students who are trying to learn something that challenges them can you effectively judge the synergy and effectiveness of your content knowledge and teaching skills.

- Ray McNulty indicates that the educator program at SNHU is grounded in "learning from actual experience." To what extent are your current professional development experiences rooted in your own classroom experience and that of your colleagues? How might you increase or deepen the capacity of learning from your current practice?
- What are your thoughts and opinions about a competency-based approach to the teaching profession? What is your position on whether new and veteran teachers should be assessed and judged based on what they can demonstrably do in the classroom as distinct from what they can demonstrate they know on a test or in writing?
- Ray writes: "Education is a contact sport, and only when you have actual contact with students who are trying to learn something that challenges them can you effectively judge the synergy and effectiveness of your content knowledge and teaching skills." How would you change your current professional learning to include peer observation to account for the "contact" nature of learning in teaching?

Teachers Have Different Starting Places

Teachers enter the profession with a range of different abilities and competencies. As they progress in their careers, their learning diverges, depending on their role, experiences, purpose, and opportunities for ongoing learning. This may result in one teacher needing to improve her skills in technology, while another needs support in developing relationships with his students. *As a learner-focused school, teacher learning at Aspire High starts where the learner is, not where the building principal thinks she or he should be.*

Acknowledging the different starting places of their Lead Learners, Aspire High professional-growth plans continue with an emphasis on developing teacher competencies. While reflection, conversation, and thinking together about big ideas are never neglected, the focus is on how to get better at what teachers *do*. Fullan and Hargreaves (2012) assert that "teaching like a pro" means teachers are continually inquiring into and improving their own teaching. At Aspire High, this includes not only ongoing development in particular content areas (in some ways mitigated by the ubiquitous nature of content) but also a stress

> **Malcolm S. Knowles** was a very influential figure in the adult education field and one of the leading authorities on adult education and training. His theory of andragogy transformed education theory.

on pedagogy. "Know-what" is available to anyone; know-how is a craft that must be repeatedly practiced. Know-what can be outsourced; know-how requires contact.

In particular, Lead Learners at Aspire High must continually develop their ability to use pedagogical approaches that personalize learning, invite students to be teachers, and support experiential, real-world, project-based learning. As we will see, individual teachers do not deliver the curriculum in disciplined silos at Aspire High. Thus, many of the skills that are refined in professional development relate to effective student-centered, team-teaching, and multi-disciplinary–based approaches.

Additionally, Aspire High develops learning and growth opportunities for adults based on research in the fields of adult and teacher learning. Adult learning highlights the need for autonomy, control, choice, and building from personal and professional experiences. Knowles (1980) asserts that adults, who have a self-concept unique from younger learners, tend to resist situations in which they feel others are imposing their wills upon them. Since teachers' experiences, beliefs, needs, and goals are diverse, professional development requires differentiated teacher learning opportunities to maximize the potential for change (Sparks & Loucks-Horsley, 1990; Truscott & Truscott, 2004). Teacher learning implies an understanding that not all teachers need to learn the same information at the same time in the same manner. Aspire High leverages these ideas so that Lead Learners have productive and genuinely meaningful experiences of professional development that clearly indicate the purpose for learning, highlight skills acquisition, and connect to each teacher's learning style.

Adult learners, like student learners, have different purposes for learning. Some adults are innately curious, while others want to learn content or skills to improve their practice. In addition, novice teachers and veteran teachers have different needs when it comes to learning. In examining self-directed veteran teachers, two types of teacher learners emerged in a recent study (Fox, 2011). One type of veteran learner is content focused: Their primary purpose for learning is to master content and skills that will help them be better teachers. These teachers are willing to learn a new idea or approach *if* they believe it will enhance their teaching practice. Another type of veteran learner is challenge focused: These veteran teachers are driven purely by the challenge and love of learning. They are constantly studying and introducing new ideas, sometimes to the exhaustion of their colleagues. Neither of these is better than the other; rather, they are unique in their needs and purposes for learning.

Understanding the purpose of teacher learning is critical at Aspire High because inspiration for learning must remain elevated for Lead Learners. It is difficult to be a role model for lifelong learning if your own course of professional study includes professional development you believe is more of a check box for the central office ("Be sure to sign in") than something you need to know to improve. We have had the sad experience of teachers telling us they attended a smart-board session when they have neither a smart board nor hope of getting one. We have heard about physical education teachers who were required to attend math PD because the person coming to lead their own PD had phoned in sick. Far too often, teachers seem to be a part of "learning" that seems to them, at least, to have no purpose. This is uninspiring, if not dispiriting, to say the least, and affects motivation:

> Motivation is the starting point for learning. For a busy and often overworked teacher to devote effort to change and new learning, there has to be a good reason for the change: some sort of catalyst or urgency—a sense that "what I'm doing doesn't seem to be working." (Stoll, McKay, Kember, Cochrane-Smith, & Lytle, 1999, para. 8)

For Lead Learners, the best source for that motivation is their own desire to get better at what they do. Reflection, dialogue, and discussion all allow the Lead Learners at Aspire High opportunities to figure out why they are learning.

Different Types of Teacher Learners

Finally, we need to understand who teachers are as learners. Included among the different ways teachers prefer to learn are reading, observing, collaborating, experiencing, attending webinars, and dialoguing. Lead Learners are free to access information in myriad ways of their choosing. Just as there is no "one-size-fits-all" approach for the students at Aspire

High, there is no single, prescribed learning regime for teachers. To be sure, each teacher must develop a personal growth plan and discuss it with the principal, colleagues, and students—not learning is not an option. But from start to finish, this plan is learner focused. Teachers are expected to collaborate, model, and coach each other in their learning journeys:

> When a teacher needs information or advice about how to do her job more effectively, she goes to other teachers. She turns far less frequently to the experts and is even less likely to talk to her principal. Further, when the relationships among teachers in a school are characterized by high trust and frequent interaction—that is, when social capital is strong—student achievement scores improve. (Leana, 2011, p. 5)

At Aspire High, collaboration flourishes in a culture of trust, responsibility, and collegiality, thus leading to better student growth.

Likewise, when teachers and students learn together, there is no one right way. In some classes, students codevelop and copresent lessons; in other classes, students learn material outside the classroom, then together with teachers in the classroom or out in some real-world setting, they apply their knowledge. At times, teachers ask questions to which students must respond; at other times, students ask questions. The key to all of this diversity of approaches is the grounding in the belief that teachers and students are partners in the learning and that the goal is to support each and every student in the development of his or her aspirations.

Many teachers learn when students provide formative assessment or feedback to them. Formative assessment for the teachers allows students to have input on their relationships with teachers, peers, content, and their role in the learning and then together consider how to improve the learning environment. In the large-scale measures of an effective-teaching study (2010), student perception results were found to correlate with other measures of teaching quality, such as observations and student learning growth. This same study concluded, "Students seem to know effective teaching when they experience it" (Bill & Melinda Gates Foundation, p. 9). Given the fact that students come to school with much familiarity at being students and thus learning, Aspire High leverages this knowledge to help teachers learn how to best support students as learners.

Taken all together, teachers-as-learners simply means that as the professional educators hired by Aspire High to lead the learning, teachers must place their own learning securely beside their students' learning as part of the profession. In order to model, guide, support, and facilitate the learning of their students, *Lead Learners must engage in an ongoing willingness to experience, wonder, understand, question, and become more and more each class, each day, each lesson, each year.*

LEARNING HOW TO LEARN

Marcel Fukayama, cofounder of Sistema B, Brazil

Interview date May 16, 2015

Marcel is a social entrepreneur, cancer survivor, and has served as CEO of CDI Global, a social-organization pioneer in digital empowerment with presence in 15 countries and 842 communities. He is also cofounder of Sistema B in Brazil, one of the leaders of the global movement of B corporations committed to use business as a force for good and cofounder of Din4mo, a B Corporation with the objective to empower entrepreneurs to develop business models that solve social problems.

The crisis [in education] is that we have globally created a generation of teachers who haven't learned how to learn. The dynamic today is completely different—we have to learn every second of every day. We have to learn from our successes and our mistakes.

We need to bring local context into learning and teaching—elements that become incorporated into local culture. In 200 years' time, Brazil's Portuguese language will be completely different from the Portuguese language in Portugal. Already, the languages are drifting apart, and it is becoming harder to move between the two.

The global movement of B (benefit) corporations is also having an impact. B corporations are evaluated on impact, governance, business model, communities, workers, and environment. New assessments could be collated with assessments in learning.

- Marcel Fukayama asserts that there is a global crisis in education tied to "a generation of teachers who haven't learned how to learn." Do you agree or disagree? What evidence in your school is there for your position?
- How could teachers' learning to learn be improved in your school? What changes would you recommend to professional development coordinators? To teacher trainers? To university teacher preparation programs?
- What are the implications of the kind of language and cultural shifts Marcel refers to (which include and are broader than the changes to Portuguese) on education generally and teacher learning in particular? How and why do teachers need to keep learning about global trends such as these?
- The B corporations referenced by Marcel strive to have a positive impact on their communities and the world. How could this impact the role of teachers as Lead Learners?

◇ What are your preferred styles/modes/methods of professional learning? How do you seek out learning opportunities that meet this need?

◇ Describe a time when you were most excited and engaged as a professional learner. What were you learning? How were others involved? What made this a rich experience for you?

◇ Discuss with colleagues the benefits of collaboration. How do teaming, peer observations, collegial conversations, coteaching, mentoring, and the like make a positive contribution to your ongoing professional growth?

◇ Seek out a colleague in a different role or who has a different viewpoint. Ask him or her to recommend a current professional blog, article, book, or learning opportunity. After reading it, engage in a discussion with him or her.

LEAD

We must question why the experience of teachers as learners is not as commonplace as the experience of students as teachers. While we have seen many instances of students presenting, teaching, and even tutoring their peers, we have not seen nearly as many examples of teachers learning from one another, effective professional development, or teachers engaged in a meaningful pursuit of ongoing professional learning. While nearly all districts provide and expect teachers to engage in PD in some form, in far too many districts it is seen by both the central office and the teachers as pro forma—something to be endured rather than engaged. There are, of course, exceptions, but they seem far too rare.

Maybe it is because most teachers already think they know more than they can use. Maybe teachers think they are done learning and that the next obvious progression is teaching. Maybe the thought of learning from students is a foreign concept to most teachers. We have heard teachers say, "I don't get it. What can a 13-year-old teach me?" Or maybe teachers have not yet realized the potential in each of the students they work with!

Students have something to teach their teachers. Teachers have something (a lot, in fact) to learn from their students. Additionally, teachers learn from their colleagues and school principal as well. Learning in this 360-degree way involves all the key people in a school environment. While traditional professional development is a matter of teachers learning from so-called experts, those who wish to lead teacher learning in an Aspire High mode recognize that the expertise is already among them!

On your mark. Get set! Go!!

PRINCIPAL

Step =====>

- *Meaningfully involve staff in professional learning decisions.* From the elementary school adage "Two heads are better than one" to the principles of total quality management, involving all stakeholders is a key to successful decision making. While most teachers understand that ultimate decision-making authority rests with administrators, most also want their voice to be valued in the process.
- *Use teacher surveys to gather their perspective on the teaching and learning environment.* There are other ways to get information about what everyone on a staff is thinking, but surveys—especially when anonymous—represent a beginning, safe step in the process of learning from your staff.

Stride =====>

- *Flip staff meetings so the focus is on learning, not announcements and updates.* Staff meetings are a lost opportunity in most schools. Staff members can read announcements on their own. Take advantage when your staff comes together to share ideas and learn from one another. Together, focus on vision, mission, and strategy.
- *Conduct staff focus groups to gain deeper insights into staff perspectives.* Taking a survey is one positive step, but having in-depth conversations with staff about what matters to them takes communication and learning to a whole new level. Set aside time for this important opportunity to learn what is on your staff's minds.

Sprint =====>

- *Provide teachers autonomy and ownership over their professional goals.* This is a simple concept that gets overlooked in our rush to make everyone accountable for everything. In order to make teachers feel valued and respected as professionals, provide the time necessary for teachers to develop professional goals that matter to them. Check in on progress toward their goals as a coach, not a supervisor.
- *Provide PD hours for teachers involved in online ed chats, webinars, and the like.* Expand the idea of what it means to be learning in your school. The days of driving to PD sessions or staying after school and sitting at desks at prescribed times to learn are no longer necessary.

TEACHERS

Step ====>

- *Join and participate in online educational chats, webinars, and discussions.* For many, this is a new concept, but if we are to expand our scope of knowledge, we must also be prepared to access information and learning in new ways.
- *Read current education briefs, journals, and news articles.* Initiate professional dialogue related to what you read at staff meetings with your colleagues, administration, and students. Do not wait for professional development to be "provided." Seek out new learning and share what you learn with your colleagues.

Stride ====>

- *Volunteer to lead a staff meeting, committee, or other professional opportunities you have not led before.* You need to push past your comfort zone if you are ever going to professionally grow. You don't know what you don't know. By volunteering for something new, you may find you have a hidden talent!
- *Develop professional goals aligned with your school mission, and track your goal progress on a weekly basis.* It is one thing to develop personal goals, but the real challenge is to hold yourself accountable. How does working toward your goal(s) improve the teaching and learning environment in your classroom?

Sprint ====>

- *Invite colleagues to observe you teach and offer ideas for your growth as a professional.* For many, this may be a daunting task. Teachers are used to being evaluated by their administrator, and increasingly, teachers realize that students are regularly evaluating their pedagogical performance and seek their input. But it is an entirely different thing to be evaluated by your peers—nor is anything more insightful, helpful, and rewarding.
- *Become actively involved in regional and/or national education organizations.* We know time is always an issue, but if you want to make a real difference beyond the walls of your own school, you must extend your horizon into the wider field of education. Become involved in regional and national educational organizations, and challenge yourself to be a presenter as well as a participant.

STUDENTS

Step ⟹

- *Learn about your teachers' passions and hobbies.* Establishing relationships is a reciprocal endeavor. Just as you want teachers to know you, your teachers really want you to know something about them. The more you get to know your teachers, the more you will want to know what they know. Ask your teachers about their interests; offer to help with something you know about.
- *Ask your teachers if you can have a role in teaching the class.* This is a pretty bold thing to do, but you are asking teachers to just give you a "role" in the teaching process—you are not asking to take over the class . . . yet!

Stride ⟹

- *Share your interests and hobbies with teachers so they can learn about you.* Sometimes it is easier to ask teachers about their interests rather than sharing your own. The truth is you need to do both! The more teachers know about you, the more they can connect what they are teaching to your interests.
- *Share with teachers interesting websites you discover related to what they teach.* Believe it or not, teachers will find your sharing this kind of information with them very refreshing and helpful. Don't be surprised if they ask you to share the information with the entire class.

Sprint ⟹

- *Teach staff on a regular basis about new learning apps and technology that you and your peers are using.* The key here is "regular basis." Work in partnership with your teachers, and share your vast wealth of knowledge—not as some kind of special event, but as a consistent part of your teachers' professional learning.
- *Create opportunities in which teachers and students work together to improve the school.* If the opportunities for partnerships do not exist in your school, then create some. From curriculum development to school beautification committees, make an effort to establish reasons to work hand-in-hand with teachers in a cooperative learning environment. Start with ideas you have for changes that would improve the teaching and learning environment for all students. Gather information. Collect other people's ideas. Then, make a difference!

Is Your School . . . ?		
TYPICAL HIGH	ASPIRE HIGH	ASPIRING HIGHER
Teachers informally seek student input and sporadically use formal means (e.g., surveys, focus groups, etc.).	Teachers regularly seek student input through formal means.	Teachers systematically use formal student feedback to inform curriculum and learning.
Staff are asked for input into important decisions.	Staff (and students) are meaningfully involved in important decisions.	All important decisions are made in partnership with students, teachers, and administrators.
Staff meetings are led by administrators with occasional teacher presentations.	Staff meetings are led by teachers.	Traditional staff meetings are replaced by various standing and ad hoc gatherings for the sake of learning.
Teachers have little time for meaningful self-reflection.	Self-reflection is expected as a learning tool.	Time is intentionally set aside for teachers' expected self-reflection.
Principals provide informal and formal feedback on lessons.	Administrators and colleagues regularly provide professional feedback.	Ongoing feedback from students, administrators, and colleagues is a way of being.
Teachers volunteer or are drafted onto school committees.	Teachers share leadership of school and local committees.	Teachers serve on regional and national boards and committees.
Teachers are team and department leaders, but they relinquish building leadership to administrators.	Teachers' team leadership involves real decision-making authority at the building level.	Teachers exercise leadership responsibility beyond the building level.
Most teachers know the school mission, but it does not drive their practice.	Teaching and learning decisions are deeply informed by the school mission.	Teachers support the positive role of the school mission in the wider community.
Teachers observe each other's lessons by request.	There is a regular practice of collegial observation and dialogue.	Teachers coteach with other teachers and model best practices for one another.
New teachers are assigned a mentor for a two-year probationary period.	The first two years of teacher training include team teaching and collegial reflection on teaching practice.	Veteran teachers lead robust partnerships with local teaching colleges that support full integration of teacher training curriculum and professional teaching practice.

(Continued)

(Continued)

Is Your School . . . ?		
TYPICAL HIGH	**ASPIRE HIGH**	**ASPIRING HIGHER**
Teachers are classroom managers.	Classroom management involves students working in partnership with teachers.	Students lead and manage classes with teachers offering suggestions and expertise.
Professional development is sporadically helpful, often redundant, and misaligned to teaching responsibilities.	Professional growth and learning are driven by teachers and informed by teacher and student needs.	Professional learning includes teaching and instruction beyond the building.
Professional development is planned by the central office and delivered by outside experts.	Professional growth is delivered internally and by teacher-invited experts.	Teachers share their expertise at the local, state, and national level.
The goal of PD is typically credit hours toward recertification.	The goal of professional growth is professional learning.	Traditional PD is replaced by continual professional growth and learning as part of one's role.
Professional development is time bound and limited to contractual agreements.	Professional growth is competency based.	Teachers and administrators codevelop the competencies on which teacher learning is based.
Professional learning communities (PLCs) are common but are directed by building administration or central-office staff.	PLCs are focused on student learning and have specific goals and outcomes.	PLCs include students and community members.
Teacher evaluation is carried out by administration in a supervisory mode.	Teacher evaluation is done by administration and lead teachers in a coaching mode.	Teacher evaluation includes efforts beyond classroom performance (e.g., community involvement, committees, etc.).
Teachers have little input into curriculum; curriculum is based on national/state standards.	Teachers and students develop curriculum based on student needs as related to national/state standards.	Fully competency-based education makes traditional curriculum obsolete.
Teaching assignments are decided by seniority.	Student learning needs dictate teaching responsibilities.	Students have a voice in choosing teachers they work with and learn from.
Teachers collaborate as needed or according to academic discipline. Teaming is not typical at the secondary level.	Teachers and students collaborate frequently in order to learn.	Teacher–student collaboration extends beyond the building (e.g., through use of social media and online tools).

Is Your School . . . ?		
TYPICAL HIGH	**ASPIRE HIGH**	**ASPIRING HIGHER**
Teachers ask parents to complete information sheets about students.	Teachers and parents partner to ensure student learning throughout the school year.	Parents and teachers are involved in reciprocal learning experiences.
Teacher–parent meetings are scheduled as needed and typically relate to student academic or behavioral deficiencies.	Teachers, students, and parents hold monthly round-table discussions to learn together.	Teachers, parents, and students are regular collaborators for the sake of student learning.
Teachers see community patrons as funders of the school budget.	Teachers and community members work together to create unique learning opportunities.	The community is fully integrated into the learning.

3

A Dynamic Role for School Leadership

Leaders are people who do the right thing;
managers are people who do things right.

—Professor Warren G. Bennis

LISTEN

The principal of Aspire High enters Steve's classroom. He greets several students with "Mr. Shipman" and "Ms. Lewis." The students greet him as "Mr. Harper." He walks over to the whiteboard and asks a student who is seated what they are learning. A young man explains. "Why?" he asks the student standing at the board. She provides several reasons.

He moves on and sits down with a group of three students having a discussion and asks them the same questions: "What are you learning?" Then, "Why?" The students explain eagerly. Before leaving that group, he puts a hand on one student's shoulder and says, "How's Dad?"

"We get to Skype with him Friday. We're not sure where he is, but it's somewhere in the Middle East."

"I'm keeping a good thought for him."

"Thanks."

Mr. Harper comes over to us and, grinning, asks, "What are you learning?"

"Well, for starters," we say, "we've learned that your school values applied learning. It seems as if the entire place is set up for that singular purpose: for students to be learning things that apply either to the present or to their futures. Students are teaching to learn better, and teachers are constantly learning to support students teaching better."

"Why?" he asks.

We think. "It's your mission: to provide students the ability to dream and set goals for the future while inspiring them in the present to reach those goals."

He stands up and addresses the whole class: "Is anyone ahead in this class?" A student sitting alone reading raises his hand. "Join us?" Mr. Harper asks. The student follows us as Mr. Harper escorts us out of the classroom.

Along the way, we learn that Mr. Harper is rarely if ever in his office during the school day. "*This* is the office of a principal," he says with arms extended as we walk down a hallway. "This." He is clearly referring to the whole building. He points to a fitness band on his wrist. "Fifteen thousand steps on an average day." He prides himself on working toward knowing the names of all his students and at least one personal fact about each of them. "How do you think I do, Mr. O'Malley?" he asks the student.

"Not bad," Mr. O'Malley says.

"I asked Mr. O'Malley along in case you want a student's point of view on anything we encounter."

As we walk down the hallway, Mr. Harper greets students he knows by name, and if we encounter a student he doesn't know, he asks for her name and a point of interest. If a student replies that he should know them, he apologizes. He uses students' names and this information as we move in and out of classes, meet students in hallways, and later, work the cafeteria lunch line—something he does every day except Wednesdays. "It's a great way for me to eyeball each kid on a regular basis," he explains. "Plus, Ms. Joyce and Ms. Alvarez—the lunch workers—love me, and I get as many homemade cookies as I want."

"What do the students think of that?" we ask Mr. O'Malley.

"They think he does it *just* for the cookies."

Sadly, the principalship as currently configured seems to be an undoable job. Once upon a time, its skill set consisted of a classroom teacher who had risen through the ranks, was backed by trusting and trusted colleagues, and had some innate leadership talents. No longer. The ability to be building manager and instructional coach, head disciplinarian and community liaison, parent complaint department chair and implementer of district initiatives, politician and professional confidant exceeds the capacity of even the most capable and committed educator. The principalship is the pressure point of our entire educational system. The weight of all the systems above the school level rest on their shoulders—district, state, and federal mandates all focus their requirements on building principals. Then, their feet are too close to fires on the ground—student discipline issues and parent concerns frequently find their way to a chair in their office. The principal's office is the place where seemingly inescapable mandates from above and relentlessly unavoidable obligations from below all come together.

To counteract this, the principal of Aspire High is first and foremost a learner, like everyone else in the building. And the special field of scholarship that he studies is systems thinking, including emerging work in the areas of networking and improvement science (see Bryk et al., 2015). In particular, Mr. Harper considers himself a master of leverage. He knows if he finds the right point of leverage in any system or subsystem—learning systems, social systems, family systems, political systems—he can effect change in that system and through that, change the way people behave and act. This is not Machiavellian; it is Archimedean ("Give me a lever long enough and a fulcrum on which to place it, and I shall move the world"). It is practical and produces results. Mr. Harper considers the building his office because he believes the highest leverage available to him is as the shaper of the school's climate and culture. Thus, he wants proactively to create the weather in his building, not simply be reactive to various storms and sunny days. This can only be done by being out in the building regularly.

High leverage points in systems are those places the system, either directly or indirectly, touches the most people. The underlying premise of Aspire High is that each person has a dream for his or her future to be inspired in the present to work toward. There is, therefore, an enormous amount of leverage in working in support of everyone's aspirations. Mr. Harper is aware of the research spanning three decades that maintains that in order to support each person's aspirations one must develop each person's Self-Worth, Engagement, and Purpose, as well as their voice.

- **Self-Worth** occurs when students know they are uniquely valued members of the school community, have a person in their lives they can trust and learn from, and believe they have the ability to achieve—academically, personally, and socially.
- **Engagement** happens when students are deeply involved in the learning process as characterized by enthusiasm, a desire to learn new things, and a willingness to take positive, healthy steps toward the future. Students are meaningfully engaged when they are emotionally, intellectually, and behaviorally invested in learning.
- **Purpose** exists when students take responsibility for who and what they are becoming. This involves not only choosing a career but also deciding to be involved, responsible members of their community. Purpose is as much about who students want to be as it is what they want to do (Quaglia & Corso 2014, pp. 23–24).

In the classrooms, corridors, and cafeteria of Aspire High, the principles that guide Mr. Harper's shaping of the school's culture are ensuring the Self-Worth, Engagement, and Purpose of every person in the building. Through the relentless daily effort to let each person know he or she is valued, to cultivate each person's active participation in learning, and to foster each person's sense of intention and commitment, he affects the very air people breathe. This in turn influences how they act. He knows that—as management guru Peter Drucker is attributed to have said—"culture trumps strategy."

While there are various points of leverage throughout the building that allow Mr. Harper to affect the school's climate and culture, a particular area of focus is what is traditionally thought of as instructional leadership. Given Aspire High's unique approach to teaching and learning, Mr. Harper trusts that teachers are learning and students are teaching and that they are mutually responsible to one another. In that context, "instructional" leadership is something of a misnomer. It is truer to say that Mr. Harper is the Principal Learner than to say he is the principal or head instructor or teacher. The classrooms of Aspire High and all the places inside and outside of the school where education occurs are a nearly constant point of contact between the young people who attend Aspire High to learn and the adults entrusted with the responsibility to guide their learning. As principal, he considers it among his primary responsibilities to ensure the quality of learning in all those settings. His questions—"What are you learning?" and "Why?"—are not mere niceties or polite throwaways such as "How are you?" They are genuine questions that make it clear to everyone that he is ever-concerned about what is being learned and for what reasons.

To exercise this responsibility, every day of the week students are in the building, he is in the building, with the exception of Wednesdays and the first Friday of every month. He spends real time in classes—not just evaluating teachers, but observing and pushing the learning. He is not just visible in the building or a class, passively observing; he is fully and actively present. He learns alongside students. He teaches alongside when asked. He participates in team meetings when they happen during the day. He serves lunch, and after serving, he sits and eats with students who brought lunch since he doesn't see them in the line. He answers the occasional urgent e-mail (prescreened by his administrative assistant) on a mobile device, but for the most part, he stays available to the building—that is, to students and teachers—throughout the day.

At 6:30 a.m., Mr. Harper arrives and deals with e-mails and paperwork until 8:30. Every morning at 8:30, he attends a staff briefing. Staff members who have the best facilitation skills lead these—Aspire High has four such staff members: two teachers, a guidance counselor, and one of the administrative assistants. They rotate this responsibility weekly. Part pep-talk, part bulletin announcements, starting the day this way—having everyone learn about what student might be off for whatever reason—is the foundation of a successful day at Aspire High. Mr. Harper "memos the memo-able" so this meeting is a far cry from the typical laundry list of what is on the principal's mind. The meeting lasts just 15 minutes.

Thirty minutes before the day ends and for another 30 minutes after that are office hours he holds for any parents or community members that want to see him. He leaves dismissal to his assistant principals, as he feels making time for parents when it is convenient for them is a point of leverage. He also lets parents know that they can call him on his cell phone during his commute home between 5:30 p.m. and 6:00 p.m. any day except on weekends. This approach leads to far fewer fires to put out, and although it seems time intensive in the short run, there is no doubt it saves time in the long run. This is another systems principle: to pay a short-term price for a long-term gain.

Wednesdays are different. The day starts and ends the same, but by 9:30, the principal is off to meetings outside the building. Depending on the week, these may be at the central office or with community members. There may be meetings with grant writers or local business-people. The principal considers this work outside the building worth 20% of his week. He believes the relationships he builds outside the building—and the learning available to him that results—benefits the learning inside the building. He paves the way for guest speakers, field trips, and the internships that are part of Aspire High's curriculum.

He is always back in the building by 2 p.m. on Wednesdays, which begins the hour devoted to meetings attended by both staff and students. The first Wednesday of the month is devoted to meetings about pedagogy. As the learning at Aspire High is project based, these are interdisciplinary and attended by students. Together, teachers and students discuss teaching and learning strategies they are using or that they might introduce. The second Wednesday of the month holds what might be considered traditional department meetings, and students also attend. They are part academic club, part subject specialization meeting. How the school makes use of particular content areas is discussed. The third Wednesday sees prescribed committee work; various policies are examined and discussed, new ideas are studied, proposals are made to change this or that procedure. The final Wednesday of the month is dedicated to a community meeting. The entire staff and all students assemble in classrooms so that various information, presentations, and new procedures can be shared using the school's closed-circuit TV system. This meeting includes an "Ask Harper" segment in which anyone can submit a question, anonymously or not, for Mr. Harper to address.

LEARN

At Aspire High, leadership looks different from a traditional school in theory and practice. While education is not a business and principals are not CEOs, there is much we have learned about organizational behavior in other fields that is applied to the leadership structures at Aspire High. Among the applicable lessons is the realization that leading and managing are two different, though related, functions. While much has been written on this subject, the short version is that *leading drives and is driven by a vision and mission*, whereas managing is about the efficient procurement of resources to achieve a vision and mission. "A mission-driven culture propels schools to new levels of excellence" (Corso, Lucey & Fox, 2012, p. 22). Although leadership's vision can be communally built and implemented, those who are school leaders are caretakers of this vision—vision keepers, if you will, rather than supervisors or overseers.

The vision at Aspire High is for every student to have the ability to dream and set goals for the future while being inspired in the present to reach those goals. While there is no doubt that principals matter and play a critical role in development of high-quality schools (Darling-Hammond, LaPointe, Meyerson, Orr, & Cohen, 2007; EdSource, 2008; Knapp et al., 2003), formal leaders alone cannot change school culture. "Few visionary leaders have had any effect on the dominant institutional patterns of American education" (Elmore, 2000, p. 2). Accordingly, at Aspire High, leadership is about more than just the head administrator, and the term *leadership* is not reserved for those in formal roles. In a large-scale study with the Pittsburgh school system, researcher Carrie Leana (2011) concluded, "The more effective principals were those who defined their roles as *facilitators* of teacher success rather than instructional leaders" (p. 11).

At Aspire High, a building full of adults and students take responsibility, make decisions, and lead the learning community toward the school's vision and an execution of the mission. Every leader—that is, *everyone* at Aspire High—comes to the role with a wealth of experience and a rich diversity of expertise. Given this approach and the uncountable other aims and responsibilities involved in education, the principal acts as a focusing mechanism. Think of a satellite dish that draws in waves from all around and centers them in a single direction. As a shaper of the school's culture, the principal maintains everyone's focus on Self-Worth, Engagement, and Purpose and sets these as the expectations that guide the learning community. Test scores, behavior, parental and community involvement, and cocurricular activities all must answer to how they support the Self-Worth, Engagement, and Purpose of every person.

- Does your behavior improve the other students' Self-Worth or diminish it?
- Does this lesson increase Engagement or reduce it?
- Will reading this book move someone closer to his or her Purpose or distract from it?

To maintain this focus, the principal and other administrators at Aspire High are expected to be, as Fullan says, "systems-thinkers-in-action" and to understand organizational and leadership theories in order to align all the moving parts in the learning community toward the common goal.

In order to bring about this degree of focus, Self-Worth, Engagement, and Purpose are used by the systems-thinking principal as levers for widely distributed leadership. These Guiding Principles are not only desired outcomes on the way toward ensuring each student is dreaming about his or her future and working toward it in the present, but they are also the means to those ends. A principal must enact, not just espouse, the values by which he seeks to shape the school. By prioritizing Self-Worth, Engagement, and Purpose in his own interactions, the principal of Aspire High maintains a leadership emphasis on what is really important, not just what is urgent or expedient. He shares leadership—that is, decision making and responsibility—with both adults and students precisely because it affirms value in the other, engages the other, and invites participation in a shared sense of purpose.

Leaders Nurture Self-Worth

Leaders build the self-worth of those with whom they interact. Toward that end, *positive relationships are a key factor.* While in many schools there can be tension or even an adversarial tone between administrators and the teaching staff (and even, at times, among staff), the principal at Aspire High maintains positive interactions with staff, as he does with students. Similar to the importance of relationships in the teaching and learning environment, relationships between administrators and staff matter. "The nature of relationships among the adults within a school has a greater influence on the character and quality of that school and on student accomplishment than anything else" (Barth, 2006, p. 6). During the first few weeks of inservice with the staff, the principal spends time getting to know people—not just their names but also their strengths, challenges, and professional aspirations. This helps the principal better support each adult as an individual. There is also a high expectation that all staff interact with one another, regardless of professional status, in a positive and healthy way. Though a large staff, all are expected to know one another's names and address each other with respect and cordiality.

Through a process of relationship building, the staff develops trust with leadership and one another, and as a result, healthy communication systems develop.

In staff surveys and focus groups, a lack of trust and effective communication are frequently cited as barriers to improvement and change in many schools, to say nothing of their smooth day-to-day functioning. Only 69% of staff report that they respect each other (*QSVNR*, 2016). Bryk and Schneider's (2003) research in Chicago public schools highlights that the quality of social relations in institutions makes a difference in how they function. The authors note that schools are networks of sustained relationships, and trust is key to school improvement.

Accordingly, at Aspire High developing others' self-worth is a *leadership function*. It improves relationships, trust, communication, and effectiveness, all of which are critical to shared decision making and being mission driven. The more the principal accepts each person for who he or she is, respects others, models expected behavior, and recognizes the effort and contribution each person is making to the school community, the more successfully he or she leads. *Developing Self-Worth is not a question of being nice or a function of emotional intelligence; it is about vision keeping.*

Leaders Foster Engagement

For the last decade, much has been written about the role of the principal as instructional leader. *Instructional leadership* is the term *de jour* in educational leadership circles, yet research has shown that direct involvement in instruction is among the least frequent activities performed by administrators. In fact, principals spent the most time on administration activities such as managing student discipline and fulfilling compliance requirements to keep the school running smoothly—about 30% of the school day (Horng, Klasik, & Loeb, 2009). Furthermore, researchers Grissom, Loeb, and Master (2013) found that classroom "walkthroughs"—the most typical instruction-related activity of principals in Miami-Dade schools—were negatively associated with student performance, especially in high schools.

Note that the operative assumption in casting a school leader in this role is that the primary purpose of schooling is *instruction*. If that is the case, then indeed, a school may benefit from having its chief administrator be an instructional leader. Whatever strategies support such a role—leading professional development, walk-throughs, observations, and so on—should be the primary tasks of someone attempting to lead in that mode.

However, at Aspire High, while instruction occurs, it is not a primary or even a secondary goal. Students' aspirations are the primary goal, and the secondary goals are Self-Worth, Engagement, and Purpose. Leadership's instructional concerns, therefore, are most directly related to engagement.

Whenever and wherever instruction occurs, it must engage the learners, whether adult or student. This approach has three implications.

First, this responsibility requires the principal to work closely with adults to understand the relationship between engagement and the choice of pedagogical strategies. Over the past few years, researchers and practitioners have amply learned how to create dynamic learning experiences for all students. While it is beyond the scope of this chapter to single out any one approach, learning through gaming, project-based learning, real-world application, and service learning, to name just a few, have each in their own way proven the efficacy of nontraditional, multidisciplinary approaches. Yet far too often, this knowledge is not shared, understood, or practiced. There are still far too many lectures, packets, seat-work assignments, and homework-as-busywork worksheets to engage students fully. This no doubt impacts the following results from the 2016 *QSVNR* (percentages reflect total in agreement):

- I enjoy being at school.   49%
- Teachers make school an exciting place to learn.   38%
- School is boring.   43%
- I enjoy participating in my classes.   54%

Neither single-subject curricula nor teacher autonomy—both mainstays of traditional schooling—drive the learning at Aspire High. *The active engagement of every student is the standard. All other standards are subject to it.* As a result, leadership expects that instructional strategies serve engagement and that engagement is never sacrificed for the sake of some instructional strategy. While ideally students are effectively, cognitively, and behaviorally engaged in their learning activities, at least one form of engagement suffices in any given learning experience. As such, there is no such thing as a universally effective teaching strategy; the effectiveness of any given strategy can only be determined by evidence of its effect on student learning (DuFour & Marzano, 2011). Aspire High focuses on engagement as a broad strategy intended to have the greatest impact on learning.

A second implication of Engagement-oriented leadership is that the principal understands that for engagement to occur in learning, the school systems must support this engagement. Again, the role of the principal is one of providing focus and coherence. To foster a community that shares engaging pedagogical practices, the principal creates time for team teaching, coaching, and mentoring. He supports and understands that the best avenue toward learning and student growth is through vibrant professional learning communities. The principal clears time and space for teachers and students to work together not just on projects and content, but on instructional strategies as well. The principal invites emphasis not only on *what* is being learned, but on *how* and *why* it is being learned.

Learning is viewed as both a personal and a social activity at Aspire High. *The principal nurtures an environment whose thriving is dependent upon both individual and community learning.* However, the latter effort—learning *together* as professionals—is primary for the Lead Learners at Aspire High. The principal of Aspire High has no interest in having a handful, or even a school full, of outstanding teachers who do not share, mentor, and coach their colleagues. As Gawande notes in his 2012 TED Talk thought experiment,

> What if you built a car from the very best car parts? Well it would lead you to put in Porsche brakes, a Ferrari engine, a Volvo body, a BMW chassis. And you put it all together and what do you get? A very expensive pile of junk that does not go anywhere.

The principal ensures that professional learning at Aspire High takes a fluid, coherent, and systematic approach geared toward student engagement and learning.

The Organisation for Economic Co-operation and Development's (OECD) Teaching and Learning International Survey published in June 2014 sought the views of 20 teachers and the school leader from 200 schools from each participating country. Eventually, 107,000 teachers responded. In most countries, between 80% and 92% of teachers demonstrate high levels of self-efficacy—in other words, they are confident in their own ability to teach. In 20 of the participating countries, it was found that teachers who agreed that staff at their school are given opportunities to participate in decision making report greater self-efficacy. Aspire High, likewise, is far beyond the self-efficacious independent-contractors-connected-by-a-hallway approach of the traditional school. At Aspire High, working together and sharing in decision making are part of what makes the adults effective educators, thus making learning engaging.

A third implication of being an Engagement-oriented building is that the principal and his or her assistants are themselves constantly engaged in learning. They regularly shadow not just at other schools but also in other organizations. The principal reflects on questions such as these: "What can I learn from the successful nonprofit?" "What can I learn from female leaders?" "How can I be more responsive to those I serve?" The principal never says, "School is different from businesses/ nonprofits/military/government," or, "Our school is different from other schools," as justification for shutting out lessons from other organizations. Just because a school is not a multinational corporation or small start-up business or a hospital does not mean school leaders cannot learn from leaders in those fields. In fact, it is often the learning outside the school environment that opens up new ideas and innovative possibilities.

As with Self-Worth, the product or outcome of an Engagement-oriented leader is a building of shared leadership. *Having a learning community that is engaged is not just better for their learning; decision making and living the school's mission are also positively impacted.* It makes little sense for the principal to be an expected expert on writing and de facto instructional leader for writing when on staff there is a member who has his or her doctorate in English, is a published author, and has made amazing gains for his students in writing. Likewise, a principal who comes to the position as a former social studies teacher can hardly have the best specific instructional strategies for his science teachers. A principal focused on Engagement is required to draw on the best thinking of everyone he serves as leader. Engagement requires team building, and team building is essential to leadership.

FLIPPED LEADERSHIP

Peter DeWitt is the author of Collaborative Leadership *(2015) and writes frequently about "flipped leadership."*

Flipping faculty meetings involves a principal recording himself or herself for what is traditionally the "announcement" portion of a staff or faculty meeting. All participants are expected to have watched the recording prior to attending the meeting.

When doing the flipped-faculty model, consider the following:

Why are you flipping your meeting?
   Don't do it because it is the new thing to do. Flip your meeting because you want to focus on a couple of topics more at length in the actual meeting.

How long do you record yourself?
   It seems like 15 minutes might not be a long time, especially when you're the one talking—it goes by fast. Unfortunately, when you're the one watching, it may seem too long. Try to keep the flipped portion down to no more than 10 minutes. Remember, the flipped portion is setting the stage for the actual meeting. It's not meant to make meetings longer but more productive.

What are you using to flip your meeting?
   Principals have to use what they are comfortable with, and I ended up using Touchcast because it was user-friendly and allowed me to write up my thoughts in a Word document and cut and paste them into a teleprompter to read when I was recording my message. The teleprompter was close to the camera, so people viewing the video really had no idea I was reading something. To make it better, Touchcast offered an option of a green screen where I could

(Continued)

(Continued)

use creative backdrops and embed pictures of students, so teachers really didn't have to see my face during the whole message. Flipping faculty meetings brought a level of authentic communication that wasn't there before because teachers could view the video before the meeting, and then we could dive into authentic dialogue during the meeting.

Who will benefit from the experience?

Both the principal and the staff should benefit from the experience. I'm not an expert because I have only done it once, but I am planning on tackling different topics in different ways through the flipped model.

What topics need more discussion?

It's easy right now to find topics that need more discussion. Annual professional performance review (APPR) and common core state standards (CCSS) are two topics I felt needed our time and effort. During a year, there are many topics worth discussing at length.

- Currently, what portion of your faculty meetings is given to announcements and administrative concerns? How much time is typically given over to professional conversations among the staff about their concerns?
- What do you see as some of the benefits of a flipped faculty meeting? What would be some of the drawbacks?
- How comfortable are you with technology? Who could you enlist to help you with the recordings?

Leaders Inspire Purpose

Developing Self-Worth and ensuring Engagement are only two legs of a three-legged stool. They must be supported and driven by a sense of Purpose. Purpose brings together intention, commitment, and a willingness to think beyond oneself (Damon, 2009). Leadership at Aspire High encourages Purpose at both the individual and the communal level. Purpose is both personal and shared. As such, the principal at Aspire High helps focus attention on each student and adult's sense of purpose, as well as how they are contributing to the overall purpose of the community of learners. He works to ensure a mutual reciprocity between each person's aspiration and the mission of Aspire High to promote everyone's aspirations. Michael Fullan (2001) writes about this function of leadership as helping people find a moral purpose in a shared activity or change process. Peter Senge refers to it as "shared vision" (1990) and considers it one of the five core disciplines of a learning organization.

The key to successfully developing a shared sense of purpose while maintaining individual purpose and of fostering an environment in which individual purpose makes a contribution to shared purpose is the concept of Voice. By encouraging and amplifying Student and Teacher Voice, and indeed, Parental and Community Voice, the principal at Aspire High shares and distributes leadership (Quaglia, 2016). As voice emerges from individuals, it is shaped by their intentions, commitments, and concern for others— that is, their personal purpose. In turn, that voice, *when amplified by the school leader*, contributes to a greater common good and common goals. Reciprocally, as individuals together move closer to common goals in community, they move closer to their personal goals. Amplifying School Voice—the voice of all stakeholders—is critical to being a successful Aspire High leader.

William Damon is a professor of education at Stanford University and the director of the Stanford Center on Adolescence. He is one of the world's leading scholars of human development. His current research explores how people develop character and a sense of purpose in their work, family, and community relationships.

In a sense, the principal of Aspire High serves as the conductor of an orchestra in which the instruments express unique voices yet together make a far richer sound. In both cases, successful leadership depends on the leader as a focal point—not in the sense of "center of attention," but rather as the guarantor of each individual making a meaningful contribution to the whole—harmonious music in the case of the orchestra and achieving the school's mission in the case of Aspire High. At Aspire High, encouraging Voice creates both personal and communal Purpose.

To do this, the principal at Aspire High develops opportunities for staff and students to share their voice in several formats. In community meetings and through surveys and focus groups, both formally and informally, the principal is always inviting feedback, dialogue, and discussion. The ultimate goal is that no person is afraid of sharing his or her ideas, as the principal is always willing to listen and is open to new thoughts. All forms of feedback help guide the principal as he strives to lead the community toward its shared Purpose.

For Reflection

◈ What leadership roles do you currently take on? If you are an administrator, how do you distribute leadership?

◈ Consider who you are as a leader in your school. What does it mean for you to exercise leadership? To have a voice? To make decisions that affect other people?

◈ Discuss with colleagues how you can support each other as leaders. How can your voices acting in harmony advance your professional aspirations more effectively than acting solo?

◈ If you are an administrator, seek out a classroom teacher or student; if you are a classroom teacher or student, seek out an administrator— ask about the other's greatest accomplishment. What did they learn? Share your greatest accomplishment and your learning as well!

LEAD

We ask principals to do it all. We expect them to know what to do and how to do it. We assume they can lead, inspire, and at the same time put out fires daily and sometimes hourly to ensure the continuous safe and effective running of a school. Principals hold the key to success, right? Not exactly. They may hold the keys, but the staff, students, and educational community hold everything else. If we have learned one thing in our work, it is that being a great principal has become a team sport.

Where and how a principal spends her or his time is indeed a complex matrix of leadership and creativity. Patience and a lot of energy are also a must. Success, however, requires something far beyond these minimum requirements. As daunting as the role of the principal has become, we believe it is *not* a solitary position. The principal must act as a player–coach: one that is surrounded with the best and brightest talent available and leads them to greatness by drawing the best out of each individual and of all as a team. By being mission driven, the principal is responsible for ensuring that the whole staff's efforts are always greater than the sum of their individual parts.

While leaders are decision makers, and while the ultimate decision of what happens may come down to the principal, *the principal lives out and models the effort to listen to others (including students), to learn from others (including students), and to lead with others (including students!).* Leading together naturally guides Aspire High to an approach of shared responsibility for the well-being of everyone in the school.

On your mark. Get set! Go!!

PRINCIPAL

Step =====>

- *Share leadership.* This is much easier said than done. As a matter of fact, sharing leadership sounds paradoxical. The key here is to find the balance between providing opportunities for others to take on a leadership role while still maintaining a level of involvement that is not intrusive. Find something to delegate.
- *Ask for feedback on your leadership.* Surveys work; however, there are more information-rich ways to gather feedback on how well you are doing as a leader. The most effective method is to conduct focus groups regularly that are supported by trust and respect. Sit down and schedule them.

Stride =====>

- *Mentor aspiring leaders.* Just like teaching, leadership is a craft that requires skill development and practice. As the "ranking" leader in your building, this responsibility is yours to take on. You need to develop leadership capacity in others to effectively achieve your school's mission. Choose two shining stars, and approach them with a plan to mentor them.
- *Be visible. Everyone knows that you can't effectively lead a school building from behind an office door.* This is easy to know and say, but it seems difficult to do. Bring a high level of intention to the need to have a presence in the hallways, the cafeteria, and most importantly, the classroom. Get up and interact with students and staff out in the building.

Sprint =====>

- *Involve students in meaningful schoolwide decisions.* Most principals are comfortable involving staff in decision making (though some rely too heavily on an inner circle). Involving students is totally different and more challenging. Be brave (and smart) and have at least two students actively participate on a hiring committee. You will be amazed at what they see that you don't.
- *Rearrange staff meetings so others lead.* It can be anxiety producing and more challenging to share control of meetings or completely turn them over. Staff-led meetings have greater value for staff. Without exception, you will see leaders emerge in your staff that will surprise you. Find willing leaders for your upcoming staff meetings, and share leadership of the meeting with them.

TEACHERS

Step ====>

- *Communicate and share concerns directly with leadership.* Granted, it is so much easier talking about leadership when the principal is not in front of you. But we all know that gossip rarely is productive, nor does it typically result in positive consequences. Make an appointment.
- *Get to know your principal's hopes and dreams as a leader.* Just as it is important for the principal to know your hopes and dreams, it is important for teachers to know the principal's. Knowing what is important to each other facilitates not only better understanding, but builds mutual respect that is of great value in schools. Ask your principal what his or her hopes are for your school.

Stride ====>

- *Actively and productively participate in professional learning opportunities.* Teachers need to take the lead for their own learning. Be proactive, and lead with your principal to determine what is best for you and the entire staff in order to provide students the best type of teaching and learning environment. Find a colleague or two who want to learn the same thing you do, and approach the principal with a plan.
- *Seek out emergent leadership opportunities.* Don't wait for someone to anoint you as a leader. Actively go looking. Feel free to step forward when the time is right, and step back again if what you have to offer is not needed. Emerge as a leader at both the building and the district level. The best way to get connected to the leadership of the building is to work side by side.

Sprint ====>

- *Enroll in leadership courses.* We are all busy, but we should never be too busy to stimulate our mind with new learning. In addition to the usual courses in educational leadership, consider taking classes in organizational change, behavioral theory, improvement science, policy development, and so on. Google them and sign up.
- *Continually hold yourself and your colleagues accountable to achieving the school mission.* Mission statements are not just plaques to be hung in the office or documents that are hauled out when there is an accreditation visit. In effective schools, everyone lives the mission. If you don't know your school's mission statement by heart, learn it. Then live it.

STUDENTS

Step ⟹

- *Introduce yourself to the principal.* Sure, that sounds a bit frightening, and when we were students, we never wanted the principal to know our name because it usually meant we were in trouble. But times have changed, and principals want to know their students. You would make the life of your principal easier if you took the initiative with the introductions. Make an appointment to introduce yourself.
- *Be supportive of school leadership rather than finding fault.* Having spent quite a few years in school, you probably know what works and what doesn't, what your school does right and what it does horribly wrong. It is easy to be judgmental, especially of the people in charge. We challenge you to consider your school with an attitude of "Why is this a good idea?" rather than "What the heck is the principal thinking?" Share with your friends and adults what you think is working.

Stride ⟹

- *Attend schoolwide/districtwide meetings.* It is impossible to be a leader in a school if you do not have a presence at the places where decisions are made. You don't need to be the star of the show—yet. But at the very least you need to be seen. Going to school board meetings (you don't need an invitation), department meetings (you might need to ask), or various other committee meetings is a good place to start. Find a meeting that interests you, and ask if you can attend.
- *Take school surveys seriously.* You need to look upon surveys and focus groups as an opportunity to share your ideas and thoughts about your school. To take your participation to the next level, ask to see the results of any survey you and your friends have taken. Then offer solutions and talk about how you are accepting responsibilities to improve the situation.

Sprint ⟹

- *Run for an elected position related to the school.* This is a daunting task, considering how busy students are with the day-to-day challenges of being a student. Nonetheless, seize opportunities to not only lead in an informal way but also as an elected school official. Your impact will be greater than you think.
- *Do your homework.* Aside from doing your homework in your subject areas, we are challenging you to do your homework on your school. Learn and understand what is happening at your school. From budgets to bus routes, make the effort to know all that you can about your school. Then be a part of the solution.

Is Your School . . . ?		
TYPICAL HIGH	**ASPIRE HIGH**	**ASPIRING HIGHER**
The principal has an "open-door policy" that few take advantage of.	The principal establishes and protects time to meet with students and staff by going through the open door.	Students and teachers arrange meetings with their administrative support as needed.
The principal, pressured from above, talks about "implementation with fidelity," but is open to new ideas.	The principal seeks out new ideas and implements them as needed.	Teachers and students drive implementation of all policies and practices.
The principal provides feedback to staff following evaluation protocols.	The principal provides ongoing formal and informal feedback to staff and students.	Feedback, supported by the principal, becomes a natural part of all that staff and students do.
The principal appoints teachers to various committees to support administrative functions.	All teachers serve on committees on a rotating basis to support school-driven goals and needs.	Teachers and students develop and serve on committees that support the work of the school.
Teachers accept responsibility for the decisions being made in collaboration with the principal.	The principal, teachers, and students share in important decisions.	As a global- and community-oriented school, the focus of decision making by the school community is outward.
The principal's primary role vis-á-vis students is haphazard and student management related.	Students initiate partnerships with the principal.	Relationships between the principal and students are deep and meaningful.
The principal leads nearly all initiatives and efforts at the school level.	Leadership is "flipped"—teachers are given responsibility for school-level decisions and implementation.	Students and teachers, supported by administration, enjoy levels of autonomy related to classroom and schoolwide decisions.
The principal mentors a self-selected one or two aspiring administrators from among teachers.	The principal coaches and teaches all staff and students in how to effectively be school leaders.	Coaching and mentoring for leadership occurs beyond the school building.
The principal's duties require significant amounts of time in the office and out of the building.	The principal places strict limitations on office and out-of-building time in order to spend the majority of time in and throughout the building.	Given pervasive sharing of leadership functions within the building, the principal's time is free for local, state, and national networking and advocacy.

Is Your School . . . ?		
TYPICAL HIGH	**ASPIRE HIGH**	**ASPIRING HIGHER**
Staff meetings are pro forma, and typical agendas are driven by administrative needs and concerns.	Regular meetings include staff and students, and agendas are driven by the concerns of the entire school community.	Regular meetings include scheduled, periodic networking with other schools to learn and advocate for best practices.
Communication from the principal seems untimely and rushed to those receiving the information.	Communication systems regularly and consistently ensure a flow of information in all directions.	Communication includes frequent and direct involvement with other schools and the community.
The principal's role with parents tends to be formally related to traditional parent meetings and informally related to reacting to upset parents.	The principal's role with parents is to encourage and invite their regular participation in the life of the school.	The principal uses technology and other means to create a school without walls. Parents and community are welcome at all times.
The principal feels like a middle manager for district-level decisions and programs.	The principal has site-based autonomy and is responsible to the district for decisions.	District personnel play a partnership role, not a hierarchical role, and are involved in learning and decision making.
Within a district or region, the principal tends to compete with other schools (for recognition and students).	The principal is highly collaborative with other administrators to learn and grow together.	The principal shares programs and resources with others schools.
The principal and central office provide professional development according to current program needs.	Internal experts—staff and students—deliver professional development based on their assessment of learning needs.	"Professional development," as such, does not exist, as everyone's ongoing learning is the nature of participation at the school.
The principal knows teachers through their required growth plan. Goal setting is a function of current, district-mandated programs.	The principal knows each staff member's professional and individual hopes, dreams, aspirations, and goals.	Staff assignments are based on a collaborative assessment of teacher and student goals.

4

Involving Parents in Meaningful and Productive Ways

Parents can only give good advice or put them on the right paths, but the final forming of a person's character lies in their own hands.

—Anne Frank

LISTEN

We realize that we have likely matched the principal's 15,000 steps as well as we follow Mr. Harper to the Inspiration Café. Along the way, Zawadi replaced Matthew O'Malley, and then Mariana replaced Zawadi. The students talked to us about what they liked best about Aspire High and what they thought could be improved. Mr. Harper asked as many questions as we did, seemingly not wanting to lose an opportunity to interact with students. At one point, Mr. Harper learned that Mariana was struggling academically as she is rethinking her career goals.

"Yeah, at first I was all over being a corporate lawyer because my mom's a lawyer and her father was one, too. But about a month ago for one of my classes—it was a business unit—we went to a law firm and spent the day, talked to a lot of lawyers . . . all who seemed to enjoy what they do. But I left not so sure anymore."

Mr. Harper said, "Better to find out now than 10 years from now. But let's make sure you're sure you're not sure. Who's your academy adviser?"

"Professor Kate."

"Let her know, and we can follow up together and with your mom."

Mariana returned to class when we arrived at the café.

The Inspiration Café is a smaller room off the main cafeteria run by parent volunteers with the help of students. We learn that culinary students frequently prepare the food offered here. "This is where I have most of my meetings with parents and community members. I have to sign it out of course, at least if we need some privacy. But I like the tone it sets—it's nonthreatening, casual, more suitable to the kinds of conversations I have with most people. It doesn't trigger all that baggage of being 'summoned to the principal's office.'" He makes the sound of the three ominous chords you hear at the end of a skit that implies threat or impending doom. "I make a lot of decisions here over a cup of coffee and a conversation. I think it's critical to hear all sides of an issue . . . parent–teacher, student–adult, student–student, teacher–teacher. I like saying, 'Let's get a cup of coffee.' Of course, some prefer tea or something cold."

The first of just two scheduled parent meetings is about to start. He says, "You can probably stay for the first one, but for the second, we'll have to see." He sends a quick text asking his administrative assistant to ask the adults waiting to talk to him if it's OK for a few people studying Aspire High to be silent observers in the meeting. "All good; they are on their way," he says.

The three parents arrive at the same time as our drinks and are introduced individually and then collectively as Parents Engaging Pupils—PEPs. "I thought of that," says one of the parents proudly. "The kids ask each other all the time: 'Anyone doing a PEP talk this week?'"

Another parent explains that PEPs was created to deal with time challenges related to parenting as it relates to school. We learn that, given the diversity at Aspire High, some students have very busy parents, some have only one parent, some live with other relatives, and so on. There are many family configurations at Aspire High. Yet homework must be monitored, cocurricular activities need transportation and sometimes oversight, social activities need to be supervised, and various parent functions (e.g., orientation, parent-teacher-student meetings, etc.) must be organized. The three people in the café today are the leadership of a multi-tier solution to aligning the needs of the school to the families of Aspire High.

There is another ring of about 30 parents around this leadership team. They provide both a go-to group of workers when needed and the first part of a two-way communication system involving all the rest of the parents. They help move information about schedules, activities, and family news (as appropriate) up and down various communication channels—phone calls, e-mails, texts, tweets, Google docs, and so on. The original working theory of PEPs was that a parental community that was robustly networked could be a far greater asset to the students and staff of Aspire High than either parents working independently or in loosely and haphazardly affiliated groups—which typically form along socioeconomic lines. "That working theory has proven itself again and again," Mr. Harper remarks.

The leadership of PEPs is checking in with Mr. Harper about the upcoming homecoming activities—a week of celebration culminating in a one-act stage performance Thursday evening and Saturday afternoon, a football game on Friday evening, and a dance Saturday night. School on Thursday will be shortened for a pep rally for both the students in the play and the football team. The meeting is brief and includes updates on the set construction and strike schedule, coverage for the concession stand at the game, and chaperone coverage at the dance. While this particular meeting is about a large-scale event, PEPs also coordinates more routine activities, such as a homework check-in system, an Aspirations Advocates program, and ride-sharing schemes. While PEPs is not the only parental group at Aspire High, it is among the most critical.

One of the underlying premises of Aspire High is that everyone aspires— that is, everyone has the ability to dream about the future and to be inspired in the present to reach those dreams. This view extends to parents as well. Not just that they, like all persons, have goals and a desire to work toward those goals, but that they have aspirations *as parents*. They have hopes for their sons and daughters. They have dreams for their role in supporting their children toward their own aspirations. And most parents are doing the best they can. Certainly, their children believe that, as nearly all (94%) agree that "My parents care about my education" (*QSVNR*, 2016). The staff members at Aspire High believe their professional responsibilities include supporting parents so they can live up to and out of that care.

Consequently, there is no conversation among the faculty or administration at Aspire High about parents who "are not doing their job"—as if anyone adequately understands the "job" of parenting in any particular family. Parents are not seen as guests or visitors or intruders. They are not clients or customers. They, like the students, are the school's partners. No matter what their circumstances, advantages, or challenges, parents are seen as assets to the school and their child's primary advocate and teacher. *Parents are most welcome and regularly sought out as allies in the mission of Aspire High.*

This does not mean that the staff at Aspire High see all parents through rose-colored glasses. It does mean that they operate out of the realization that none of their students selected her or his parents. Each student, therefore, deserves professional educators who are willing to build a relationship of trust, expectation, and support with the adults at each student's home. Developing that relationship involves a realistic and judgment-free assessment of each family's capacities. The staff devote professional development time to learning about family systems in general and to getting to know the particular families of the students in their care. Just as we will see when we discuss the curriculum and the world, the professional staff members train to see the walls between school and home as porous and permeable, not made of stone.

Building a learning community this broad must be achieved; it is not automatic. Despite the orientation material, not every parent that sends his or her child to Aspire High at first understands what is expected of him or her. While there is no set number of hours or activities any parent or caregiver must contribute, each one must stay engaged with the school in some capacity. The options and opportunities for this are numerous and range from weekly volunteer work to one-time participation in a major event. All of these expectations and opportunities are articulated to parents by parents. While school administration stays involved and itself develops relationships with parents and families, for the most part, parents at Aspire High set these expectations and provide the needed support to meet the expectations for one another.

Beyond this level of involvement in the school as a community, all parents and caregivers are expected to stay involved as their son or daughter's primary learning advocates. There are various ways parents can access student academic work and outcomes. However, beyond that traditional approach of parent-as-homework-supervisor-and-report-card-signatory, parents are expected to learn alongside their children. The curriculum involves parents and entire families in various ways from interview subjects to coresearchers. Aspire High is a learning *community*, and insofar as parents are integral members of the community, their role as colearners is essential.

LEARN

How and why does parental and caregiver involvement really matter in school? This is a question Aspire High ponders regularly. Aspire High does not just involve parents because it seems right; rather, educators know that parental and caregiver support helps the school meet its mission of supporting every student to reach his or her fullest potential. Routman (1996) provides examples of the need to include parents: "Partnerships with parents are an absolute necessity for successful [school] reform efforts. We are naïve if we think we can make changes in our teaching without support of the parents" (p. 64). Parents have a voice at Aspire High. They are not teachers and they don't advise on pedagogy, yet their support and involvement is crucial to building a successful school.

While some educators may debate if parents really care about education, *the reality is that parents do care about their child's education and future.* Even though parents may not show care in the ways teachers want—for students to arrive at school on time or for them to oversee homework completion and attend parent conferences—most parents do the best they can. Although some research questions whether parental participation matters (Robinson & Harris, 2014), many studies support the need for parental involvement in our schools.

- Regardless of family income or background, students whose parents are involved in their schooling are more likely to have higher grades and test scores, attend school regularly, have better social skills, show improved behavior, and adapt well to school (Henderson & Mapp, 2002).
- Parental involvement was found to improve academic and emotional functioning among adolescents. In addition, parental involvement predicted adolescent academic success and mental health both directly and indirectly through behavioral and emotional engagement (Wang & Sheikh-Khalil, 2014).
- Working to include parents is particularly important as students grow older and in schools with high concentrations of poor and minority students (Rutherford et al., 1997).
- Students with parents who are involved in their school tend to have fewer behavioral problems and better academic performance and are more likely to complete high school than students whose parents are not involved in their school (Henderson & Berla, 1994).
- A recent meta-analysis showed that parental involvement in school life was more strongly associated with high academic performance for middle schoolers than helping with homework (Hill & Tyson, 2009).

Aspire High operates under the premise that parental/caregiver involvement and voice is important. Given this premise, Aspire high has a threefold strategy to connect with parents: develop positive relationships with parents, establish meaningful parental engagement, and build a school that supports students and families to lead healthy, positive lives. All three of these strategies align with the mission of Aspire High.

The Power of Positive Relationships

The first tactic used at Aspire High to build positive relationships and foster community for parents is to understand and know who the parents are each year. Over the summer (staff are on a year-round contract), Aspire High staff work with local officials to learn the current demographics of the community. There are years when the surrounding areas gain an influx of new citizens due to resettlement issues or housing changes, and accordingly, this can alter the socioeconomic status (SES) and ethnicity of the students. Aspire High teaches and believes in all students' potential; however, in order to facilitate their mission the staff must connect with parents in an open and welcoming manner. That means sometimes meetings and parental communication are in Spanish or any of the dozen other native languages of students who attend the school. Lead Learners also take the time to know if their students reside with caregivers, grandparents, relatives, foster care, or, sadly, are homeless. Adults at Aspire High are aware that the number of homeless children in public schools reached a record national total of 1.36 million (3%) during the 2013–2014 school year (http://www./ed.gov). Each year there is an unfortunate expectation at Aspire High that some students may not have a home or adequate shelter. The school works proactively with social service agencies to mitigate this and considers the impact of these circumstances on student learning.

Additionally, given that Aspire High is a public high school, on the occasion that a student is transitioning from a juvenile detention center to Aspire High, the principal takes the time to meet with the student, teachers, experts from the detention center, and parents/caregivers in order to establish connections and develop opportunities for success. Aspire High leads the reentry planning that begins before a student is discharged from his juvenile justice placement; continues with regular communication and collaboration between the educational and correctional systems, the student, and his family; and involves an interagency transition team that has clear roles and responsibilities (Feierman, Levick, & Mody, 2009). Aspire High also works closely with social work experts to provide wraparound services to meet the student's non-school-related needs. *These living and social realities affect a student's ability to be present in and attend school, as well as achieve his or her aspirations.*

Another tactic Aspire High employs to build relations with parents and caregivers is through consistent communication. At the start of the school year, Lead Learners and administration venture into the community to do home visits and introductions. As Thomas Barone (1989) puts it, most educators "have lost the ability to reach out and honor the places (whether the barrio, the ghetto, the reservation, the Appalachian holler, or simply the peaks and pits of adolescence) where our students live" (p. 151). But at Aspire High, home visits build relationships and trust. Staff prioritize meeting with new students or students in danger of not returning to school. In particular, education researchers have discussed the importance of visiting with immigrant families to discover these families' strengths and talents (Ginsberg, 2007; Lopez, 2001; Moll, Amanti, Neff, & González, 1992). All staff members divide up these responsibilities and make welcome calls as needed.

Additionally, parents are regularly invited to complete surveys, participate in focus groups at the café, and have lunch with the principal and the students he is sitting with that day. The principal and staff communicate with parents through e-mails, voicemail, class web pages, and a variety of other technological means. As stated earlier, the principal provides his cell phone number for parents to call him during a specific time block. At the end of the year, the staff send thank-you notes to parents for their help and support. As with home visits, staff divide the student population to conquer this task.

A third tactic Aspire High uses to build positive relations is to draw on the skills and talents of parents. The outreach and communication in the first two strategies inform this third strategy. The staff of Aspire High *know* their families, their capacities, their resources, their strengths, and their talents. The school web page regularly posts upcoming assignments and activities for which parental help is needed. For example, a biology Lead Learner may post a lesson that relates to using a microscope and may put out a request for any parent who uses microscopes in their profession. This parent is then invited to share his or her work and the various ways learning about microscopes relates to his or her career. Alternatively, Lead Learners reach out to particular parents they know have a specific talent or can fill a specific need. Perhaps an economics unit requires learning about recessions. The Lead Learner contacts parents who are known to be bankers, businesspeople, or even managers of a food pantry to share the realities of recession on their jobs and the people they serve.

BEYOND TOKEN INVOLVEMENT

Mike Gibbons, former head of a succession of successful schools in England and Belgium, and then lead director of the Innovation Unit at the Department for Education and Skills in London

If you want parents' engagement and involvement in school life to go beyond a token involvement, it's a tough business. Helping out, raising funds, and attending and supporting events is token involvement. Participating in setting, monitoring, and adjusting vision, policy, and strategy is authentic involvement. Cosmetic engagement can be easy but ultimately only ticks boxes with no appreciable benefit in terms of culture or helping the school work better and more effectively.

When starting out with parents' engagement as a new endeavour, you should work on the basis that the school needs to think anew, to start again. Then undertake real and committed consultation. Consultation should involve all those steps and stages that real commitment to Student Voice entails. It means research to gather parent views and reach a broad, representative cross section of opinions and ideas. Research can mean use of questionnaires as well as conversations with groups of parents to reach deeper into the reasons behind concerns, aspirations, hopes, and fears. That consultation should start with the

(Continued)

(Continued)

overarching vision for the school, and then it can move on to examining and reflecting on the school's work on a subject-by-subject basis.

It should include discussion of and implementation of communications such as the school's website so that the site provides parents with real and helpful information. Parents may wish to have up-to-date information on what's coming up at school and on the homework given—all provided in a parent-friendly form—to ensure that information can be relied upon to be available and current, as well as be something that parents can search for, find, and use easily.

At one of [our] schools, each class elected a parent representative who met regularly with school staff to review issues associated with strategy and planning. The meetings encouraged airing of issues that could be discussed and addressed, more often than not, before they could become problems. This approach worked well because all parties engaged maturely in the meetings, and parents took positive approaches because they were being taken seriously and listened to.

At another school (one in which there had been some challenges), when I met parents for the first time things went awry. Parents were agitated and loud in their assertions. Under pressure, with a poorly organised and chaired meeting, I found myself seeking to rationalise with some and making up answers on the hoof. One thing I did promise was a second meeting six weeks later.

I organised the second meeting differently. Parents sat at round tables and were asked, through well-structured questions, to reflect on the last six weeks and what had worked and what had not. Some more strident voices were moderated by the group process. Discussion became less about individual gripes and more about organisation and strategy. When the tables came through with conclusions, responses were considered, and no false or risky promises were made. The conditions allowed greater trust and maturity, and I observed that nobody lost his or her dignity at that second meeting, in contrast with the events of the first.

All of this points to the importance of commitment to Parent Voice, its effective management and support, and the benefits and challenges associated with parental commitment to school beyond tokenism.

- Mike Gibbons states, "When starting out with parents' engagement as a new endeavour, you should work on the basis that the school needs to think anew, to start again." What parts of your current parent practice do you believe would benefit from starting again? Why?
- How do you currently research parents' opinions, thoughts, and ideas? What more might you do to expand or deepen feedback from parents?

- How could your parent meetings be improved to make them more engaging and participatory rather than simply informational?
- What is the greatest benefit of having robust parental involvement? What is the greatest challenge or risk?

The Effectiveness of Meaningful Engagement

Engaging parents if they do not attend meetings or read or listen to communication sent home is challenging. To ease the initial hurdle of getting parents into a high school setting, meetings at the beginning of the year for parents are held at both the high school and the local feeder schools. Parents attend at whichever location is more convenient. There is a two-fold reason for this approach to parent engagement. First, high schools tend to have lower parental involvement than elementary and middle schools, as many parents recall their own high schools negatively. In fact, a 2012 *Child Trends* report states that 89% of students in Grades K–5 were represented at parent–teacher meetings, compared with just 71% of middle school students and 57% of high school students (www.childtrends.org). By meeting in a familiar environment, parents get to know the principal and staff prior to having to navigate a large high school building .Second, transportation is a challenge for many parents due to lack of a vehicle or the financial costs of taking public transportation to a high school, whereas many middle schools are closer to the neighborhoods of students and their families.

Staff and administration at Aspire High are cognizant of the time demands on parents. Accordingly, they strive to make parent interactions meaningful. During all parent meetings, a cheat sheet of educational acronyms is available. As hard as the staff try not to talk in the alphabet soup of educational jargon, terms such as *SAC*, *PET*, *BLT*, and so on unintentionally slip into the conversation. The school also provides translators during all meetings. When possible, the translators are students. A second tactic used to engage parents is that, as with staff meetings, parent meetings do not review dates or any information that can be read or listened to or viewed as podcasts or prerecorded videos. Parent meetings are opportunities to learn from parents, answer questions, and create action plans related to parental involvement. Meetings are held in the café, and either the school makes a spaghetti-type dinner or the community organizes a potluck—both of which are greatly appreciated by parents coming straight from work.

Parents are also meaningfully engaged through a program called Aspirations Advocates. This program trains community members to mentor students at the school. The mentoring program is not a tutoring scheme; rather, the goal is to make sure as many students as possible have an extra, caring adult in their lives. Advocates must attend training to learn about supporting Self-Worth, Engagement, and Purpose for students. The program also pairs one adult with two students in order to foster peer relationships. Thus, when adults attend Aspiration Advocates meetings, they are fully engaged in the learning and the project at hand.

The Ultimate Open-Door Policy

A final tactic related to meaningful parental involvement is that Aspire High is a school open to the local community—a place where community services are housed and community activities are welcomed. According to the Coalition for Community Schools, community schools are places where "schools and communities connect, collaborate, and create. Children and families have an array of supports from community partners right at their school. Communities and schools leverage their shared physical and human assets to help kids succeed" (n.d.). On any given night, a visitor may see adults playing basketball, Junior Achievement meetings taking place, or voters registering. To encourage community use, the school facilitates evening classes for parents. Classes include everything from ESL to practical how-tos for parents to help navigate financial applications for college. As long as there is demand, the school helps to organize the class. If there is a request to learn about something and the school has student experts, then the students lead the learning. Aspire High also partners with local agencies to provide health and housing services located in or near the school. Parents welcome the opportunity for school to be a hub where they can have many of their questions answered and services provided.

Related to this communal approach, administration and staff at Aspire High advocate and speak up about issues related to parents that affect the education of students. For example, if the city is considering rezoning housing districts or rerouting bus lines, school staff demand a voice on how this will affect the current and future education of students. When budgets are discussed related to organizations such as the local YMCA or other places students and parents attend, a school representative shows up to support the need for such services for families. *Parents and caregivers know that the educators at Aspire High are on their side when it comes to wanting their children to reach their hopes and dreams.*

COMMUNICATING FOR COMMUNITY

Andy Torris, Director of the Universal American School in Dubai

Andy's administrative career has included work as an elementary vice-principal, middle school vice-principal, elementary principal, PreK–12 principal, and middle school principal. The Universal American School in Dubai is an internationally accredited IB World School, offering a high-quality education to a student body of 1,500 that represents 75 nationalities.

The school has a unique set of community opportunities. The students' parents are professionals with busy lives. Their children, while a priority, are often taken care of by domestic helpers (e.g., nannies, tutors, etc.). This leads to the parents assuming that the school will provide the same level of support in lieu of parenting. This assumption initially led to a lack of parent engagement.

In an effort to counterbalance this concern, we took the opportunity to move beyond the "open-door policy" and opened up the entire organization. Rather than wait on them to take the initiative, we invited parents, whose experiences in schools were much different than in our American school in Dubai, to visit the school. Our first step in this effort was to increase communication coming out of the school. We shared our stories about things that parents find compelling and invitational.

Next, we focused on personal relationships, which are key to gaining support in our school culture. Our leadership team stepped out in front of our community and, more importantly, into the midst of our parents. We believe we're a learning community and that we must learn and teach each other. This required that we become open to the inevitable criticisms that followed.

We now open up school initiatives to discourse about specific programs, as well as engage with outside experts who can support our school reform efforts. Additionally, we gather our school parent leaders in small, intimate forums where we simply listen and acknowledge their ideas, criticisms, and celebrations. It is through making ourselves open and vulnerable that we hear the voices of the community most clearly.

- What is unique about your parent community (e.g., in the Dubai school, it is the presence of caretakers) that you need to consider as affecting parental partnership?
- What improvements to communication systems might lead to better outcomes? How is what you are sharing with parents "compelling and invitational"?
- Discuss what it would mean to be vulnerable and open to your parent population. How can you develop the needed organizational readiness to take parental critiques constructively?

For Reflection

⬥ What are the best examples of parental partnership you have seen? How did these develop? Why were they effective?

◇ Consider a time you made an effort to understand a student's home life. What was the impact of that effort on your approach to teaching and learning with that student?
◇ Debate and discuss the following statement with colleagues: "Parental involvement in their child's education is 'icing on the cake'—it's sweet, but not necessary."
◇ Discuss with a group of parents their current satisfaction with how the school involves them. What could be improved?

LEAD

Of all the complexities in our educational system, one of the biggest challenges involves the role of parents. We stand up at the beginning of every school year, asking parents to "come visit the school," saying things such as, "The school is yours," and, "We want you here as much as you can be." While the sentiment behind these invitations may be heartfelt, we wonder whether there isn't an underlying hope that most parents, if not all, will not take the invitation seriously. Of course we want parents to be involved with their child's education, and of course we want them to feel a sense of ownership and pride in the school. But do we really want them coming in and out of school all the time?

In our experience, most teachers and administrators see parental visits as more of an intrusion than a support. Can you imagine 10 ninja mothers—or worse, grandmothers!—visiting your school on a daily basis? If you can imagine it, the thought will probably keep you up at night! Virtually everyone is in agreement that having a positive role model at home to support and encourage learning is important. And we understand and appreciate that, as we have seen, almost *all* students believe their parents care about their education. But how do you channel the potential energy of parents into something meaningful for the entire student body?

Being a parent is certainly more than being on a booster club and raising money or volunteering one's time at some event. *The role of the parent in a student's education can be critical; however, schools have yet to capitalize on that parent potential and turn it into meaningful action.* Parents have a more purposeful role at Aspire High, but it is up to the important players *inside* the building to set the stage for it to happen.

On your mark. Get set! Go!!

PRINCIPAL

Step ⟹

- *Communicate with parents in their native language.* Sending out information (phone calls, e-mails, newsletters) doesn't help if parents don't understand what you are saying. Communicating in their language not only allows parents to know what is going on but also shows they matter to you. Additionally, consider delivering parental information at events they attend (e.g., athletic events, a theater, etc.). As long as you have a captive audience, you should take advantage of that.
- *Survey parents.* Don't let the typically low-return rates on parent surveys discourage you. The trick, as with all surveys, is to have a plan for doing something with what you learn. Take action on survey results, and you will build confidence in your future use of surveys. The key is to start the habit.

Stride ⟹

- *Hold monthly luncheons for parents with a focused topic for Q & A.* Everyone appreciates a good meal. Most parents would welcome the idea of coming to school for a lunch. Just make sure it does not turn into an opportunity for you to lecture. Informal dialogue will build trust and stronger relationships between you and the parents.
- *Regularly conduct focus group sessions with parents.* It takes time, but sitting down and having a meaningful conversation with parents is critical. Keep in mind that these sessions are not designed for parents to come and complain; rather, they are an opportunity for you to get input from them around issues you are considering.

Sprint ⟹

- *Offer evening learning opportunities for parents.* Staff, community members, other parents, and students could teach various topics. The best way to get parents to school is make sure you are providing *them* with something useful. Offer classes that are of interest to the parents and other adult family members—maybe even a GED course or something that will help them reach their aspirations.
- *Commit to calling a dozen parents every week to provide updates about their children.* The key is to call with good news, not bad news. Let parents know you care about their children, and share something the parents should be proud of.

TEACHERS

Step ===⟶

- *Respond to all parent e-mails in a timely manner.* This is simple and obvious maybe, but at the same time critically important. Whether it is good news or bad, parents want information in a timely fashion. Waiting a day or two for a reply to an inquiry about their child can seem like an eternity to a parent.
- *Offer suggestions, ideas, and tips on how parents can help their child be successful in your class.* Most parents want to help their children in school but don't know how. Regularly sending home a few tips on what they can do at home to promote learning would go a long way in building relationships—not to mention, help you and their child!

Stride ===⟶

- *Volunteer with parents at school events.* It is one thing having parents volunteer for school events, but it is quite another for you to show up and show your support and appreciation for what they do. Working beside parents gives you an opportunity to interact with them on their terms.
- *Take pictures to show parents what their children are doing in school.* Use various forms of technology to highlight the work of the students in your classroom. We are not suggesting making public posts of student pictures, but instead, send pictures of their children directly to parents. Parents love getting photos of their children when they are in school, and images cut through language barriers.

Sprint ===⟶

- *On a weekly basis, commit to calling at least one parent per class with good news about his or her child.* Certainly, this is not the easiest thing to do, but it is a surefire way to not only let parents know what is going on in your class but also to give them a reason to be proud of their children! A win-win scenario for sure.
- *Write a personal note each marking period to your students' parents.* There is no question that this is a daunting task, but if you want to get connected to the parents, *you* need to take the initiative. Sending home a personal note will certainly let the parents know you care about their children. It does not have to be long—a sentence or two goes a long way.

STUDENT

Step ⟹

- *Share what you learn at school each day with someone at home—not your grade on a test or assignment, but what you* learned. Talk, talk, talk—let your parents know what is going on, and share with them one thing you learned that they don't know. When they ask, "How was school?" go beyond "Fine."
- *Bring home school communication.* It is impossible to expect your parents to be supportive of you in school if they don't know what is going on. Dig paperwork and announcements out of the bottom of your backpack, and make sure they get them the day they are given to you.

Stride ⟹

- *Arrange to attend teacher conferences with your parents.* The truth is that most parents don't like going to parent–teacher conferences. But going together will be less painful for everyone—especially your parents! The grown-ups will be discussing *you,* after all!
- *Ask your parents or grandparents about their experiences in school and what they would do differently if they could go back in time.* The key here is to have conversations with your parents. Shift the conversation to them, and ask them about their school experiences. Chances are you may have more in common than you think.

Sprint ⟹

- *Volunteer at a school event with a parent.* It is great if your parents have time to volunteer at your school. If they do, go with them. As they show support for you and your school, you need to do the same for them.
- *Attend a school board meeting or school committee meeting with your parents.* Sure, there are more exciting things to do with your parents, but having a voice at your local school board meeting is important. Challenge each other to ask a question or speak up on an issue that concerns you. Discuss your perspective on the meeting on the way home.

Is Your School . . . ?		
TYPICAL HIGH	**ASPIRE HIGH**	**ASPIRING HIGHER**
Selected parents are sporadically involved in school decisions.	All parents are meaningfully involved in school decisions.	Parents are a regular part of decision-making processes and committees.
Parent meetings are rare, poorly attended, and largely informational.	Parent meetings are held on a regular basis and are learning oriented.	Parent meetings are led by a diverse group of parents, students, and school staff with the goal of supporting all students' learning.
Parents have access to their children's grades—typically online.	Communication with parents includes narratives and progress updates.	Communication feedback loops between teachers, students, and parents become a natural way of being.
Available parents volunteer to serve on designated school committees.	Opportunities are created for *all* parents to participate in school life in different capacities, roles, and at convenient times.	Parents take the lead in promoting their children's school in various public forums.
Parents group informally according to cocurricular participation or certain "special-interest" groups.	The school arranges parent groups that are positive and build greater awareness of parenting challenges and solutions.	Parents invite other parents from neighboring districts to participate in forums, discussions, and other school-related experiences.
Parents typically side with their children against teachers and administrators.	Parents work in partnership with teachers and administrators to achieve their children's best interest.	Parents advocate for school improvements that benefit all students.
The most vocal parents typically drive agendas and have disproportional influence.	The school has systems and structures for all parents to have an equal voice.	All parents feel comfortable initiating important issues to be discussed.
The school acknowledges a variety of family structures.	The school actively supports the different needs of students, depending upon their family structure.	The school staff seek opportunities to learn about and conduct research on the connection between family structures and student learning.
The school accommodates a variety of ethnic, racial, and cultural family backgrounds.	The school celebrates and leverages the diversity of its student families.	The racial and ethnic demography of school families shapes the curriculum.

Is Your School . . . ?		
TYPICAL HIGH	ASPIRE HIGH	ASPIRING HIGHER
The school is generally indifferent to, unaware of, and at the mercy of local municipal policies that affect families.	To support parents and families, the school studies and attempts to influence local policies that affect them.	The school community advocates for local policies (e.g., housing, bussing, shelters, etc.) that affect their parents and students.
Other than for sanctioned cocurricular activities, school closes at the end of the school day.	The school is open in the evenings and on weekends for family and community use.	The school uses community spaces (e.g., churches, libraries, community centers, etc.) as learning venues for students and the community—and vice versa.

5

Policies That Advance the Mission

> *If the structure does not permit dialogue,*
> *the structure must be changed.*
>
> —Paulo Freire

LISTEN

After checking with the next-scheduled parent, Mr. Harper asks us not to sit in on the second meeting. He offers no explanation, but we take it that something is to be discussed in confidence, and we gladly exit. We decide to go to the media center, as we know a group of students and teachers is meeting there to do some extra work on a policy project. While Aspire High has had peer mediation for a number of years, they are considering a peer adjudication policy. The thought is that for certain levels of student misconduct, peers—following guidelines developed by a committee of teachers, students, parents, and administrators—would "hear the case" and determine what consequences should be enacted.

After we are introduced, one student explains, "Last week we visited a school about an hour's drive away that has peer adjudication."

Another student chimes in, "We talked about what we learned a little bit on the van ride home, but we haven't had a chance to meet since then."

Paulo Freire's work has widely influenced people working in education, community development, community health, and many other fields. One of his most well-known and influential books, *Pedagogy of the Oppressed* (1972), highlights the need for dialogical methodology to education. A typical feature of Freire's approach to education is that people bring their own knowledge and experience into the process.

A teacher adds, "We want this as a policy at Aspire High, but we need to discuss implementation." They know there will need to be training, and they must consider how to have the panel of peer judges rotate and not be the same from year to year—as in a club or other cocurricular activity.

"We don't need a group of Judge Judies," agrees one parent.

After bringing us up to speed, they continue debating the length of the term of the panel and whether or not the entire panel should turn over at the same time or whether there should be some sort of staggering and overlap. The dialogue is lively. A teacher explains that they are under no pressure to come to a conclusion today or even this month.

It almost goes without saying that all policy at Aspire High is made by committees of students, teachers, and administrators, and, as needed, parents. Typically, when a policy is taken up for change or alteration or a new policy is considered for implementation, a team of interested adults and students is convened to study it. They conduct research online, interview professionals and authors of books on the policy's topic, and visit nearby schools that already have such a policy in place. If there is no school nearby that has a comparable policy, they find a way to videoconference with staff and students from a school that does.

One critical feature of this multiperspective approach is a willingness to stay in dialogue about the ideas being proposed for as long as possible before coming to a decision. While debates sometimes are required near the end of the process, the majority of the time is spent making sure that all who are participating feel they have been adequately heard and understood. This process includes everyone on the committee knowing they are fairly representing not just their own point of view but also that of their peers not on the committee. This means that an important responsibility of being involved with policy decisions is polling "public opinion" on the particular issue in question. Committee members use a variety of techniques from short surveys to focus groups to informal conversations to town-hall-type meetings.

Policy at Aspire High is always made with reference to the school's mission. Although we missed it for coming late to the conversation about peer adjudication, every policy meeting begins with this assertion: *This policy must contribute to the goal of each and every student developing the ability to dream and set goals for the future while being inspired in the present to reach those dreams.* Each meeting also ends with the committee checking in with the question "Do you believe the policy we are moving toward will contribute to each and every student's ability to dream about the future and be inspired in the present to get there?" Each member must answer "Yes" or "Not yet." While this mission frame sometimes feels rote, it is never neglected.

All policy decisions adhere to the Aspirations Framework that is Aspire High's underlying structure (see Quaglia & Corso, 2014). Policy must advance the Self-Worth, Engagement, and Purpose of anyone and everyone—students, staff, administrators, parents—that the policy may affect. These are the three Guiding Principles of the Aspirations Framework and, as such, are the governing principles of all policies that govern the learning environment at Aspire High. The fundamental shape of all policy must accomplish the following:

- *Promote a person's positive valuation of himself or herself.* This does not mean that the policy must make a person *feel* good about himself or herself. Rather, the policy must have the ability to support a person in gaining greater clarity about his or her self-worth and value as a person. Toward that end, all policy must promote these Conditions:

  - *Belonging*, not alienation
  - Being a *Hero* to one another, not a power trip
  - A *Sense of Accomplishment*, not frustration

- *Encourage a person's meaningful engagement in learning.* With learning at the center of Aspire High, all policy must consider the impact on student learning. Behavior that disrupts the learning environment is not tolerated by school policy, but neither are consequences that diminish the learning of a student who has offended. Toward that end, all policy must encourage these Conditions:

  - *Fun & Excitement*, not boredom or apathy
  - *Curiosity & Creativity*, not indifference or one-size-fits-all
  - A *Spirit of Adventure*, not fear or anxiety

- *Develop a person's ability to reflect on his or her intentions, commitments, and ability to think beyond himself or herself.* Decisions at Aspire High are deeply informed by a desire to help all affected by a policy to consider his or her own purpose and how adherence to or violation of a particular policy contributes to or diminishes that purpose. Toward that end, all policies must develop these Conditions:

  - *Leadership & Responsibility*, not drifting or lack of personal accountability
  - *Confidence to Take Action*, not uncertainty, passivity, or a victim mentality

The Aspirations Framework—from the school's mission to promote each student's aspiration to the Guiding Principles and into these 8 Conditions—drives policy creation and change at Aspire High. The work of the committees is to figure out how a particular policy or set of policies concretely enacts an element of the framework. Will the proposed changes to the school dress code create a greater sense of Leadership & Responsibility? How does the recommended new advisement policy advance the cause of Engagement in learning? What will be the impact of peer adjudication on the view of students as Heroes to one another?

LEARN

Policies in any organization are designed to provide *direction*, while procedures are the *actions* one takes under the guidance of the policies. These terms are subtly different, often erroneously interchanged, and yet worth distinguishing. Consider that policies are a map, whereas procedures are a vehicle for accomplishing a journey. No doubt the final destination may influence the choice of vehicle. To get from Boston to Bermuda, you may want to fly rather than take a boat or swim. But the map does not determine the choice of vehicle. You can cruise to Bermuda from Boston (or swim, for that matter) if you have other goals than simply to arrive.

Let's consider policies and procedures as they relate to testing. Traditionally, schools are "high performing" when tests scores reach or exceed a certain state-determined, standardized threshold. Accordingly, there are state and local *policies* related to assessment that provide direction for hitting the mark. In addition to the mandated high-stakes tests themselves, these policies often include end-of-course (EOC) exams. EOC exams typically also have a designated passing mark, and some policies dictate that the EOC must be a specific percentage of a student's final grade. In Florida, for example, EOC assessment scores count as 30% of students' final course grades (www.fldoe.org)—among the highest of any state. All of this "mapping" is set by policies.

The *procedures* for preparing for EOC exams may include pacing guides, practice tests, and tutoring, along with myriad questionable pedagogical practices such as overreliance on lectures to cover material, memorization of terms without understanding application, and, unfortunately, cheating. However, other procedures for achieving state targets on tests may include mastery, collaboration, use of technology, formative assessment, and other strategies designed to foster twenty-first-century skills. Such is the distinction between policies (which map a course) and procedures (which are vehicles for following the map) in a school whose policies and procedures are all about state-mandated tests.

At Aspire High, developing and sustaining a school with a focus on helping each student reach his or her fullest potential requires a different set of policies and procedures. As a result, assessment policy at Aspire High encompasses multiple evaluative measures of academic success, as well as personal, social, and emotional success. No student at Aspire High "fails" based on policy that mandates the passing of a single EOC. No student sits through hours of mandated standardized tests based on a regime designed to hold teachers accountable for teaching and learning. According to the National Center for Fair Testing ("Fair Test," 2012), "Already tens of thousands of students who have met all other high school graduation requirements are denied diplomas each year based solely on their scores on a state standardized test." This is an impossibility at Aspire High.

Accordingly, the procedures at Aspire High that follow a policy supportive of multiple measures of success require teachers to develop opportunities for formative assessment, student self-assessment, portfolio assessment, assessment through demonstration, as well as some traditional testing. These all become factors in judging student learning and progress. *At Aspire High, test scores are just one, and by no means the only, indicator of high performance.* Policies and procedures supportive of healthy self-awareness, positive relationships, meaningful engagement, thoughtful application, hard-earned mastery, contributory citizenship, Student Voice, and effort toward personal aspirations are all as important in the governance of *academic* matters at Aspire High, as is academic performance on tests.

The Aspirations Academy Trust (AAT; www.aspirationsacademies .org) in England oversees a consortium of schools that have all adopted the Aspirations Framework as a core set of principles for policies and procedures. The trust has identified four key areas of strategic focus: School Culture, Systems and Structures, Teaching and Learning, and High Aspirations. Each of these is tied to the Aspirations Framework in meaningful and appropriate ways. The AAT school improvement plan (2016) insists,

> The Aspirations Framework should influence the operation of the systems and structures at work in the school, as well as being a critical element in the teaching and learning process. The Three Guiding Principles and 8 Conditions that Make a Difference should be fully embedded into every aspect of the school—in the culture, the systems and structures and in the teaching and learning. (p. 3)

At AAT schools, all policy decisions refer to the overall goal of helping students dream about their futures and inspiring them in the present to work toward those dreams. The beneficial outcome of this approach has been proven insofar as all the schools that have been assessed by their national accrediting agency have achieved an increased performance rating. This includes several schools that were failing at the time the Trust undertook work with them (that subsequently achieved the highest rating).

Given that schools, districts, and states have dozens of nonnegotiable policies, this chapter focuses on five malleable policies primarily related to student learning. Policies concerning safety, educational statutes, negotiated contracts that involve hiring and retaining personnel, and the like must all follow required local, state, and even federal policies. While the effectiveness of Aspire High is meant to inspire change at those higher levels, the following policy conversation is meant to inspire change in your school. When policies that can be changed are transformed to support students' aspirations, energy and time can be focused on what really matters for student learning. Furthermore, improved state- and federal-level policies alone will not develop a climate supportive of improved teaching and learning; no matter the federal, state, or local mandate, implementation is ultimately the key to any policy's effectiveness. Despite the often high-stakes machinations of policy makers, there simply is no way to "teacher-proof" any policy. At Aspire High, Lead Learners discuss strategies for adhering to required policies while not negatively impacting student learning.

As a critical secondary consideration (the mission is primary), all policies at Aspire High are based on research as related to student learning and the Aspirations Framework. For example, although a policy preference for small class sizes seems to be enjoying popularity, at Aspire High teaching and learning takes precedence over small classes. In fact, the Program for International Student Assessment (PISA) results show no relationship between class size and learning outcomes, neither within nor across countries (www.pisa.oecd.org). A blanket policy capping off class size does not exist at Aspire High because it is not supported by research. An ineffective teacher is bad for students no matter how many are in his class. It is not that Aspire High policy supports large classes; Aspire High does not support any policy not related to its mission. Since there is not a research-based relationship between small class sizes and students reaching their full potential, procedures in a class of any size involve student learning and engagement as a priority, not a student-to-teacher ratio. A great Lead Learner can engage 100 students as well as 10.

Similarly, policy related to technology usage is only as effective as the teacher and students' understanding of technology as a learning tool. Simply having an open-access policy or one-to-one policy does not ensure better learning. Policies related to student Internet safety and privacy are necessary; however, policies that dictate usage are irrelevant at Aspire High. Each Lead Learner and her or his students decide the best way to access and engage information with a device (or not). In some classes, this may require using a free online university course to supplement learning, while another class may find very little use for technology as a learning tool, given the course goals.

What follows is a sample of policy considerations at Aspire High as an outline for thinking about policy development in a unique way. These scenarios are by no means exhaustive; rather, they are meant to inspire reconsideration of policies at your school that are flexible and locally set.

Scenario 1: Start of School Day

Many high schools start as early as 7:00 a.m. For years, teachers and parents have heard countless reasons for an early start time—sports, bus schedules, energy use, building usage, and so on. However, at Aspire High what works best for adolescent learners dictates the start of the school day. Research on this topic includes these points:

- In March 2014, researchers from the University of Minnesota's Center for Applied Research and Educational Improvement (CAREI) analyzed data from more than 9,000 students at eight high schools in Minnesota, Colorado, and Wyoming and found that shifting the school day to later in the morning resulted in a boost in attendance, test scores, and grades in math, English, science, and social studies. Schools also saw a decrease in tardiness, substance abuse, and symptoms of depression. Some even had a dramatic drop in teen car crashes.
- In a policy statement published online August 25, 2014, the American Academy of Pediatrics (AAP) recommended middle and high schools delay the start of class to 8:30 a.m. or later.
- The Center for Disease Control and Prevention (CDC) recommended on August 6, 2015, a start time of 8:30 a.m. or later. According to Ann Wheaton from the CDC, "Most US middle and high schools start the school day too early. Students need adequate sleep for their health, safety, and academic success."
- Sleep researcher Mary Carskadon's (1999) research showed that "the biological clock of pre-teens shifts forward, creating a 'forbidden' zone for sleep around 9 or 10 p.m. It is propping them up just as they should be feeling sleepy."
- According to *Scientific America*, "Biological research shows that circadian rhythms shift during the teen years, pushing boys and girls to stay up later at night and sleep later into the morning. The phase shift, driven by a change in melatonin in the brain, begins around age 13, gets stronger by ages 15 and 16, and peaks at ages 17, 18 or 19" (Fischetti, 2014).

In addition to research, Student Voice and students' Self-Worth deeply inform policy at Aspire High. Regarding the start time of school, student and staff discuss students who are likely to be chronically late in an early start to the school day. Late students cause obvious frustrations for Lead Learners and peers, yet there are many reasons why students are late other than laziness. Conversations with students support the biological basis for a later start as suggested by research but also reveal responsibilities toward siblings in the morning, public transportation obstacles, and late evenings at necessary jobs. Beyond creating a convenient bus schedule, the matters of respecting adolescent students, their biological processes, and their often-complex lives are a policy consideration. The goal at Aspire High is not to alienate students with policies that bar them from entry into class because they prepared breakfast for their younger brother and made sure he got to school safely. Starting the school day at 7:00 a.m. is frustrating, despite a sleepy teenager's best effort to overcome his or her internal clock. A concern for Belonging, Heroes, and Sense of Accomplishment influences the schedule at Aspire High.

School start time also clearly affects Engagement. Whether engagement is measured by student attendance or student attention, sleep matters to an adolescent. Sleepy, diligent students may arrive on time, but they might be ill-prepared to be emotionally, cognitively, or behaviorally engaged. A student unable to generate enthusiasm, form a coherent question, be creative, or be intellectually challenged is a source of frustration for teachers and peers alike. One student's lack of engagement affects all students at Aspire High. A concern for Fun & Excitement, Curiosity & Creativity, and Spirit of Adventure influences the schedule at Aspire High.

A sense of Purpose vis-à-vis students' aspirations also determines the schedule policy at Aspire High. While actual classes begin later in the morning, the school is open at 7:00 a.m. for sports, clubs, group projects, mentoring, leadership, relationship building, and breakfast. Students, while not necessarily expected to be firing on all cylinders, are expected to be responsible for commitments to school activities that do not require heavy intellectual lifting. Students also have an opportunity to interact with community services and various volunteers at this earlier time. Many visit a nurse or dental hygienist, see a counselor or social worker, or take advantage of the fitness facilities to get in a workout. All of these responsibilities belong to the students. The adults' responsibility is to support policies that encourage Leadership & Responsibility and Confidence to Take Action.

Given these *policy considerations*, at Aspire High the building opens at 7:00 a.m. and classes follow a flexible, sliding schedule. Classes can be taken from 8:30 a.m. until 3:30 p.m. or from 9:30 a.m. until 4:30 p.m. It is a student's responsibility to choose a schedule that accommodates all of his or her responsibilities—academic, family, cocurricular, and the like. Lead Learners, too, welcome this flexibility and plan their schedules accordingly.

Scenario 2: Homework

The research related to the effect of homework on academic outcomes is inconclusive. Whether one examines homework's relationship to academic achievement or learning, research can be found on both sides of the issue.

- Fifteen years of meta-analyses indicated the limitations of K–12 homework to influence achievement (Cooper, 1994, 2001, 2007). Yet Cooper, Robinson, and Patall (2006) noted, "With only rare exceptions, the relationship between the amount of homework students do and their achievement outcomes was found to be positive and statistically significant. Therefore, we think it would not be imprudent, based on the evidence in hand, to conclude that doing homework causes improved academic achievement" (p. 48).
- In a comparison of 50 countries, research shows that the highest-achieving countries actually do less homework than lower-achieving countries (Baker & LeTendre, 2005).
- There is no research to support that homework promotes responsibility or discipline in children (Kohn, 2006).
- Education scholar Denise Pope found that too much homework has negative effects on student well-being and behavioral engagement (Parker, 2014).
- Students in Japan and Finland are assigned less homework but still out-perform U.S. students on tests (Organisation for Economic Co-operation and Development, 2004).
- Some research suggests that the positive relationship with student achievement weakens when middle school students spend more than one hour on homework per day (Cooper, Robinson, & Patall, 2006).

> **Alfie Kohn** writes and speaks widely on human behavior, education, and parenting. His best-known book *Punished by Rewards* (1993) caused educators to rethink the role of rewards in learning.

Given this mixed bag, Aspire High policies related to homework move beyond available research and focus more on the unique requirements of learners and learning projects. While the generic value and benefit of homework is questionable, schools rarely reflect on a coherent purpose for homework when developing generic policies such as a zero tolerance of late assignments. As Aspire High's policies support Self-Worth, which is frequently fostered through the lessons learned from struggle and failure, there is a policy of forbearance around late assignments. The established purpose of homework at Aspire High is to provide students opportunities to demonstrate current knowledge, go deeper with what is already known, or share what they don't understand. Therefore, homework is graded for effort, not necessarily academic correctness. Students are given several opportunities to correct wrong assignments and improve their understanding, as homework is about learning and not grades. Additionally, students are encouraged to collaborate on homework assignments—not to copy each other's work, but rather to work together to find solutions to complex problems. This all creates a greater sense of accomplishment for not-in-the-classroom assignments and keeps them from being mere repetition of what was done in class or busy work.

Homework at Aspire High is also about quality, not quantity. High-quality homework is engaging and serves a purpose. If there is a zero-tolerance policy at Aspire High, it is that all homework, if assigned, must be completed: Willingly accepting a zero for noncompletion is not an option. A student who turns in a late assignment may get less credit if the Lead Learners are assigning a grade; however, she or he must still do the assignment and is expected to do it to the best of her or his ability. Homework assignments, particularly those involving collaboration, are also a great opportunity to challenge students beyond their capacity. By creating a supportive peer homework experience, Lead Learners stretch students in a way that does not induce homework panic.

Student Voice also plays a role as homework is designed by Lead Learners in partnership with students. Students are encouraged to pose questions in the margins of the assignments or when appropriate develop alternative assignments to demonstrate their understanding. It makes little sense to a Lead Learner at Aspire High that all students are assigned the same homework, as students may be at different places in their understanding and interest in a particular subject, project, or unit. Homework intentionally challenges students and expands what they may think they are capable of doing.

Homework at Aspire High involves responsibility and choice. Expectations are high for all students, including the expectation that homework is completed and returned in a timely manner despite the allowed flexibility. Students are responsible for knowing about assignments and deadlines, as they are involved in developing both of these with the Lead Learners. Some students may feel the need to better prepare for upcoming state exams or advanced courses. These students work together with Lead Learners to develop assignments they *both* feel make sense for their growth and learning.

THE ASPIRATIONS ACADEMY TRUST

Steve Kenning, founder and chief executive of the Aspirations Academies Trust

Steve, as an educational innovator, devised the Space Studio and Post 16 Leadership Incubator Programme concepts.

Education in England, and in many other parts of the world, requires an upgrade, a new operating system, perhaps "OS21," designed to provide relevance to the twenty-first century. In an era when the English education system produces over 1 million unemployed under-21-year-olds and companies cannot find the highly skilled workers they require, strategically thinking educational entrepreneurs are required to stimulate and develop sustainable school improvement. In a country such as England, with its traditional target-driven and knowledge-based educational constraints, innovative and enterprising approaches are not easily employed. Instead, the challenge is to improve schools through finding entrepreneurial approaches to education that result in the high-quality outcomes that not only satisfy the requirements of the rigid examination system but also develop in young people the skills required for success in the world today. The Aspirations Academies Trust (AAT) school improvement model aims to achieve these combined outcomes.

For sustainable, highly effective school improvement, the starting point needs to be a thorough and deep analysis of the whole school in order to identify, in particular, the issues that are possibly restricting development, before then prescribing the way forward. Following this in-depth analysis, the AAT formula for continuous sustained school improvement can then be applied. We are committed to raising students' aspirations so that all young people reach their fullest potential and achieve the success they desire. This is our "Sense of Purpose," our aim, and the basis of our philosophy. As a result, the Aspirations Framework forms the centrepiece of our schools' culture. To achieve our aim, each Aspirations Academy needs to achieve "Outstanding Practice." This is achieved by having a very strong purpose driven by highly effective leadership. Outstanding educational practice can then be achieved in a series of interrelated stages, which include the following:

- Being centred on the Aspirations Framework
- Reviewing, renovating, streamlining, and possibly replacing the systems and structures to be coherent with the Aspirations Framework
- Developing the foundations and platform to enable the school to focus on the main task of teaching and learning
- Using innovation to create "next" practice
- Requiring continuous review, relentless monitoring, and incremental change

- Steve Kenning indicates that the Aspirations Academy Trust strives to combine the governmental policy requirement for target-driven, knowledge-based outcomes with the more innovative, entrepreneurial policies required in a changing world. What is the current state of this debate in the policies of your school/district? How does it affect your classroom policies and practices?
- The AAT's adherence to the Aspirations Framework drives all policy consideration at their schools. What drives policy considerations at your school? How are students' aspirations and personal goals a part of policy decisions?
- "Outstanding Practice" in the classrooms of AAT schools flows from the coherent alignment of systems and structures at the school level. What school or district policies support your own outstanding practice? Which interfere? How can these interferences be addressed?

Scenario 3: Student Management/Suspension

Policies that dictate the exclusion of students from a class or school are reactionary and not what guide student management at Aspire High. Of course, immediate safety concerns would require student removal from class and school settings. There may be times when removing a student is a benefit to the student, as he or she may need time to regroup, reflect, and then reengage as a learner. At other times, a student may need peer mediation to work through an issue or problem. Research supports such approaches.

- Pamela Fenning and her colleagues (2012) noted most school districts continue to use out-of-school suspensions even for minor disciplinary issues even though they tend to actually exacerbate problem behaviors and also may lead to academic problems.
- Recent research showed that being suspended even once in ninth grade is associated with a twofold increase in the likelihood of dropping out, from 16% for those not suspended to 32% for those suspended just once (Balfanz, Byrnes, & Fox, 2013).
- Frequent use of suspension as a disciplinary practice is predictive of higher dropout rates for both White and Black students and is not explained by other school demographics or by student attitudes that are associated with breaking school rules (Talisha et al., 2011).
- School-related disciplinary events have also frequently become precursors to juvenile court involvement, placing students in the school-to-prison pipeline (Skiba et al., 2003).

- Exclusionary discipline, or discipline that removes students from classrooms and/or schools as a punishment, has become the most common punishment in secondary schools across the United States, with educators' use of out-of-school suspension doubling between 1973 and 2010 (Martinez, 2013; Rafaelle Mendez, & Knoff, 2003).

Digging more deeply into this last set of statistics from a policy point of view brings up the need to get to know students—including how race affects who a student is—called for in the first chapter. Absent such an understanding, a school runs the risk of having student management policies that sort students by race in obvious and unacceptable ways. Studies have shown that African American students are three-and-a-half times as likely to get suspended for the same first offense as White students, are more likely to be repeatedly sanctioned (U.S. Department of Education, 2012), and receive harsher sanctions than their White peers for similar behaviors (Skiba et al., 2011). Racial differences in school discipline are widely known, and Black students across the United States are more than three times as likely as their white peers to be suspended or expelled, according to Stanford researchers (Okonofua & Eberhardt, 2015). Students of Latino and Hispanic, Native American, and Native Alaskan heritage fare no better. "American Indian and Native Alaskan students are also disproportionately suspended and expelled, representing less than 1% of the student population but 2% of out-of-school suspensions and 3% of expulsions" (U.S. Department for Civil Rights, 2014). Aspire High student management policies are not color-blind; they are color conscious in accordance with the absolute requirement of getting to know students.

Assuming that there is no immediate safety concern to a student or his peers, the policy preference of Aspire High is to keep students *in* school. This accounts for many of the procedures at Aspire High that create a welcoming and friendly school environment, but such a paradigm also influences policy itself. Student management policy at Aspire High is grounded in developing mutual respect for one another, both adult to student and peer to peer. As a community of learners, all students grow to feel valued at the school. A visitor to Aspire High will rarely, if ever, see a Lead Learner yelling at students or embarrassing them in front of peers. Since no adult would want to be treated in a disrespectful manner, Lead Learners do not treat students disrespectfully. This is as much as a matter of teaching by example as following a golden rule.

Because academic policies place a premium on Engagement in the classroom, disruptive behavior is a rarity. *Engaged students do not act out because of boredom.* However, at Aspire High all learners are responsible for the learning, so occasions to behave in a disruptive manner are kept in check by peers. Students who require removal from a classroom have opportunities to continue their learning in another environment. No student can sit in an in-school suspension (ISS) room and do nothing or listen to music or text their friends or sleep or watch TV or do meaningless repetitive worksheets, all of which only serve to have students fall further behind their peers—thus, inevitably setting up a reinforcing loop of more acting out.

The primary goal of student management policy at Aspire High is to develop young adults who are responsible to themselves and their peers. To this end, students actively develop classroom rules and procedures together with Lead Learners. Students decide the classroom climate as well as the consequences for interrupting the learning of others. Practices of restorative justice and peer mediation that help students understand how their behaviors affect those around them are regularly employed. As we saw, a committee at Aspire High is currently weighing a peer adjudication policy.

Scenario 4: Dress Code

One might think that learning, assessment, or even student management are the most-often-discussed issues in staff meetings. Regrettably, year after year, experience shows that dress code discussions, frustrations, and disagreements permeate most high schools and are the largest single drain on staff time, energy, and morale. Whether a debate over hoodies, hemlines, or heels, this appears to be a perennial annoyance. To some, a dress code seems insignificant as a policy issue in the face of so many other learning challenges. To others, it is the critical first line of policy defense on the slippery slope that is adolescent defiance of adult authority. Research makes the following contribution to the conversation:

- According to Educational Partnership, Inc., "No large scale studies have demonstrated a conclusive link between school dress codes or school uniforms and student achievement" (Johnston, 2009).
- According to Long Beach (CA) Unified School District officials, uniforms were successful in reducing violent crimes (theft, weapons possession, and assaults) by 36% in the three years after the district began requiring students to wear uniforms (Mancini, 1997).
- Brunsma and Rockquemore (1998) found that school uniforms do not have a direct effect on behavioral or academic outcomes of students. They concluded that adopting a school uniform policy is largely symbolic. They wrote, "Instituting a uniform policy can be viewed as analogous to cleaning and brightly painting a deteriorating building in that on the one hand, it grabs our immediate attention; on the other hand, it is only a coat of paint" (p. 60).
- Wade and Stafford (2003) found that although teachers in schools with uniforms perceived significantly lower levels of gang presence, students did not report any differences.

- Dress codes are increasingly being implemented predominantly to combat school violence and increase school safety (Workman & Freeburg, 2006), although there are no strong findings to support this belief that school administrators have.

Policy development related to dress code at Aspire High first and foremost involves students, who dress themselves and come to school every day. At the end of every year, students review both school and national research related to dress codes. They debate the pros and cons of dress code, uniforms, skirt length, dress-down days, dress-up days, and so on. This all gets filtered through a Belonging bias that must weigh wardrobe as individual expression over clothing as a uniform expression of community and teamwork. Those working on this standing policy committee (dress code at Aspire High is reviewed yearly as styles, student attitudes, and school needs change) consider community factors, such as poverty and gangs, and whether these should affect dress code. Respect for oneself, others, and adult sensibilities are factored.

Dress code affects Engagement. Comfort and the absence of distraction are considerations. Students review options with adults and debate, question, develop, and even create alternatives. This all happens in a way that promotes Curiosity & Creativity in the process as much as it is hoped that this Condition will be supported by the policy outcome. To the extent that risk-taking is involved at all, students remind each other that Spirit of Adventure only involves *healthy* risk-taking.

The dress code, once chosen, is entirely the responsibility of the students. The adults at Aspire High are not Dress Code Cops. Students call each other out if there are violations, which are rare because students themselves are involved in developing the policy. The expectation is that students will adhere to the policy, and when they don't, a simple reminder from a peer sends them looking for a remedy in their own locker, a friend's, or the office. This works because the entire culture of Aspire High is based on trust and responsibility (which most young people crave), not on command and control (which most resist). What seems like a Stepford-like adherence to the dress code is simply one, albeit obvious, example of Aspire High's entire approach.

One final note is that adults at Aspire High adhere to whatever dress code is set by the dress code committee. If in any given year, the committee decides that jeans are not "up to code," the adults do not wear jeans to school; if there is a uniform, adults wear the uniform.

Scenario 5: Cocurricular Participation and Academics

Which comes first? A student does well in school and so earns the right to participate in a sport, or a student finds meaning in sports and so engages in school? Athletic, band, drama, and art coaches can all attest to the stories of a "failing" student who finds a sense of accomplishment, heroes, and even a purpose in a cocurricular activity. This purpose, in turn, drives the student to stay in school and reengage in learning. Numerous studies point to the positive results—academically, behaviorally, and in terms of personal development—of having students involved in cocurricular activities.

- Research suggests that participation in extracurricular activities may increase students' sense of engagement or attachment to their school and thereby decrease the likelihood of school failure and dropping out (Finn, 1993; Lamborn et al., 1992).
- Eccles and Barber (1999) found that participation in activities tends to increase achievement and reduce student engagement in risky behavior—with one exception. Participants in team sports are some-what more likely to engage in drinking alcohol than students engaged in music, academic clubs, or service organizations.
- The College Board report *Everyone's Game: Extracurricular Activities* (2012) holds that nationwide, students who participate can see a jump in their SAT scores.
- Marsh and Kleitman's study (2002) shows that extracurricular school activities (ESA) have equal if not greater benefits for disad-vantaged students. The authors' findings support the conclusion that ESAs foster school identification and commitment that benefits diverse academic outcomes.

Given the benefits of student cocurricular participation, Aspire High has a door-wide-open policy when it comes to sports, clubs, and student activities. Students are encouraged to participate as their time and interests allow. Because all policy at Aspire High is grounded in Self-Worth, and because many students experience Self-Worth outside of academics, there are no "threshold" academic requirements for participation. Students are expected to attend and make progress in all of their classes. A struggling student, who would traditionally be excluded from participation, must work out a plan of action with a Lead Learner and an upper-class peer involved in the cocurricular activity they wish to be a part of. As long as the student is faithful to the plan, she or he may participate; a student is not required to complete the plan *before* participating.

The cocurricular policy also supports Engagement. The very choice of the word *cocurricular* instead of *extracurricular* at Aspire High indicates a belief that students are *learning* during these experiences and not sim-ply having fun outside of or beyond the classroom. Many young people derive their fun and excitement, their ability to create and innovate, and their willingness to challenge themselves in their cocurricular experi-ences. Losing track of space and time during a game, practicing a new technique in a sport or a new instrument in band, and taking a risk playing a different kind of part or entering a longer race are all valued at Aspire High as learning experiences for students.

In addition to traditional programs such as basketball, theater, robotics, French club, and the like, Aspire High has a new sport/club application process. With three other students and a Lead Learner or other adult staff member, any student can start a club or sport. The responsibility that comes with the application process falls on students to hold meetings or practices for at least six weeks. After that time, the group may continue or choose to disband. Students are responsible for learning about and, with the help of adults if needed, meeting all financial and safety requirements for their venture. This expansive approach to cocurricular policy at Aspire High maximizes opportunities for students to learn and practice leadership skills—one of the major strengths of this aspect of school life.

In the previous five examples, we have not sought to dictate, or even to suggest, what your school policies should be as related to schedule, homework, student management, dress code, or cocurricular activities. And obviously there are many areas of concern for policy that we have not addressed. Rather, Aspire High invites an approach to policy making that allows decisions to be made at the lowest practical level. Students should be involved in all policy decisions that directly affect them. Classroom policies should be set in classrooms, not by the school or district. School policies should be determined by the school, not the district or state. And so on.

Additionally, all policy decisions must be informed by research, not based on "what we have always done" or on a popular ideology or as a reaction to a handful of irresponsible students. Nor is the most vocal person to show up at a school board meeting a firm foundation for a successful school policy. At Aspire High, national research as well as locally collected data combine with the professional expertise of resident educators and the experience of students and their families to make or change policy.

COMMUNITY AND POLICY

The British Education Communications and Technology Agency (BECTA) was the lead agency in the United Kingdom for promotion and integration of information and communications technology (ICT) in education. Established in 1998 through the reconstitution of the National Council for Educational Technology (NCET), its strategic objectives were "to influence strategic direction and development of national education policy to best take advantage of technology" and "to develop a national digital infrastructure and resources strategy leading to greater national coherence." Before it ceased operations in 2011,

(Continued)

(Continued)

BECTA developed a self-review framework for schools that has since been adopted by the National Association of Advisors for Computers in Education (NAACE).

BECTA developed a self-review framework for schools that has been adopted by the National Association of Advisors for Computers in Education (NAACE). The early self-review framework provided a set of questions for schools to reflect on in areas that included leadership management, planning, learning, assessment of ICT capability, professional development, and resources. While some school leaders might have reflected on this themselves, they were encouraged to include their entire school community and together reflect on the questions that ultimately led to a score for the school in each area. The intent of this community-wide approach was to lead to future plans for school improvement. When used well, this approach involved all of the school community in policy making.

For example, the second area of the self-review framework covers planning and in these four sections:

- Plan for the development of pupils' ICT capability.
- Plan the use of ICT to support the curriculum and respond to new technologies.
- Ensure pupils' ICT experiences are progressive, coherent, balanced, and consistent.
- Identify and evaluate the impact of ICT on teaching and learning.

Discussion with the entire school community may lead to the conclusion that the current plan for ICT capability is poor and does not enable the school to meet statutory requirements. Policies would then be put into place to improve students' ICT capacity. The critical benefit of the tool is the opportunity to engage all school stakeholders in assessment of how well the school is doing, which, when looked at across all the areas of the self-review framework, paints a picture of policy priorities.

- Aspire High uses the Guiding Principles and the 8 Conditions as a framework for setting policy. BECTA provides those responsible for setting technology policy in Great Britain with a framework that includes leadership and management, planning, learning, assessment of ICT capability, professional development, and resources. What ideas frame policy considerations in your school or district? What are the principles or values that form the foundation upon which policy is built or renovated?
- The school community planning process places a heavy emphasis on broad community involvement in setting policy. How can you expand policy involvement widely in your community? What are the benefits of doing this?

- As part of the effort to involve the community meaningfully in policy decisions related to ICT, tools and resources were developed to help participants—some of whom may have had no expertise in ICT—question, ponder, and even evaluate various policy considerations. What resources can be provided to ensure that policy discussions at your school are professional, informed, and fairly assessed?

For Reflection

◊ What policy in your school or district makes the least sense to you? What research or practical experience is your disagreement grounded in?

◊ Describe your district/school's current process for policy development. How could educators be more involved in this process? How could students be more involved?

◊ Discuss with colleagues a policy you agree should be removed, changed, or added. Be sure to get at why you believe this about the particular policy.

◊ Engage in a conversation with a member of the school board about the effects of the latest state or national policy on your school/classroom.

LEAD

On the very first day of school, whether you are a teacher or a student, parent or principal, you are given a set of policies for the school. Policies affect all that we do in schools. School policies come in all shapes and sizes and have varying levels of influence and control. From homework to fire drills to dress codes, there seems to be a written policy for everything. At their best, policies guide the procedures and behaviors of an organization in ways that ensure the general well-being of all concerned. At their worst, policies are narrowly focused and driven by various interest groups. *In schools today, most policies are based on "common practice" not "common sense."*

At Aspire High, the entire school community collaboratively, not competitively (special interests), establishes policies. The policies represent what is best for everyone with an equal concern for what is right for each one. Above all, policies at Aspire High are emphasized by a greater sense of responsibility, representing the unifying mission of the school: everyone's present and future matters. Since policies are for the good of the entire educational community, each member plays an important role, either directly or indirectly, in the development and implementation of school policy. No one makes policy for someone else at Aspire High.

Most traditional school policies have two overriding concerns: safety and academic performance. Over time, these have been appropriately adapted as new safety concerns, and changing academic standards have emerged in our schools. But between the first-and-foremost concern for safety, and the last-but-not-least concern for positive academic outcomes lies a vast region of policies that seem impervious to changes in our world and students' mindsets. This is not the place to debate all of them (though we want to encourage you to have those debates with your colleagues, community, and students). What leadership must call into question is whether the discipline, dress code, hiring, and homework policies of yesteryear are suitable today.

While schools will inevitably, and perhaps appropriately, remain hierarchical for the foreseeable future, policy development and implementation need not stay top-down. We see no reason why policy conversations cannot occur up and down the "chain of command." Many similarly hierarchical management structures—corporate and even military—have approaches to policy that have been adapted by input from front-line workers. Increasingly, businesses shift or change policies based on input from clients and customers. And while we are not proponents of the if-it-works-in-business-it-will-work-in-schools approach, there is no arguing that the world has grown much "flatter" and that much of this has been positive or at least personalizing (Starbucks anyone?) in its effect.

School leadership that seeks effective policies that are not dismissed as irrelevant or out of touch with those they serve wisely seeks input from those the policies will most directly affect. In a school, that clearly means students and staff. Beyond that, parents are also affected by policy. All policies should routinely be reviewed against the school's vision, mission, and core values. Aspire High has stuck its policy stake in the ground of ensuring the Self-Worth, Engagement, and Purpose of all its members. At your school, you might ask: Do command-and-control discipline policies really teach students the responsible citizenship professed by the mission statement? Do zero-tolerance homework policies unwittingly promote copying? Does the out-of-school suspension policy lead students to cut school so that that they can then be *told* to stay home?

While many policies still in place once made sense in a world where authority was seldom questioned, that is not the world we currently live in. The challenge for leaders is to not pretend at democratic processes because people expect more of a voice today. We believe it is possible to provide students, teachers, and parents with a voice and still have only a select few designated leaders ensure the community is effectively living up to the policies it helped create. *Rather than being driven from the outside or above by testing and accountability, such an approach to policy is driven from within by trust and responsibility.*

On your mark. Get set! Go!!

PRINCIPAL

Step ⟹

- *Understand the long-term outcomes of policies.* Enacting dozens of policies is relatively easy; however, taking time to research and understand both the immediate and future implications policies have on students is critical. Policies frequently have unintended consequences. Do your best to foresee the most obvious of these (e.g., capping ISS at 10 days typically leads to some of the most challenging students becoming emboldened once they hit the cap).
- *Involve students and staff in policy discussions.* Policies are established for the well-being of the entire school community. Those affected by the policy must be involved in developing, implementing, and even enforcing the policy. All violations of policy should include review or adjudication by a peer group.

Stride ⟹

- *Insist that all policy aligns with the school's mission.* Take the time to ensure that your policies complement the mission and goals of the school. This alone could help make policy discussion and development more manageable. Most policy manuals read as though they were written by a law firm—our litigious society perhaps makes that inevitable. However, the core of our policies should support our mission as a school.
- *Document and analyze the effects of new policy initiatives.* After adopting a policy, make sure you set up a way to assess the impact the policy is having on the school. Decide ahead of time what metrics and data you believe will be most affected by the new policy. Keep track. Report findings. This will ensure the policy is doing what it was designed to do.

Sprint ⟹

- *Use your voice.* Challenge district and state policies that make no sense for your students or your staff. Too many policies exist because they are driven by common practice and not common sense. Stop accepting "because they said so" as an answer.
- *Use students and staff to write policy.* Writing policy is a demanding task indeed and needs to be done by someone who knows how to write policy. However, students and staff must participate in that process, not only as a great learning experience but also as the best path to policy acceptance and adherence.

TEACHERS

Step ⟶

- *Learn about policy development.* Policy is like a multifaceted form of art, and as with all things that are complex, it takes time to master but once understood can be powerfully influential. If you are to be meaningfully engaged in policy, you must first study the dynamics of policy development.
- *Sign up to be on policy committees.* Since virtually every school policy involves teachers in one form or another, get involved. Granted, a policy meeting may not be the most fun event in the world, but for your school, it is one of the most important.

Stride ⟶

- *Implement new policies with professionalism and commitment.* Developing new policies can be quite contentious, and that is not necessarily a bad thing. In a pluralistic community, debate is healthy. However, once the community comes to consensus, implementation must be done with loyalty and trustworthiness. "Voting" after a policy is adopted by failing to implement it is unprofessional. The time to object occurs further upstream.
- *Discuss, debate, and analyze new policies with your students.* Discussing policies with students is always time well spent. One of the best ways is through debates as they look at both sides of an issue. By involving them in a deeper understanding of school policies, there is a greater likelihood that they will feel connected to them—rather than put out by them.

Sprint ⟶

- *Attend school board meetings.* It is shocking to us how few teachers we see at school board meetings. School board members must be held accountable for establishing reasonable policies to which you are responsible to adhere. Your voice cannot be heard from your living room or the teachers' lounge.
- *Use your voice on a bigger stage.* Speak out statewide or nationally about educational policies that do not benefit students. The time to sit back and implement policies that you as a professional educator know are damaging to students is over. If there are policies that make no sense, then teachers must stand up and let people know. Eliminate "But they . . ." and finger pointing from your thinking and vocabulary.

STUDENTS

Step $\Longrightarrow$

- *Ask questions about school policies.* If you don't understand something, ask! Policies can be incredibly confusing and in some cases contradictory to other policies. Ask questions and seek answers on policies that affect your learning.
- *Learn about policies.* Policies are around you in every aspect of your life. You may know them as "rules" or "expectations," but they are a necessary part of any community. Understand the reasons why policies exist in schools, government, and corporations. Most importantly, understand how policies affect you.

Stride $\Longrightarrow$

- *Join a policy committee.* Granted, this is not like joining a spirit committee, but for students, it is every bit as important. Since policies developed in school are designed to have a positive impact on you, your involvement in the process is critical. Instead of complaining or doing your best to get away with breaking a school policy you don't agree with, work to change it.
- *Share your ideas.* Use social media to share your ideas and perspectives about school policies. Writing an old-fashioned letter to the editor of your local paper would work, too! If you find polices that are not in the best interests of students, offer solutions or alternatives. If there are policies in school that you find useful, share them with others.

Sprint $\Longrightarrow$

- *Lead a policy committee.* If you have an idea that would benefit others at your school, don't be afraid to start your own policy committee. In doing so, make sure you invite all the parties that will be affected by the policy you are studying or looking to develop. See what other students, teachers, administrators, and parents are willing to work with you to rewrite or create new policy that will improve the safety or school climate or learning for all students.
- *Get involved in policy development in your community.* Policies are in place in every aspect of your life. School is one place to start working on and learn about policies, but take your involvement to an even greater level by participating in the development of community and state policies or even laws that affect your school.

Is Your School . . . ?		
TYPICAL HIGH	**ASPIRE HIGH**	**ASPIRING HIGHER**
High-level policies are generally determined by academics and politicians who have little experience within school settings.	Students and staff have input on all policies that affect the school.	Students and staff regularly participate in local, state, and national policy discussions and debates.
District personnel, with a select few from building leadership, determine school policies. Building leadership is responsible for "enforcement" of these policies.	The entire school community is involved in determining, implementing, and being responsible for adherence to all school policies.	School policies involve input from thinkers beyond the school's local community. Best practices are sought from among those available globally.
Whole policies that affect all students are often created for a select few challenging students.	All policies are adopted with the well-being of each and every person in mind.	The centrality of learning and its effect on school culture reduces the need for and number of policies to the minimal few required to ensure safety.
Students have little to no role in developing or implementing policy. Their role is strictly one of compliance.	Students are intimately involved in the development and implementation of school policies.	Students accept full responsibility to ensure policies are adhered to.
Policies appear to have little or no relationship to the school mission statement or district mission statement.	Policies are purposefully aligned to the school's mission.	Polices take into consideration broader educational purposes at national and global levels.
Implemented policies are seldom tracked for impact and only revisited if a crisis occurs.	Policies are reevaluated yearly, and impact data informs decisions.	The school carries out a research agenda related to policies and publishes its findings widely.
Opportunities for learning about policy development and implementation are rare.	Professional learning in the area of policy development is provided regularly to all stakeholders.	The administration, staff, and students lead learning sessions and debates on various school policies at local through global levels.
Policies are mostly decided in closed committees or in open session with few attending beyond those creating the policy.	Policies are widely and openly discussed and shared.	Policies are communicated with other schools in order to share best practices.
The school board dictates district and school policy with little input from teachers or students. The tendency is an us-versus-them dynamic.	The school board (which has students with voting membership) ratifies policy decisions brought forward by the teacher–student committees that work on policy.	There is no school board (as traditionally understood). Professional educators in partnership with their students and the local community set policy.

6

A Pedagogy With Purpose

I never teach my pupils; I only attempt
to provide the conditions in which they can learn.

—Albert Einstein

LISTEN

Having sampled Aspire High on our first day, our second day involves sitting in on an entire class. We settle in to the room in which Steve Lewis is the Lead Learner today. His specialization is English language arts, but much of the curriculum at Aspire High is interdisciplinary. After the transition year, there are few classes in separate disciplines. These, we learn, are mostly for advanced students who are already leaning toward a particular college major or have a particular career focus. In most classes, Lead Learners, along with students, collaborate around a particular topic, theme, or project. When projects are designed, the goal is to include all the disciplines when possible.

The current class is learning about World War II. With Steve, they are studying the rise of science fiction as a genre before, during, and after the war. The timeline from yesterday is still on the board and shows various historical events from 1930 to 1955 above the line and the publication dates of several classic science fiction books below the line. A different group of students than the ones we encountered yesterday are reviewing this time-line. In addition, we overhear a group of students watching and discussing a Skype interview one of them conducted with a World War II veteran—an increasingly rare breed. Another group is using Google Earth to fly over Pearl Harbor and sketch battle scenes from their imaginations.

We sit with two students, Allison and Jamal, who are studying a spreadsheet with the header *Army Cargo Shipped Overseas*.

"This was part of our math homework," Jamal says.

Allison explains, "We are trying to figure out how to get food supplies to the American troops about one month after they land in Normandy. I never really thought about that before . . . needing to feed everyone in the middle of a war."

They point to a historical map of France on the table and indicate problems of topography that have to be dealt with. Jamal says, "Actually, that's not our problem. We have to deal basically with numbers: numbers of men, meals per day, clean water needed . . . that sort of thing. One kind of sucky thing to work out is what to do with oversupplies due to soldiers dying. We are trying to not have those just go to waste. The group over there is working on the bridges to get stuff across this river."

"Physics geeks," Allison whispers.

Most Aspire High classes follow a similar format. Some have a historical basis like the one we were in. Others are grounded in more contemporary issues. One popular class studies the stock market, including the way public perceptions and confidence, election cycles, and world events influence market reactions. Another class is centered on a robotics project. Yet another has a media basis in which students learn to critically view and analyze a variety of forms of media.

While the bulk of classes offered at Aspire High are of this type, the backdrop of all classes is a somewhat nontraditional curriculum and scheduling system that is beyond the scope of this book. While those logistical considerations provide underlying support for the type of pedagogy we are exploring in this chapter, the pedagogical approach used at Aspire High is available in more traditional settings. That approach is to learn through real-world, interdisciplinary, and project-based experiences rather than in the artifice of the academic disciplines. Aspire's distinctive schedule just makes it work buildingwide.

To begin with, the first year at Aspire High is unique. Aspire High assumes that most students are coming from a variety of more or less traditional middle school experiences. This transitional year exposes new enrollees to Aspire High's students-as-teachers approach and works to level out any gaps in reading or mathematical knowledge and skills. After placement testing, this is accomplished through traditional single-subject courses in English language arts (ELA) and various levels of mathematics.

Peer tutoring plays a major role in that leveling process. In addition, all first-year students are enrolled in a Teaching to Learn course where they learn the basics of research, curriculum design, pedagogy, and how to use presentation tools. The first-year schedule is filled out through electives in science, information science and technology, history, foreign language, arts, health education, and so on. There is also the option to take accredited online classes.

In their second year at Aspire High, students begin to take more interdisciplinary classes such as the ones described earlier. Choices of what to take are directed by each student's aspirations. Within each selected class, baseline academic test data are used by Lead Learners to guide assignments and support each student's academic and skill growth. This responsibility is the first of the main learning tasks of the Lead Learners at Aspire High—that is, learning about their students (as outlined in Chapter 2) is their main job. Content learning is the responsibility of students. In each class, then, through multiple, ongoing, formative, summative, and self-assessment strategies, Lead Learners keep learning about individual students so that refinements to assignments and tasks are continual, and trends toward continuous learning emerge. For example, in Steve's class, the two students building bridges are capable of higher-level math than the two students figuring out troop supplies—each pair is doing math at levels that suit them and help to grow their math skills.

Second-year students are also required to choose an area of intensive study that connects to an aspiration—whether personal or career oriented. This selection is the beginning of a multiyear intensive study in a particular area. These "academies" range from carpentry and culinary to marine biology and media graphics. This concentrated study into an area of passion connects a student to the same Lead Learner who oversees that academy for the duration of their participation in it. Whereas all Lead Learners are expected to learn about all of the students they work with, academy Lead Learners become "experts" in the students in their academy.

Through these courses and the individualized nature of the pedagogical approach at Aspire High, students move toward proficiency on state-mandated tests. *State testing is a reality at Aspire High but by no means central, nor does it drive the curriculum.* Lead Learners are cognizant of the requirements of state and local mandates; however, passing these tests is used as a means to achieve students' aspirations rather than a goal in itself. Beyond the walls of Aspire High, Lead Learners, as well as students and parents, advocate for and work toward an approach to school that is not as test oriented as the current regime. Within the walls of Aspire High, Lead Learners prepare for the inevitable future when schools will not be as test driven as they are today. This proactive approach to teaching and learning is part of the culture of Aspire High.

Most of the curriculum at Aspire High was and still is initially designed by Lead Learners. As courses unfold, student input shapes and guides subsequent iterations of the course. Over time, it is truer to say that course offerings each year are codesigned by Lead Learners and students. Student Voice shapes the curriculum, and later, students benefit from the input and ideas for improving courses of their forerunners. A simple example would be an algebra class influenced by student requests for more cross-discipline application. Subsequent classes would go on to consider concepts such as constants and variables in music and in history. A more challenging example would be a World History class that had been narrowly focused on European history but increased its scope to include African and Asian history at the suggestion by students that the world was a lot bigger than Europe. In addition, most classes at Aspire High have a much greater use of technology than originally planned, all due to student influence.

The curriculum strives to meet the needs of both the school's mission and various nonnegotiable state and federal mandates. Tasked by local authorities to fulfill their mission, the former is given priority over the latter, but for the most part, both goals are obtained. In the overall offerings—through traditional, single-subject classes as well as interdisciplinary, project-based classes—every effort is made to ensure everyone can take three courses each term that relate to their goals and dreams or to some other area of interest.

Students and Lead Learners also have the option of proposing new courses. A new course must be submitted near the start of the term prior to its being offered so that an entire term can be spent in development. Lead Learners and upper-level students collaborate when developing any new course. The new course must fulfill a need to support a group of students' aspirations, but not be so narrowly aimed as to serve only those students. During the term prior to the course being offered, time is spent in the academic interest groups designing the new class. Recall these academic interest groups are facilitated by academy Lead Learners who specialize in that discipline. These groups meet and function during the school year in the same way academic departments do in a traditional school. Early in the term, all academic interest groups learn of the newly proposed class and, as part of their agenda, consider if and what contribution that discipline might make to the new course. For example, a new course in game development might draw obvious interest from the IT academic interest group for programming, but also from ELA (for writing the story), science (for getting the game physics right), fine arts (for graphic design), and social studies (for geography and the game setting). If the course also intends to end up with a marketable product, business may be involved, as well as marketing, and so on. Students and Lead Learners work together in their interest groups for half the term to research, plan, and create the parts of each course that relate to the discipline they represent.

In the second half of the term, Lead Learners who have an interest in being part of the class and students interested in taking the class gather regularly to review the work of the interest groups and assemble the various parts into a coherent whole. The parts are connected, relating the chosen elements from the disciplines to one another in meaningful ways and sequencing lessons, projects, and assessments. Although Lead Learners will move in and out of classes, depending on the needs of the curriculum, a single Lead Learner is chosen to oversee each new course. The course is then listed as an option for the next term, and, if successful, subsequent terms.

All advancement at Aspire High is competency based. Students are not promoted, nor do they move on to either higher-level classes or subsequent years without demonstrating ability and mastery in the classes in which they are currently enrolled. This process includes passing through various academic and performance "gateways." The gateways ensure a proper balance between academic proficiency and the high level of engagement connected to learning rooted in real-world application.

The highest-level classes offered at Aspire High are of two kinds. Both are intended to fulfill the mission of involving students in learning experiences in the present that help them achieve who and what they want to become in the future. First, there are academic subjects offered at advanced and college levels. Through a partnership with a local college, students may also earn university credit by taking certain upper-level classes. In addition to several of these courses being offered at Aspire High, students can take online classes through an accredited online secondary or tertiary institution. Second, there are upper-level courses offered at Aspire High that involve internships and real-world experiences. These are typically multidisciplinary but may also include a specialization in a particular area. For example, a student interested in writing may take a journalism internship. While the focus will be on becoming a better writer, the learning will also include interview skills, social studies, sports, graphic design, and the like. A student interested in business may do an internship in a local small business to learn about entrepreneurship as well as psychology, advertising, management, and other appropriate topics.

The most significant underlying feature of Aspire High's curricula—in addition to being project based, interdisciplinary, real-world applicable, and aspiration oriented—is that *learning is the constant and time is a variable.* This is different than in a traditional school where time is a constant (e.g., periods of the same length, a school day of the same length, semesters of the same length, school years of the same length, all culminating in the same four-year completion period) and learning is a variable (e.g., some students picking up material more slowly, others more quickly).

Truth be told, the fixed nature of time and the variability of learning in the inherited industrial model of school may be the single biggest impediment to schools becoming places where all teachers and students can experience success. "I/we don't have time" is the most frequently given response to why educators feel they cannot be more creative, include more projects, be more relevant, invite greater student participation, or stray from the prescribed curriculum to follow students' interests. The sense of an impending academic apocalypse seems to hang over principals' and teachers' heads throughout the year. But why have schools become places where learning has an ending time—be it day, term, or year?

High-stakes testing is clearly a part of this equation because there seems to be much greater freedom to have engagement in learning (to say nothing of an increase in field trips) *after* some high-stakes test has been administered in the late spring. Students have remarked that they are mystified as to why they must stay in school for a year or two after passing a 10th or 11th grade so-called "graduation" test. It is a legitimate question from a student's point of view to which any educator, hopefully, would give a "But the learning isn't over" answer. Yet that student musing is something the current way we do school gives rise to. Unfortunately, in many schools, learning appears to end, or at least break, for the weekend, a holiday, the summer, or to start one's "real life."

At Aspire High, every student's efforts to strive toward his or her dreams is paramount. As a result, the learning necessary to fulfill students' aspirations drives the curricula, not time (or its attendant, pacing guides)—from choices about what to study to when and for how long to study it. While the logistical puzzle this creates for the schedulers at Aspire High is a knotty one, it is not an impossible one. And while the resulting schedule each term may not be a model of factory efficiency, it is always as effective as it possibly can be for helping each student achieve her or his goals.

LEARN

The term *pedagogy* admits of diverse and at times discrepant definitions and explanations. The simple definition of pedagogy as "the art, science or profession of teaching" (*Merriam-Webster*, 2015) tends to focus merely on teaching. From this perspective, pedagogy is a skill set that can be taught and mastered. Numerous schools of education take this approach. Budding pedagogues learn the profession's skills and how to impart knowledge and instruct students.

A broader view of pedagogy espoused by thinkers such as Freire (1972) and Giroux (1981) considers critical pedagogy and going beyond instruction toward designing educational experiences that are transformative.

Ladson-Billings (1994), too, broadens the scope when she writes about culturally relevant pedagogy that must take account of the learners and not just the material to be delivered. These educators and founders of pedagogical theories and movements put pedagogy in a larger, societal, democratic, and relational context. Aspire High adopts this approach. Pedagogy at Aspire High refers *not* to a set of strategies and skills used by adults to impart predetermined subject matter to students; rather, *pedagogy is the purposeful coteaching and colearning that occurs through all of the meaningful educational activities and daily interactions that take place.*

> **Henry A Giroux** is one of the foremost contemporary writers on critical pedagogy, schooling, higher education, neoliberalism, and the condition of vulnerable young people.

As we have seen, prior to any teaching and learning experiences at Aspire High, relationships are built and continually revisited. There is no learning, no teaching, no meaning-making unless teachers know their students. Far too much evidence and research supports the need for relationships as the foundation of pedagogy, not a nice "extra." Hattie's (2009) research shows that teacher–student relationships have a .72 effect size on student achievement. Noddings (1999) notes this in support:

> First, as we listen to our students, we gain their trust and, in an ongoing relation of care and trust, it is more likely that students will accept what we try to teach. They will not see our efforts as "interference" but, rather, as cooperative work proceeding from the integrity of the relation. Second, as we engage our students in dialogue, we learn about their needs, working habits, interests, and talents. We gain important ideas from them about how to build our lessons and plan for their individual progress. Finally, as we acquire knowledge about our students' needs and realize how much more than the standard curriculum is needed, we are inspired to increase our own competence. (p. 4)

Aspire High takes this a step further. While developing relationships with students gains us their trust, provides us personal knowledge of them, and inspires us to improve, the effect Noddings is describing remains centered in "us"—the teachers. At Aspire High, the *mutuality* of relationships is the far-deeper basis of the pedagogy. *Lead Learners and students are equals in Aspire High's classrooms—not in experience or even knowledge—but equals in that the Lead Learner does not wield power over students or design learning experiences based on mere compliance.* This relational equality—that all are equally *learners*—informs Aspire High's entire pedagogical approach.

With this understanding of learning partnership as the basis of Aspire High's pedagogy, and given the mission to help students find their aspirations, several common pedagogical components emerge. While not all-inclusive (entire books have been written and careers built on each of these), these components—interdisciplinary learning, metacognition, self-assessment, and mastery-based learning—provide an indication as to why pedagogy looks different at Aspire High: Classrooms are filled with problem solving, hands-on learning, real-world inquiry, debates, questioning, collaboration, critical-thinking skills, blended learning, creativity, and consistent challenging of current knowledge.

Interdisciplinary Learning

Long gone are the days when learning made sense in individual classrooms, studying discrete subjects. Yet this persists in many schools due to inertia. At Aspire High, connecting subjects is not a luxury to be entertained when time allows. Lead Learners are required to guide learning and discoveries in an interdisciplinary manner. A longtime proponent of interdisciplinary learning, Sir Ken Robinson (2009) shared this:

> I want, really, to get away from the idea of *subjects* and I think *disciplines* is a much better idea. A discipline suggests something which is a kind of an amalgam, a mixture of concepts, of practical skills, of techniques, of ideas, of data. I mean, mathematics isn't really a subject. It's a whole series of different sorts of disciplines. And I think that's true of music. Music isn't really a subject, but practicing music involves extraordinary levels—different levels—of ideas, of practical skills, of sensibility. (para. 18)

In fact, given the thematic nature of classes at Aspire High, a student learning about a single subject in isolation is nearly impossible. Jacobs (1989) defines an interdisciplinary curriculum as "a knowledge view and curriculum approach that consciously applies methodology and language from more than one discipline to examine a central theme, issue, problem, topic, or experience" (p. 8). Rowntree (1982) defines the interdisciplinary approach as "one in which two or more disciplines are brought together, preferably in such a way that the disciplines interact with one another and have some effect on one another's perspectives" (p. 135). Unlike a curriculum that supports the memorization of discrete pieces of specialized information, interdisciplinary education readily facilitates the development of "structural knowledge," leading to an understanding of higher-order relationships and organizing principles (Goldsmith & Johnson, 1990). This approach, given primacy by Aspire High, can be distinguished from both multidisciplinary and cross-disciplinary learning.

- Multidisciplinary learning is parallel learning. Perspectives of multiple disciplines are used to explore a topic, but no effort is made to integrate the perspectives. We can study World War II from a political science perspective or from a literary perspective in parallel.
- Cross-disciplinary learning involves using one discipline as a lens on another. We can understand religion through a political science lens or literature through the lens of history. There is no attempt at integration.
- Interdisciplinary learning examines a topic from multiple perspectives and disciplines and attempts a synthesis of those perspectives to arrive at a coherent understanding of the topic under consideration. Integration is the point.

Many authors and researchers highlight the learning outcomes of interdisciplinary learning. Research continues to emerge in education that articulates the view that learning about or forming connections between fields of knowledge is an essential need for success in the twenty-first century (Boyer, 1991; Caine & Caine, 1991; Dwyer, 1995; Jacobs, 1989; Martinello & Cook, 1994; Nielsen, 1989). While no age is too early to begin developing twenty-first-century skills such as critical thinking, collaboration, and creativity, adolescence—with the development of formal operational thinking, peer group adhesion, and increased ability to think divergently—is an especially ripe period to intensify such efforts. Additionally, Lake (1994) argues that learners in interdisciplinary programs are guided beyond simpler forms of knowledge acquisition to a deeper assimilation of cross-disciplinary concepts. One of the critical skills needed today is the ability to think and integrate knowledge across disciplines and to understand the relations between fields of knowledge (Frodeman, 2010). Finally, attendance, graduation, and college attainment rates are positively impacted through integrated studies (Catterall et al., 2012; Furco, 2010; Hughes et al., 2002).

Repko (2009) asserts that interdisciplinary instruction fosters advances in cognitive ability. Educational researchers (Field et al., 1994; Kavaloski, 1979; Newell, 1990) have identified a number of distinct educational benefits of interdisciplinary learning, including gains in the ability to (1) recognize bias, (2) think critically, (3) tolerate ambiguity, and (4) acknowledge and appreciate ethical concerns. Other positive outcomes associated with interdisciplinary learning include an increase in the ability to make decisions, think creatively, and synthesize knowledge beyond the disciplines (Aschbacher, 1991; Beane, 1991; Burns, 1995), as well as the increased ability to identify, assess, and transfer significant information needed for solving novel problems (Beane, 1991; Davenport and Jaeger, 1995; Dwyer, 1995; Harter & Gehrke, 1989). Interdisciplinary integration also enhances critical-thinking skills (Billig, 2010; Furco, 2010).

Given the strength of this testimony, making a case *against* interdisciplinary learning in high school is challenging, if not impossible. While there is an argument that posits interdisciplinary learning does not allow learners to go deep enough into single subjects, Aspire High graduates experience deep, single-subject learning in their postsecondary choices. They can also experience single-subject learning if they choose AP courses or an online course to supplement a current interest. *If the goal of any school—and most certainly the goal of Aspire High—is to develop meaningful engagement, relevant learning experiences, real-life applicability, and students' lifelong success, an interdisciplinary pedagogy is the only sensible path.* Admittedly, interdisciplinary learning requires planning, time, and resources—all of which are perennial school challenges. The restructuring and repurposing of the traditional school that would be required may seem daunting. An interdisciplinary approach also threatens many teachers who have grown comfortable with their autonomy and expertise in a particular subject area. However, given the research, Aspire High's pedagogical approach could be no other.

REAL-WORLD LEARNING

North East Surrey College of Technology (NESCOT), located in Surrey, United Kingdom, has become one of Further Education's success stories as it progresses toward being recognized as outstanding.

The Premier League is the organizing body of the Barclays Premier League in England, with responsibility for the soccer competition and its rule book.

More than 10 years ago, NESCOT Community College engaged in contracted work with a number of London's professional soccer clubs to provide education programmes for their young professional players. Thanks to the enthusiasm and support by staff in the Business, Management and Information Technology Department, these programmes proved successful. The Premier League then contacted the college to discuss providing support to players in all their clubs. Eventually, the college was awarded the contract to build a full e-commerce system to support all the clubs, on the basis that the system would be built and managed by technology students. The college–league partnership employed the students to do this work and also recorded it as part of their learning.

The students who became engaged in this work raised their efforts magnificently, as did the staff supporting them, to build a system that eventually became premierleaguelearning.com. The students had full responsibility for running the system in the early years. Those involved with the work report how extraordinary it was to see the motivation in the students, their hunger to do a great job, the creative designs they produced, and the overall success of the project.

Students and staff worked together as colleagues in an enterprise to build and then manage the system over a number of years. Such is the value of real-world and authentic learning.

- What local organizations could your school connect to in order to develop real-world learning for your students? Seek these groups out, and start a conversation that leads to a win-win like the NESCOT example.
- What is it about real-world learning—as distinct from something being "merely an academic exercise"—that makes such work more engaging for students? How can you adapt your curriculum to create more real-world application and, so, greater engagement?
- Note that the real-world learning effort led to a greater collaboration between school staff and students. What are the benefits of adults and students at your school working "shoulder to shoulder" with one another, rather than across a desk from one another? How can you introduce more experiences like this into your school or classroom?

Metacognition

Among the most important pedagogical processes that take place in classrooms at Aspire High is metacognition. *While all learning seeks to engage students, ultimately all learning activities strive to develop metacognitive skills.* Metacognition is often simply referred to as "thinking about thinking." It is the intellectual process used to plan, monitor, and assess one's understanding, judgments, and performance. This includes an awareness of one's thinking and learning and a consideration of who one is as a thinker and learner. The antithesis of metacognition is rote memorization. Gourgey (1998) states,

> Whereas cognitive strategies enable one to make progress—to build knowledge—metacognitive strategies enable one to monitor and improve one's progress—to evaluate understanding and apply knowledge to new situations. Thus metacognition is vital to cognitive effectiveness. (p. 82)

Metacognition, therefore, refers to awareness of one's own knowledge—what one does and doesn't know—and one's ability to understand, control, and manipulate one's cognitive processes (Meichenbaum, 1985). Flavell (1976), who first used the term and continually refined his thinking, offers the following example: "I am engaging in Metacognition if I notice that I am having more trouble learning A than B; [and] if it strikes me that I should double check C before accepting it as fact" (p. 232).

Metacognition supports academic growth at Aspire High. Zhang and Richards (1999) note that positive relationships have been demonstrated between metacognitive skills and academic achievement, characterized by strengthened abilities to reason, think, and make decisions. The ability to control one's cognitive processes (self-regulation) has been linked to intelligence (Borkowski et al., 1987; Brown, 1987; Sternberg, 1986). In *How People Learn*, the National Academy of Sciences' synthesis of decades of research on the science of learning, one of the three key findings is the effectiveness of a "'metacognitive approach to instruction" (Bransford, Brown, & Cocking, 2000, p. 18). The study finds that metacognition is the secret to and driving force for all effective learning. In fact, according to Hattie (2009), metacognition strategies have a .69 effect size on student achievement. Research further shows that metacognitive skills can be taught to students to improve their learning (Nietfeld & Shraw, 2002; Thiede, Anderson, & Therriault, 2003).

Metacognition also supports students knowing themselves as learners, including being writers, readers, mathematicians, and scientists. Students who know their strengths and weaknesses in these areas will be more likely to "actively monitor their learning strategies and resources and assess their readiness for particular tasks and performances" (Bransford et al., 2000, p. 67). Weimer (2012) asserts this:

> [I]t is terribly important that in explicit and concerted ways we make students aware of themselves as learners. We must regularly ask, not only "What are you learning?" but "How are you learning?" We must confront them with the effectiveness (more often ineffectiveness) of their approaches. We must offer alternatives and then challenge students to test the efficacy of those approaches. (para. 8)

Classes at Aspire High support metacognition through a relentless *reflection* on learning—not just learning itself. Directly and indirectly, sometimes explicitly and always tacitly, learners examine their thinking using a variety of techniques and strategies. Lead Learners, as a matter of pedagogy, assume primary responsibility for this effort, given that it is an acquired skill that requires modeling, coaching, and guidance. Most students can articulate their thoughts and opinions, but it takes practice to learn to articulate why and how one came to those thoughts and opinions. For example, when a student shares his or her highlights from a reading assignment, a Lead Learner asks, "What about that section made you highlight it?" When a student says, "I think X," a Lead Learner replies, "Why do you think you think X?"

As students acquire and grow into this approach, they begin to take ownership of these actions:

- Correcting and understanding mistakes
- Assessing pre- and postknowledge
- Developing a plan before approaching a learning task
- Learning to ask robust questions
- Comparing and contrasting thoughts and ideas
- Acknowledging and clearing up confusions
- Recognizing growth in thinking
- Writing reflective journals about thinking
- Evaluating thinking after task completion

The purpose of this approach to pedagogy, as distinct from mere content delivery, is to help students at Aspire High become lifelong learners. *To learn how to learn is the surest way to guarantee students are prepared to take steps toward the goals they have set for themselves.* As students learn to "externalize mental events" (Bransford et al., 2000, p. 67), they employ these skills spontaneously and, as they teach, make liberal use of them in conversation and discussion. In a sense, metacognition is the most relevant learning Aspire High imparts, as it creates the capacity for ongoing learning no matter what situations, future schools, careers, or challenges an Aspire High graduate encounters.

Self-Assessment

Though self-assessment is a form of metacognition, it is given special emphasis at Aspire High as the chief pedagogical approach to evaluating student performance, understanding, and mastery. In addition to its relationship to metacognition, self-assessment is an essential component of the cognitive and constructivist theories of learning and motivation that are the backdrop of Aspire High's approach to education in general. McDonald and Boud (2003) define *self-assessment* as "the involvement of students in identifying standards and/or criteria to apply to their work and making judgments about the extent to which they met these criteria and standards" (p. 209). At Aspire High, self-assessment is a dynamic process in which students self-set standards, self-monitor progress toward those standards, self-evaluate, and self-correct to learn. To support this process, students use rubrics they codevelop during planning and preassessment.

Self-assessment occurs when students think about and judge their work to improve understanding and performance as they identify discrepancies between actual and desired processes and outcomes. *Note that self-assessment is a skill that must be taught, practiced, and learned.* Self-assessment practices include formative assessment and self-regulation (Wiliam, 2011). At Aspire High, self-assessment makes positive contributions to students' mastery and motivation. Motivation theorists suggest that student self-assessment contributes to feelings of control over one's own learning, of choice and of agency, and of self-worth (Covington, 1998). In addition, the National Council of Teachers of Mathematics' (NCTM) Assessment Standards for School Mathematics (1995) recommend student self-assessment as part of a total assessment plan to foster student confidence and independence in learning math. Students who are able to use self-evaluation increase their competency in mathematics (Ramdass & Zimmerman, 2008).

Mastery Learning

All learning at Aspire High strives toward mastery. However, since Aspire High personalizes learning, every mastery strategy may not be the right fit for *all* students. The concept of *mastery learning* is not new (mastery learning is also often referred to as *competency-based* or *performance-based learning*). In fact, some principles of mastery learning originated with Aristotle and other ancient Greek philosophers. Most current applications of mastery learning stem from the work of Benjamin S. Bloom (1971, 1976, 1984). More recently, instructional approaches— including differentiated instruction (Tomlinson, 2003), understanding by design (Wiggins & McTighe, 2005), and mastery orientation (Dweck & Legget, 1988)—support the idea of mastery learning. *The process of mastery learning leads to better student engagement due to the customization of learning.* Learning is relevant to each student and his or her unique learning needs. Mastery learning also provides students more choice over what they learn, when they learn, and how they show mastery. Schraw (1998) states, "Students with mastery orientation seek to improve their competence. Those with performance orientations seek to prove their competence" (p. 122).

Mastery is a theory about learning and an accompanying set of instructional strategies. Some of these strategies include classroom formative assessment as learning tools, individualized learning, enrichment activities, "corrective" activities, sequencing, and, most importantly, time as a variable in learning. Feedback is always a part of mastery learning when students are given an opportunity to practice what they have learned and are given corrective feedback (Motamedi & Sumrall, 2000). Bloom (1968) explained further:

> There are many alternative strategies for mastery learning. Each strategy must find some way of dealing with individual differences

in learners through some means of relating the instruction to the needs and characteristics of the learners. . . . The nongraded school (Goodlad & Anderson, 1959) is one attempt to provide an organizational structure that permits and encourages mastery learning. (pp. 7–8)

Many examples of schools that have changed their structures to support a mastery approach can be found in a report titled *Inside Mastery-Based High Schools: Profiles and Conversations* (www.springpointschools .org). At Aspire High, formative assessment is an ongoing practice of mastery learning. Both Lead Learners and students use formative assessment. Black & Wiliam (1998) define *formative assessment* as follows:

We use the general term *assessment* to refer to all those activities undertaken by teachers—and by their students in assessing themselves—that provide information to be used as feedback to modify teaching and learning activities. Such assessment becomes formative assessment when the evidence is actually used to adapt the teaching to meet student needs. (p. 140)

Students use formative assessment as part of their ongoing efforts to uncover gaps in their learning, and redesign educational experiences to fill in those gaps. Lead Learners use formative assessment to assist their efforts to coach and guide the learning. There is substantial evidence that appropriate formative assessment activities relate positively to student motivation and achievement (Black & Wiliam, 1998). Both Sadler (1989) and Black and Wiliam (1998) contend that self-assessment is essential to using feedback appropriately. Indeed, according to Black and Wiliam, it is "a *sine qua non* for effective learning" (p. 26).

When compared with students in traditionally taught classes, students in *well-implemented* mastery learning classes consistently reach higher levels of achievement and develop greater confidence in their ability to learn and in themselves as learners (Anderson, 1994; Guskey & Pigott, 1988; Kulik, Kulik, & Bangert-Drowns, 1990). Contrary to some arguments that mastery learning is too remedial, studies have shown mastery learning to be effective when used for learning that focuses on higher-level learning goals such as problem solving, drawing inferences, deductive reasoning, and creative expression (Arredondo & Block, 1990; Blakemore, 1992; Clark, Guskey, & Benninga, 1983; Kozlovsky, 1990).

Achievement is also positively affected through mastery learning. A long-term, 18-year study by Whiting, Van Burgh, and Render (1995), which gathered data from more than 7,000 high school students, showed mastery learning to have a remarkably positive influence on students' test scores and grade point averages as well as their attitudes toward school and learning. An even-larger meta-analysis review of the research on mastery learning by Kulik et al. (1990) reported positive results as well:

> We recently reviewed meta-analyses in nearly 40 different areas of educational research (J. Kulik & Kulik, 1989). Few educational treatments of any sort were consistently associated with achievement effects as large as those produced by mastery learning. In evaluation after evaluation, mastery programs have produced impressive gains. (p. 292)

Although mastery learning and the purpose of Aspire High involve learning and growth, traditional measures of achievement are not ignored. Students do pass state exams, college entrance exams, and demonstrate growth through mastery learning.

At the heart of Aspire High's pedagogical approach is student engagement. There really is no need for students to be bored by their educational experiences. Learning can be inherently engaging if one's sources of motivation are not standards, grades, and external rewards, but rather the internal drive to move in the direction of one's dreams. Given the pedagogy at Aspire High, engagement is the standard and learning the reward.

BEYOND TESTING

The Academy for the Arts, Science, and Technology is a 9–12 STEM school in Horry County, South Carolina, and is organized around career majors. The school is open to students from the district's nine attendance areas.

Beth Havens has served in a variety of roles in the school over its 20-year history, including as a teacher, team leader, and district consultant.

For 20 years, a small school in South Carolina has embraced the notion of learning as a rich and constantly evolving collaboration between students and teachers. The Academy for the Arts, Science, and Technology opens its doors to students from high schools throughout its district and enrolls students in a combined program of academics and career majors, including preengineering, education, advanced visual arts, digital communication, entertainment technology, premedicine, theater, and dance. Students at the Academy spend their senior year engaged in senior exhibitions—a year-long process that involves research on an issue or problem related to their major, a product or project or performance, and a presentation. Because each student proposes and develops her or his own idea based on individual interests, career goals, and passions, every senior exhibition is unique and deeply owned by the student.

The senior exhibition calls for new learning driven by the student, and quite often, it requires fresh learning for the teacher as well. This is a small sample of projects:

- Developing new robotics solutions
- Coding
- Testing new techniques for autistic children
- Writing and producing plays
- Designing and teaching STEM lessons to engage at-risk youth
- Developing and marketing new apps

These senior exhibitions are as diverse as the students who develop them, and throughout the year, students and teachers are engaged in sharing ideas, brainstorming strategies, consulting experts in the field, overcoming setbacks, working in internships and field experiences, and learning together.

In the weeks before graduation, each senior presents his or her research and shares the product, project, or performance to a panel of parents, teachers, peers, and community members. These presentations and the senior exhibition process itself embody exactly the experiences that teachers at the Academy seek to offer their students and to participate in themselves: a deeply engaging collaboration in a community of learners, a demonstration of the importance of lifelong learning, an opportunity to pursue personal passions and interests, and a celebration of each student's unique potential to make a contribution to the community.

- What are the pros and cons of introducing "career majors" at the high school level? How do you think this might support student engagement? What, if any, are some of the drawbacks?
- Exhibitions, which require new learning and exhibition by seniors (no coasting during senior year!), are a significant feature of the pedagogy at the Academy for the Arts, Science, and Technology. How could you make public exhibitions and the invitation to be innovative a part of your current classes?
- The approach Beth Havens is describing calls for a high degree of student–teacher partnership, which in turn often requires new learning for teachers. How do you see this fitting into the way you currently teach? Would the price that needs to be paid in time be worth the benefit to students? Why or why not?

For Reflection

- What are your experiences with metacognition? How, in your experience, does helping students "think about their thinking" improve their learning?
- Describe a time you took a project-based approach to learning. What were the benefits? What worked? What didn't work?

◇ Discuss with colleagues the possibilities and the promise of interdis-ciplinary teaching and learning. How would your students benefit from such an undertaking? Would it be worth the learning-and-engagement bang for the time-intensive buck?
◇ Learn from students firsthand what most engages and excites them vis-à-vis their educational experiences. What makes them push themselves academically? What makes them want to work hard?

LEAD

When most people think of *pedagogy*, they perceive it simply as "teach-ing." A pedagogue is, after all, a teacher. But those that teach understand and appreciate that great teaching is more of a dialogue with one's stu-dents than a monologue. At Aspire High, teaching goes beyond mono-logue and instruction. *Pedagogy at Aspire High is about designing and supporting the conditions in each learning environment that will promote crea-tivity, inquisitiveness, and the desire to learn more and to never stop learning.* As a result, pedagogy at Aspire High is something students and teachers do together.

School leaders—and by now it should be clear that we mean adults *and* students at your school—have a responsibility to create the pedagogical conditions favorable to learning *together*. So-called "lesson planning" either by a lone teacher or a team of teachers is not pedagogy at Aspire High. There is virtually nothing related to teaching and learning at Aspire High that Lead Learners do apart from their students. Planning, designing presentations, creating rubrics, revising, and assessing are all done in partnership.

At Aspire High, teaching-and-learning becomes natural and fluid and is not dictated by bells or an arbitrary schedule based on the typical aca-demic year. Artificial time constraints cannot be imposed on a curriculum that is interdisciplinary, project based, and applicable. The simple fact of the matter is that if we are to lead schools of and for the twenty-first century, we must have pedagogical practices that reflect the world as it is. That world is one in which people are judged and promoted, hired and fired, fail and succeed based on their ability to adapt and learn, to inno-vate and create, to be masterful in the tasks assigned to them, to make relevant connections, and, above all, to be self-reflective about those very capacities.

On your mark. Get set! Go!!

PRINCIPAL

Step ⟹

- *Provide time for teachers to observe and offer each other feedback.* One of the most effective pedagogical improvement strategies to implement is to create time for teachers to observe one another. Teachers also need time to debrief, ask questions, and offer suggestions to each other. Both new and experienced teachers should view each other as resources.
- *Promote the use of creative and performing arts in classroom practices.* Recognizing that success in school is not solely measured by how high you score on a standardized test (or the football field) is long overdue. The arts must be encouraged and celebrated as classroom practices. In fact, according to many, the future belongs to entrepreneurs and innovators (Zhao, 2012) and those able to think and act creatively and with "a whole new mind" (Pink, 2006).

Stride ⟹

- *Replace report cards with portfolios and demonstrations.* When a parent gets a report card, that is exactly what it is—a card of paper with a report of student grades on it. It provides no insight into the student's interests, accomplishments, or effort. And other than the occasional "good attitude" selected from a drop-down menu, report cards convey nothing about who a child is or is becoming. Portfolios and demonstrations allow students to show off who they are and what they know.
- *Provide teachers ample time to master new programs, initiatives, or skills.* Leadership needs to balance the need for results with the time required to effectively implement new pedagogical practices. When expecting teachers to implement new teaching strategies or skills, build in the time needed to learn and understand those skills before expecting positive outcomes.

Sprint ⟹

- *Support interdisciplinary learning in all subjects.* Given the inertia of schools teaching in the silos of the academic disciplines, this artifice is difficult to overcome but needs to be removed. Schools need to get real—*life is interdisciplinary*. Ensure that different content areas work together through joint projects and paired teaching.

- *Use student engagement as a benchmark for success in the classroom.* Every principal has an approach to teacher assessment, but add one more variable: engagement. See who is making eye contact with the teacher and who is not. Check out how many questions and what kinds of questions are being asked. Keep track of how often students (and teachers) are looking at the clock. Evaluate teachers based on what the *students* are doing.

TEACHERS

Step ⟹

- *Coteach with students and colleagues.* This sounds simple, but it is not. First, you need to find the time to plan with the students. Second, it is going to always take more time than you think. However, we promise you that your students will surprise you with what they can do and how well they do it. We can also promise you that when students reflect over the year and think about their greatest learning, it will be coteaching!
- *Incorporate real-life examples into all classes.* This seems to slip away from most teachers when in actuality nothing could be more important or easier to do. Pick up the newspaper before school or open up your computer and check out a few headlines, and then ask the students how the headlines of the day relate to what they are learning. They will always come up with something.

Stride ⟹

- *Let students assess their level of engagement.* There are certainly formal ways you can assess engagement, but you will be amazed at how open and honest students are about how engaged they are. More importantly, if the students trust you, they will tell you why they are or are not engaged—now *that* is formative assessment!
- *Provide ways for students to implement new knowledge and skills.* You can have students teach each other, but go beyond that. Establish partnerships with local organizations where students can apply what they are learning. For English class, head to the local newspaper. For math class, head to an engineering firm. For history class, head to the town hall. If there is nothing around you, find a professional willing to meet online. We get asked to Skype with students all the time, and the students think it is pretty cool—we do, too!

Sprint ⟹

- *Value and use student self-assessment.* Self-assessment is as important to student growth and learning as teacher assessment. The goal is to keep student self-assessment simple and meaningful to the student. Ideally, students need to self-assess in real time. Additionally, let students develop a few assessment questions for themselves regarding their level of participation.
- *Develop interdisciplinary units with colleagues.* Although this is a "sprint," given the typical starting line, you may want to start slowly: Find ways to combine science and history or math and science or English and social studies. Then, challenge yourself to connect English and algebra or earth science and Spanish. Connect everything, and you arrive at Aspire High!

STUDENTS

Step ➡️

- *Come to school prepared and willing to participate.* There is no doubt teachers can provide an environment in which the best learning can take place, but if you don't come to class prepared and willing to learn, there is nothing teachers can do to make the learning engaging. You must accept responsibility for your own learning, and you must come into school with high expectations for yourself and your teachers.
- *Be open to working collaboratively with peers, regardless of whether they are friends.* Some students love working with other students, and others dislike it. The reality is that most people need to work with other people in life, unless you are being trained to collect money at a toll bridge. Learning is a social event, work is a social event, and thus living is a social event. Get used to working collaboratively with others. You will be amazed by what you will learn if you are open.

Stride ➡️

- *Develop global awareness.* We travel all over the world, and two things consistently impress us: first, how similar students are regardless of their location, and, second, how open students are to meeting others from different cultures. Commit to learning what is happening outside your country by reading a reputable online news source or watching the news on a regular basis.
- *Consistently reflect on your learning and how you learn.* Everyone learns differently. It is important that teachers know how you learn best, but it is also important for you to know as well. Figure out what bores you in school and why, as well as what excites you and how you can get more of that in your classroom. Your teachers work hard to establish the best learning environment possible, but you, too, play a critical role in the process.

Sprint ➡️

- *Redo tests and assignments that don't represent your best work.* Getting a poor grade or negative comments on an assignment should not be perceived as "I failed." Instead, whether required to or not, learn from your mistakes. Figure out what you did wrong, correct or improve it, and hand that work back to your teacher.
- *Demonstrate your learning and understanding of information through multiple measures.* A single test is usually not representative of what a person knows or can do. Yet in schools, that is the most common form of assessment. Show what you've learned by using various forms: slide decks, movies, performances, drawings, speeches, essays, blogs, podcasts—the list is as long as there are ways to communicate.

Is Your School . . . ?		
TYPICAL HIGH	**ASPIRE HIGH**	**ASPIRING HIGHER**
Teachers have to find time to plan lessons together.	Time is set aside for teachers and students to plan lessons together.	Lesson planning and revision is an ongoing and continual process.
Teachers plan lessons that may or may not be of interest to students.	Lessons are designed to be mutually interesting to students and teachers.	Teachers and students work together to engage in learning that addresses concerns of interest to the local community.
Subject matter is taught independently of other content areas.	Interdisciplinary units are the norm.	"Interdisciplinary" includes the involvement of other schools and the community.
Global awareness is often patched onto the social studies curriculum.	Global awareness is built into all curricula as a required fundamental skill.	Communication between students and teachers from other countries happens regularly.
Pacing guides and grade-level instruction dictate teaching.	Learning for mastery dictates teaching.	Application of knowledge and skills occurs and is judged in the real world.
Student learning is restricted to content knowledge and varies in depth of understanding. Self-reflection is rare.	Students thinking about their thinking is a priority.	Students and teachers are encouraged to consider the social and ethical implications of mindsets, paradigms, and conceptual frameworks.
Teachers assess the performance and knowledge of students based on normative guides and rubrics.	Students work with teachers to assess their own learning and performance and that of their peers.	Feedback from community members and experts is a part of self-assessment and evaluation.
Learning is based in the academic disciplines and follows guidelines set by curriculum developers.	Problem-based learning pervades the approach to teaching and learning. Learning about a particular subject is always for the purpose of solving a project problem or narrowing into a field of interest.	The school solves real-world problems brought to it by the community or that result from investigation of needs beyond the local community.
Real-world examples are used sporadically and are typically a function of an engaging teacher.	Real-world examples and applications drive the learning.	The real world is integrated into the curriculum through internships and other work-related schemes.

(Continued)

(Continued)

Is Your School . . . ?		
TYPICAL HIGH	**ASPIRE HIGH**	**ASPIRING HIGHER**
Creativity is scarce as part of the pedagogical process. End products may be considered more or less creative.	Creating, building, and designing are fundamental principles of the learning process.	Creativity and innovation are for real-world purposes.
Students are the beneficiaries of the well-meaning work of educators.	Students are fully partners of educators in the development of all aspects of the teaching and learning experience.	The learning partnership between students and adults extends to the local community and various experts from around the world.
Students work collaboratively with one another on various projects.	Students, teachers, and community members work collaboratively on projects both in and out of school.	Collaboration encompasses national and international projects.
Student engagement plays little to no role in assessment of the effectiveness of pedagogy. To the extent that engagement is considered, it is judged from teachers' point of view.	Student engagement is a benchmark for measuring the teaching and learning environment. Students and teachers judge levels of engagement together.	Students are solely responsible for their own levels of engagement.
Report cards are provided to parents for the purpose of recording and reporting students' academic outcomes. Online systems have made access to student grades more frequently available.	Portfolios and demonstration of knowledge and skills are the basis of student evaluation.	The success, mediocrity, or failure of real-world solutions, products, and ventures is the measure of student learning.
Technology has had little or no impact on teaching practices. Smart boards become glorified whiteboards, and slide decks are the new filmstrip.	Technology is fully integrated and understood as a learning tool.	Students create learning apps and discover new ways to leverage technology into learning applications.

7

Technology as the Amplifier of Learning

The illiterate of the 21st century will not be those who cannot read and write, but those who cannot learn, unlearn, and relearn.

—Alvin Toffler

LISTEN

After spending the day in Steve's class, we find ourselves back at the school later that evening for a special community event hosted by the World War II class. This experience represents one of the major exhibitions for the class, and the main event is the premiere of a one-hour video created by the students. The class also coordinated with the Culinary Academy to provide food that soldiers would have eaten during the war. Attendees understood that there would be Spam, lima beans, crackers, peanut butter, and other fare typically found in an army mess kit of that era. Most ate dinner before they came.

Jamal, whom we met earlier, welcomes the 50 or so fellow students, parents, teachers, and community members in attendance. He explains that the event is the final project for a unit the class has worked on in the use of modern technology to do historical research. He points out five stations in the room: two related to the war in the Pacific and three related to the war in Europe. The stations are staffed by students from the class and

137

include hand-drawn maps, photo displays, poster boards, and a variety of interactive experiences for those in attendance to engage in. One station is set up so that visually impaired students and participants can have displays described to them.

Jamal explains that guests will have 30 minutes to visit these stations and that this will be followed by a video that is the result of several months of interviews with World War II veterans, a conversation with the military adviser to the movie *Saving Private Ryan*, and clips edited from that movie as well as several documentaries. In addition, the class visited a local veterans' home and used video equipment to record two men and one nurse who had been part of battles in both Europe and the Pacific.

For this project, they used tablets (every learner at Aspire High has a tablet) as well as video production and editing software. Much of the research was done on the Internet, including videoconferencing with former veterans and using Google Earth views of battlefields and cemeteries. Students also used project planning software and Google docs to work together both during and after school. Those documents were also shared with community members, who provided input and feedback. It was clear throughout the evening that students had been thoroughly engaged by this project and had learned about particular aspects of World War II in some depth. Following the movie, there was a short question-and-answer session. One question the students couldn't answer on the spot was immediately looked up on a smartphone and an answer provided to the questioner. Following the event, we sat in as Steve and the students debriefed and assessed their work.

Technology is a tool at Aspire High; it is not an end itself. It is an amplifier, not a driver. Most students come to Aspire High already well versed in the world of the Internet, personal smart devices, apps, and social media. In fact, it is all Lead Learners can do to keep up with everything their students want to teach them on this front. Each student is provided with a tablet that is theirs to use at school and at home for as long as they are at Aspire High. Students are trusted to take care of their device and to use it appropriately. A student must replace a lost or carelessly damaged device. Some choose to purchase the insurance offered by the company that provides the devices.

Robust Wi-Fi is present throughout the building, and each learning space has a whiteboard that can receive a signal from anyone's device to share or show presentations. Students and Lead Learners make use of the Internet for both research and delivery. Students learn how to assess the reliability of information they obtain and cross-check references. TED Talks, instructional YouTube videos, Khan Academy, MIT's Open Courseware, and numerous other free online learning venues are culled for both learning and teaching purposes. Webinars are scheduled as needed with experts in various fields.

Videoconferencing software is used liberally. Throughout the day, students may be meeting virtually with students in other schools, experts from around the world, local and national politicians, university professors, journalists, researchers, community leaders, and so on. A student who is not feeling well enough to be in school or who is sick with something contagious may also use videoconferencing to participate in a class from home if he or she feels up to it. Though this is not expected, often students do not want to miss what is planned on a day they are out. Similarly, if school is closed due to inclement weather, students are expected to carry on with their work, including videoconferencing with one another and Lead Learners.

There are no bans on personal devices or blocks to social media sites, as students are trusted to be on task. Aspire High recognizes that prohibiting often only tempts with "forbidden fruit" and that such restrictions rarely achieve their goal in any case. Students often use Facebook, LinkedIn, Twitter, Instagram, YouTube, Blogger, and other social media sites to publish what they are learning and interact with experts and other students. Each course sets up its own YouTube channel to record and archive the lectures and presentations of a curriculum so that these can be reviewed as needed. These recordings range in quality from mere documentation of what took place videoed by someone's tablet to full-fledged productions created and edited using video production software. In addition to being review material for the class, these latter are often published for public use.

Students are also expected to introduce whatever latest software, apps, and technology might advance the cause of learning at Aspire High or support peers in moving closer to their aspiration. Several learning games have been introduced to Aspire High in this way. The current "bleeding edge" of tech learning at Aspire High is in the field of design and 3-D printing. Several new classes are integrating design thinking and 3-D manufacturing (a 3-D printer was donated by a local high-tech firm) into their learning experiences. An economic unit in a global-marketing class frequently discusses the implications of being able to make single components, whereas more traditional manufacturing methods require runs of thousands. Students studying an anatomy unit in the Trends in Health Care class had the option of designing prosthetics as a midterm project. In this and in similar use, design is discussed from a variety of viewpoints, including functionality and aesthetics. Students critique each other's ideas and final products.

There are both blended and full-fledged online classes offered at Aspire High. This supports the school in the challenging task of tuning their course offerings to all students' aspirations. It would be impossible for the adult staff to cover all the learning students need, given their myriad aspirations. Rather than considering this a defect of their mission or faculty, combined committees of students and Lead Learners spend time scouring the Internet for courses that fill the gaps. Staff members of Aspire High do not believe they need to be all things to all students. As Lead Learners, their role is to facilitate the learning, not necessarily provide all of it. Students are involved with online learning during the school day, not just as homework.

Another technological tool used at Aspire High is a real-time voting system. Students use their tablets to answer a question—typically multiple choice or true/false—given by another student or Lead Learner as a means of formative assessment. As errors in thinking are uncovered, students work to correct one another before proceeding. This technology is also used at particular forks in the road for a lesson or curriculum. After discussing choices to take the learning in this or that direction, students vote and agree to follow the path selected by the majority or debate to build toward consensus.

For all its widespread use at Aspire High, technology is merely a means to the ends of learning and the school's mission. It is not an end in itself. As we saw in both the class and the exhibition, hand-drawn maps were also part of the World War II class. Many students use pens and paper notebooks. The bridge builders were using Popsicle sticks, not the 3-D printer. Students and Lead Learners choose the tool that is appropriate to the learning. Technology does not replace discussion, writing, lab work, field trips, painting, sculpting, role plays, demonstrations, and the like. This prevents technology itself from being disengaging and avoids the pitfalls of a smart board as a glorified blackboard, a presentation slide deck as a fancy film-strip, and a tablet as simply paperless paper.

LEARN

Technology is not the panacea to our educational woes—it will not miraculously engage students, develop metacognitive skills, or provide a competitive advantage. Tablets and the Internet do not instill twenty-first-century skills by osmosis. While the goal of worldwide access and connectivity is necessary for today and tomorrow, Internet access and usage remain, unfortunately, a challenge for many students. The proportion of children in the United States with home access to computers in 2012 was 85%; however, only 64% of Black children and 62% of Hispanic children have home access (Child Trends, 2015). According to the 2012 Pew report *Digital Differences* (Zickhur & Smith, 2012), only 62% of people in households making less than $30,000 a year used the Internet, while the usage rate among families making between $50,000 and $74,999 was at 90%—yet another gap in education.

Another eye-opening statistic for those living in a First-World context from the management consulting firm McKinsey and Company (2014) is that 4.4 billion people across the globe, including 3.2 billion living in only

20 countries, are not connected to the Internet. Although it is beyond the scope of this book to tackle global issues of connectivity and access, many educational practices must change in order to effectively use technology as a learning tool applied to teaching and learning overall. Simply having new technology or new textbooks does not create more engaged, meaningful, and personal learning. "The introduction of computers into schools was supposed to improve academic achievement and alter how teachers taught," said Stanford University education professor Larry Cuban. "Neither has occurred" (as quoted in Harod, 2015).

Far too many classrooms simply replace the outdated 50-minute lecture with a 50-minute slide presentation. Clearly, teachers' attitudes toward and expertise with technology are key factors associated with its use in the classroom (Inan & Lowther, 2010; Sandholtz et al., 1997; Zhao & Frank, 2003). One theme that has emerged from the research to date is that simply adding technology to K–12 environments does not necessarily improve learning. A 2011 study of 1,000 high school teachers, IT staff members, and students conducted by CDW Government LLC found that 75% of teachers reported they regularly use technology to teach, but just 41% of the students indicated they are encouraged to use technology throughout the day. A large-scale one-to-one endeavor was the Texas Technology Immersion Pilot. Even with significant financial investment ($14.5 million), there was still also no evidence that student performance or satisfaction with school had increased (Weston & Bain, 2010). Additionally, a 2015 report from the Organisation for Economic Co-operation and Development (OECD) indicates something similar:

> The results also show no appreciable improvements in student achievement in reading, mathematics or science in the countries that had invested heavily in ICT for education. And perhaps the most disappointing finding of the report is that technology is of little help in bridging the skills divide between advantaged and disadvantaged students. (p. 3)

Since there are many examples of varying levels of academic success within schools implementing one-to-one computer usage programs, it seems clear that simply giving a child a computer will not automatically guarantee academic improvement (Higgins, Xiao, & Katsipataki, 2012).

Even given the varying outcomes associated with technology, for district leaders or classroom teachers to ignore the potential impact of technology as a learning tool indicates a lack of understanding of twenty-first-century learners and the future they will work in. There exists much research supporting one-to-one initiatives, computer programming, and all the amazing ways teachers are using technology to enhance learning. Due to society's fast-paced adoption of technology, information about technology is doubling every two years (Gantz & Reinsel, 2011). Prensky

(2010) asserts that the current generation of young learners will live in a future where technology will be over a trillion times more powerful and influential than it is today. According to the International Society for Technology in Education (ISTE),

> Rapid advances in technology have led to profound shifts in how we live, communicate and work. To prepare our students for the world they will soon enter and for a future we cannot yet imagine, education must not only adapt to these changes but innovate.
>
> Innovating education goes far beyond just learning how to use new tools. It requires us to rethink how we teach and learn. And it calls on us to re-engineer our districts, schools and classrooms for the digital age. (para. 1)

Marc Prensky is an internationally acclaimed thought leader, speaker, writer, consultant, and designer in the field of education. He is well known as the inventor and popularizer of the terms *digital native* and *digital immigrant*.

While some research indicates that specific uses of technology can improve student academic results, availability of technology in the classroom does not guarantee a positive impact on student outcomes (Dynarski et al., 2007; Wenglinsky, 1998). Despite these findings, when used appropriately technology can help to improve students' performance on achievement tests (e.g., Kulik, 2003; Wenglinsky, 2006). Wilson (2002) envisions technology as offering endless possibilities to enhance educational experiences, expand academic opportunities, and develop critical employment skills.

Lead Learners and students at Aspire High realize that specific technologies can and do support meaningful learning when students learn through the use of the technology, not merely from it. Reading a newspaper article on a website is no different *as a learning experience* than reading it on a printed page. At Aspire High, all Lead Learners and students discuss and understand the potential pitfalls and responsible use of technology. The OECD (2015) findings that show little improvement in achievement lead the authors to think that among the reasons for the lack of improvement is that "we have not yet become good enough at the kind of pedagogies that make the most of technology; that adding 21st century technologies to 20th century teaching practices will just dilute the effectiveness of teaching" (p. 3).

Mark Barnes is a leading expert on student-centered learning. Mark has helped thousands of educators build digitally enhanced, project-based, no-grades classrooms. In addition, he is the publisher of the *#HackLearning* education book series.

Technology should never be employed for its own sake; rather, technology should be used as a *medium* of access, analysis, or presentation. For example, Mark Barnes (2014) shares the importance of content curation as integral to teaching and learning. This is a specific skill required for understanding and teaching in the digital age. "We are obligated to teach our students how the information they curate may ultimately define them and may impact innumerable people in their society" (p. 12). When used in particular ways like this, technology advances and enhances learning. At Aspire High, technology is predominantly used for specific purposes in the following three ways: Collaboration, Anytime Learning, and Creation. Each of these is a low-tech pedagogical best practice that technology amplifies.

Collaboration

Lead Learners and students at Aspire High view technology as a means of cooperation and collaboration. Technology can create venues that challenge, expand, and extend projects for learners. It creates spaces to discuss, argue, and build with peers both locally and within the global community. In traditional face-to-face classrooms, the effectiveness of cooperative learning is a well-established fact (Slavin, 1995). Collaborative learning involves a joint intellectual effort by groups of students who are mutually searching for meanings, understanding, or solutions (Smith & MacGregor, 1992). In both traditional and online classroom environments, interaction and collaboration are identified as a major factor in successful learning outcomes (Bonk & Zhang, 2006; Martinez-Caro, 2011).

Aspire High uses technology specifically to amplify this effect of collaboration. Studies show that the higher a learner perceives the level of collaboration, the more satisfied he or she is with e-learning overall (Diaz & Entonado, 2009; Er et al., 2009). One benefit of collaboration through online means is that participation in computer-mediated groups tends to be more equally distributed, whereas face-to-face groups are more easily dominated by a single or few individuals (Finholt & Teasley, 1998, p. 45). Thus, using technology to collaborate not only makes possible connections that would not otherwise exist, but it also enhances the outcomes of learning in a collaborative mode. Technology itself can also be viewed as an intellectual partner (Jonassen, 2000).

Anytime Learning

Students typically engage in many learning activities in real time, or what is commonly referred to as *synchronous learning*. In synchronous learning, students and teachers work together at the same time—typically a class period framed by bells—and, usually, in the same place—whether the place is a bricks-and-mortar school environment or a virtual classroom. *Students at Aspire High are encouraged to be neither time-bound nor place-bound, but rather to learn anytime and anywhere.* In an asynchronous learning environment, students are able at any time to actively participate in their own learning, giving them the opportunity to interact with their peers, provide peer feedback, and reflect on the status of their personal learning goals and outcomes (Er et al., 2009; Harris et al., 2009; Simonson et al., 2012).

In asynchronous learning, students work at their own pace and place, yet they complete coursework within defined time limits. Students and Lead Learners at Aspire High are not necessarily interacting in real time, but they are working toward real self-imposed deadlines. While learning is not exclusively asynchronous at Aspire High, students do have occasions for in-depth learning or, at times, college-level learning through the use of online courses, webinars, or other archived resources. Asynchronous learning technologies are a personalized learning tool (Lorenzo & Ittelson, 2005). Research shows that the technologies associated with both synchronous and asynchronous learning can improve the quality of student–teacher interactions, foster increased student engagement, and improve learning outcomes (Hastie, Hung, Chen, & Kinshuk, 2010; Simonson et al., 2012). Information and communications technology (ICT) devices bring together traditionally separated education media (books, writing, audio recordings, video recordings, databases, games, etc.), thus extending or integrating the range of time and places where learning can take place (Livingstone, 2011).

Learning games can be a form of asynchronous as well as competency-based learning, as students participate at their own pace and progress through levels as the gaming platform assesses their abilities and offers new challenges. Games are seen to be fun—not only motivating, but ensuring full engagement, particularly through reflection and discussion, on which constructive learning depends (Booker, 1996). Students and Lead Learners at Aspire High make use of and develop learning games using available technology. Game-based learning (GBL) places a strong emphasis on mastering a skill. As learners gain new abilities, they have higher status and greater access. Such platforms frequently use "badges" to certify certain learning achievements. Badges may also be used as alternative assessments—students receive a badge once they reach a specific learning level. According to Cathy Davidson (2012),

> There are many different kinds of badging systems out there but the ones I like best recognize competencies, skills, training, collaborative abilities, character, personal contribution, participatory energy, leadership and motivational skills, and other so-called "hard" and "soft" individual and cooperative talents. (para. 8)

At Aspire High, games are typically integrated into a particular course or unit rather than used in a stand-alone manner. Emerging studies around gaming and rewards show that gaming positively affects learning.

According to research from Deakin University, incorporating games in the curriculum dramatically alters students' attitudes about math. Games are not perceived as boring and repetitive by the students and therefore have the potential to overcome their negative attitude toward mathematics (Bragg, 2016, p. 6). Students understand that they are in school to learn and easily distinguish between learning games and games that are merely for entertainment. Aspire High has just begun to tap the vast potential of learning through gaming.

PROJECT ASPIRE

Don Acker, school counselor and educator, Oklahoma City (OK) Public Schools. Don has been an avid learner in Project Aspire.

Project Aspire *is an online professional learning experience designed by the Quaglia Institute for Student Aspirations (QISA) that allows educators to complete learning quests of their choosing. The theory behind this approach is to extend to professional educators the opportunity to shape their own learning experiences. The preferred learning modality, asynchronous nature of the platform, and variety of learning quests (e.g., videos, podcasts, journal articles, research, etc.) suit the needs of busy educators.*

My career within the educational world began just a few years ago. This is a second career adventure after 30 years in my previous career. I did not attend college/graduate school intending to enter the educational setting, so I seek numerous ways of developing student success. I invest time to improve my skills through studying materials that empower me to be an effective educator, but without a background as a professional educator, it is a challenge to know where to look for those skills. For that reason, completing the quests through *Project Aspire* accomplishes those challenges.

Project Aspire provides learning quests that cover a wide range of material. The material is useful for both novice and experienced teachers and counselors. I serve as a school counselor for three schools and provide classroom instruction concerning social skills. The quests I have selected enhance my own understanding of QISA's Aspirations Framework and the importance of Student Voice. Additionally, I have selected quests that I can apply directly to my work with students. These many engaging, student-related activities have been fun for my students and eye-opening for me.

The use of *Project Aspire* has been instrumental in my development as both a counselor and an educator. The books on the reading list have opened up whole new ways of communicating with students and staff and motivating them. I know the time I invested in the quests has been multiplied back into my professional readiness.

- Don Acker is relatively new to the profession of teaching and so is keenly aware of his need to improve his pedagogical skills. If you are a new teacher, what skills are most in need of development for you? If you are a veteran teacher, what skills that used to work for you need refurbishing?
- *Project Aspire* involves a great deal of learner selection. What would you choose to learn if professional development were entirely up to you? Why?
- What experience have you had with online or blended-learning experiences? What is effective about such approaches? What areas of the teaching profession are most difficult to learn about online?

Making and Creating

At Aspire High, technology is used specifically as a tool and means for creation of both knowledge and actual products. Knowledge creation may be in the form of movies, slide decks, songs, multimedia presentations, interviews, articles, books, and the like. Unlike traditional classrooms that must rely on limited material supplies and time, students and Lead Learners realize that what can be created using technology and the Internet is virtually limitless. At Aspire High, knowledge creation also involves using technology to support the demonstration and assessment of learning. Since there are no blocked sites, students are free to access any material that helps them learn and demonstrate their learning. As students did in the pre-Internet age, students at Aspire High learn about plagiarism, reliability, and ethics as it relates to accessing and quoting published material—though now most of that material is found online. Newer copyright arrangements such as Creative Commons are also studied and employed when knowledge is generated and shared.

The idea of using technology in assessment schemes is seen on a national level in Denmark where Danish students were among the first ever to complete their exams with the aid of Internet access. The auditors called the 2010 experiment a success, and the Minister for Education, Tina Nedergaard, was excited to extend it:

> I am happy that we as the first country in the world had the vision to let students use the internet during their exams. The internet is an integrated part of students' everyday lives and education so this development is natural. The experiment shows there is a range of positive effects. Therefore, we have so far decided to extend the experiment to include summer exams in 2011 as well. (Danish Ministry for Children, 2010, para. 3)

In addition, a study by Jaleel and Verghis (2015) concluded that e-learning environments provide a rich variety of experiences that help in enhancing creativity and thereby aid in knowledge creation process.

Another significant aspect of the use of technology in the creation of knowledge at Aspire High is that students are involved in the Makers Movement, described in *AdWeek* (2014) in this way:

[The Makers Movement is] the umbrella term for independent inventors, designers and tinkerers. A convergence of computer hackers and traditional artisans, the niche is established enough to have its own magazine, *Make*, as well as hands-on Maker Faires that are catnip for DIYers who used to toil in solitude. Makers tap into an American admiration for self-reliance and combine that with open-source learning, contemporary design and powerful personal technology like 3-D printers. (Voight, 2014, para. 2)

According to *USA Today* (2013), Makers fuel business with some $29 billion poured into the world economy each year. Students in art classes make and sell products for Etsy, while other students post their creative ideas on Pinterest. The Makers Movement capitalizes on the do-it-yourself (DIY) explosion over the past decade. On a regular basis, students share their DIY projects.

Ultimately, what the Makers Movement at Aspire High supports is the idea of trying, failing, and trying again. Any home inventor or creator knows that nothing is created on one's first attempt. Tony Wagner (2012) notes, "The long-term health of our economy and a full-term economic recovery depends upon creating far more innovation" (p. x). At Aspire High, the desired outcomes of learning include creating, designing, building, innovating, and showcasing as replacements for memorizing, multiple-choice tests, guess-what's-in-the-teacher's-head questions, and other forms of information regurgitation.

In the past, education was about teaching people something they wouldn't have otherwise had access to. Schools, their teachers, their books, and their curricula transported people to places they never could have gotten to without the school as a vehicle. Now, education must be about helping people develop a reliable compass and the navigation skills to find their own way through an increasingly uncertain, ambiguous, and, at times, volatile world. Students unable to navigate through our complex digital landscape will be unable to participate in our economic, social, and cultural life. The world no longer rewards people for what they know; instead, it rewards them for what they *do* with what they know and how quickly they learn when they don't know. Classes in the use of technology may help students develop a capacity to use technology, but that is not nearly enough. It is the actual use of technology in learning settings for learning purposes that creates the potential for new ways of thinking and working.

Just as with pedagogy, entire books have been written about the effective use of technology in the classroom and schools. The previous list is by no means an exhaustive articulation of the use of technology at Aspire High, to say nothing of its successful uses in other educational settings. In addition, in the spirit of the very Internet that has been one of the most significant technological advances in human history, there are a plethora of free, high-quality resources available for exploiting technology's many potential contributions to learning. While infrastructure concerns obviously must be addressed, once a school is connected, the intentional and thoughtful use of technology for learning and the transformative impact technology can have on pedagogy holds the promise of closing gaps and reducing the inequities that seem limited by resources or location.

Additionally, technology has an amazing capacity to span nations, cultures, and time zones. In both real time and asynchronously, Aspire High learners can work on French with students in France or explore the holdings of the Guggenheim from a computer. A live webcam on the Galapagos Islands can be part of a science unit. A remote village in Africa can be part of an ethnographic study. Students may even work with and help solve real-world problems for people halfway around the world, whether those problems are chronic (e.g., a lack of clean water) or caused by a recent natural disaster (as with a flood or earthquake).

Even for all the promises of technology, Aspire High does not imagine a world without Lead Learners. Young people will always need coaches and guides, those who can challenge and also support having the benefit of longer or broader experience. The previously established value of intergenerational relationships is no less in play in an asynchronous experience or a virtual classroom. Learning still must be facilitated, scaffolded, personalized, and assessed. Technology is a support to all of this, not a replacement.

For more examples of interesting and innovative uses of technology for learning, use an online search engine to find the following resources:

- *Designing the Future Classroom* (FCL), European Schoolnet (pdf): eun.org
- National e-Learning Strategy, SmartLearning, Malta (pdf): eun.org
- "Ten Opportunities for Technology to Transform Teaching & Learning" in the *Ed Tech Developer's Guide*: tech.ed.gov
- KhanAcademy.org
- *Badging From Within* by Paul Fain, January 3, 2014, a digital badging project at UC Davis: insidehighered.com
- San Diego's High-Tech High: hightechhigh.org
- 3-D Game Lab (videos, student-created comments, classroom examples, etc.): rezzly.com

MOBILE LEARNING TECHNICAL SUPPORT

Jim Wynn, former principal of the John Cabot School in Bristol, United Kingdom

The John Cabot School is now an academy. As principal, Jim (now CEO of Imagine Education) introduced a range of opportunities for students to contribute to the running of the school and beyond. Some opportunities involved development of the use of technology for learning, and many led to real benefits for the wider community as well as student learning.

At John Cabot, we had an IT help desk that was run entirely by students during nonlesson time. It was there to help and support staff and students alike. The students invented and introduced a ticket system to record and track issues and to help fix them. Some of the students joined the school's IT committee, which advised on all manners of IT issues. Those issues weren't merely technical and detailed; they were strategic and curriculum based as well.

One of the amazing things the students did was to organise training sessions for our local primary schools. Some were for primary school teachers and others for primary school students. Our students took full responsibility and were supported by our staff. Sometimes their initiative took us by surprise. I recall a coach turning up one day to a room full of primary kids there for an IT training session. Whilst this great work was overseen by our teacher, Colin Coles, the students had organised everything from advertising the course to arranging the transport, refreshments, and food—the whole thing, from beginning to end.

That culture of taking responsibility spread into other things. After John Cabot School had entertained a choir from a township in Johannesburg, we found CDs of the concert on sale in our school shop alongside a cookery book. The book and concert had been specially produced and recorded and put on sale to raise funds for our visitors' school in South Africa. The only school staff who knew anything about this initiative were those that the students had asked to help them with specific tasks.

I still have a copy of that CD—it is amazing!

- Jim Wynn encouraged the employment and application of the IT skills of students in practical ways to the benefit of the school and the wider community. How might you use students' skills and technology to similar effect?
- Whether in working to support local primary schools or in recording and selling goods to support the school in South Africa, students employed collaborative behaviors and skills to complete a

real outcome. How might you encourage students to work together and collaborate while integrating technology in their work and learning?

- Ask your students what they think about your school's current policies about technology. Do they believe the policies support learning? Consider working with them to have policies revised.

For Reflection

◇ What do you see as the potentials and pitfalls of technology in education? What technological resources have you taken most advantage of? Which have you deliberately ignored and why?

◇ Describe how you have used technology to amplify your own learning. What online and digital resources have most benefited your professional growth in the last several years?

◇ With a colleague, select one of the links at the end of the previous section; together, explore and discuss what you learn from the information you discover.

◇ Have students share with you the latest trend in the digital world. Also ask them what trends or apps or devices they would welcome in the future.

LEAD

Some worry about what technology is doing to our minds—we hope it does something to our minds, otherwise we aren't learning! There is no escaping the fact that we live in a technology-infused-and-influenced world. Computers, tablets, and smartphones connect us to information at a volume and velocity that is unprecedented in human history. Round-the-clock access to databases, course materials, and 24-hour news cycles make the idea that education happens from 8 a.m. until 3 p.m. Monday through Friday between September and June in rooms called "classes" in a building we call "school" a quaint, if not utterly obsolete, notion.

We are going to state this as boldly as we have stated anything else in this book: Schools that deny their students access to technology (smartphones, the Internet, etc.) during the school day through no-use policies rather than developing proper-use policies are out of touch. They are out of touch with reality, out of touch with a great many educational resources, and, worst of all, out of touch with their students. Rather than teaching appropriate and applicable use of mobile devices in a school setting, schools that take the lazy way out into outright bans are simply irrelevant in the eyes of their students.

Yes, technology can be a distraction for students. It can be for us! But so can pen and paper. "But students will text!" Students will pass notes. "But students will not pay attention!" Students will doodle. "But students will surf the web!" Students will surf their daydreams. Technology is not a drug or weapon that needs to be banned from our schools; instead, it is a tool that needs to find a proper use.

Nor is any of this about the technology per se. We love the programs that put a device in every student's hands that are referred to not as "one-to-one" (one student connected to one device), but as "one-to-world" (one student connected by the device to the entire world). This is the shift in thinking that results in technology leadership that makes sense in the current common world. Certainly, we must take our head out of the sand of "we-learned-just-fine-without-the-Internet" thinking. We must acknowledge that technology can amplify good and bad. And we, with our students, must take responsibility for using all the tools of education to advance their aspirations.

On your mark. Get set! Go!!

PRINCIPAL

Step ⟹

- *Ensure all students and teachers are trained to effectively use technology.* We believe this is a basic and fundamental challenge, and one that commonly gets overlooked. How many times are we expecting teachers to do something differently without the support to do so? If we expect the educational community to use technology, we must first make sure they know how.
- *Communicate agendas, memos, and other routine information through technology.* Aside from saving trees, you need to lead by example in this basic way. Please understand this does not mean you can hide in the office and not have face-to-face conversations anymore! Proper use of technology to bulk communicate should open up more time for you to actually have individual conversations.

Stride ⟹

- *Work with students and staff to create a policy that values mobile devices and tablets as learning tools.* There are many schools that ban technology because it is being misused, but consider that if students abused the dress code, you would not ban clothes! Instead, you would establish better guidelines. Taking away students' mobile devices is like stripping them of their attire. Students are more likely to bring a mobile device with them to school than a coat.
- *Provide teachers opportunities to observe their colleagues who successfully integrate technology into teaching.* It is one thing to tell people how to use technology, and it is another to watch someone putting it into action. By observing others, teachers will be able to see that using technology is a process, not an event. More importantly, they will learn it is nothing to fear.

Sprint ⟹

- *Support full integration of technology as a learning tool.* The technology train has left the station, so you need to ensure that the school community is on the train. Technology is *not* going away, as some veteran educators tried to tell us. Granted, technology is going to look different in the future, but you can bet your rose-gold Apple watch we are going to be inundated with more technology in the future, not less.
- *Require all students to graduate high school with necessary computer skills to be life ready.* Yes, this involves a bold policy that ensures each student has the skills and knowledge to be technologically literate. However, since technology is here to stay and will become even more prevalent in our lives, it only makes sense that our graduates are prepared to use technology for their benefit.

TEACHERS

Step ═══⟹

- *Work with students to integrate technology into teaching.* Young people today no longer look at technology as simply a tool, but as a natural part of their day. In most schools, that natural way of being is disrupted, and students become less and less engaged. The truth is, students will be your greatest resource on how to incorporate technology into your teaching. All you need to do is ask!
- *Use the Internet to help students find real-time connections to what they are learning.* One of the easiest ways to engage students is by connecting what you are teaching to real-world issues in real time. The majority of students say school has no relation to their everyday lives. Simply "Google" what you are teaching, and they (and you) will see the connections.

Stride ═══════⟹

- *Ensure students complete a range of assignments using multimedia techniques.* Students love to impress peers with something in technology they have mastered before anyone else. Asking students to be technologically creative with assignments outside of school will turn home*work* into "home*learning*."
- *Develop a classroom web page.* This is an engaging and relevant class activity. The learning opportunities are endless and vary from designing a logo to writing policies and procedures to writing short bios about everyone in the class to posting assignments. Make students responsible for checking the web page daily.

Sprint ═══════════⟹

- *Connect students with learners from around the world.* Develop connections between your students and students from other countries. Create a challenge that must be solved by a global network of students. Ask your students to take the lead. Using technology to establish international connections will open up new learning and new perspectives.
- *Have students become technology designers.* We have no idea what the next app, gadget, or tech innovation will be, but your students might! Carve out time to have your students become not just consumers and users of technology, but creators as well. Robotics and coding classes are all the rage. Find a way to have students invent technology for your class purposes.

STUDENTS

Step ⟹

- *Appropriately use technology during the school day.* Be responsible when it comes to using technology in and outside of school. Technology is a tool and needs to be used appropriately. Do not let the abuse of technology by some students spoil it for the rest.
- *Use resources available online to support and deepen what you are learning in school.* Don't let your learning stop at the end of the school day. You know as well as any adult that you can learn anything online. Once you find the proper resources that advance your learning, share them with your teachers and other students.

Stride ⟹

- *Teach adults about new ways to learn with technology.* This is your opportunity to shine and to take the lead. Become a teacher of teachers! Ask to be scheduled for a brief time at every staff meeting so you can share with the entire teaching staff something new going on in technology—your school's IT director will probably be glad for the support.
- *Use social media as a means to have your voice heard for positive change.* One of technology's greatest uses is how it amplifies people's voices. Go viral with a positive or inspirational message. Using technology as an amplifier of who you are, what you value, and what you believe can and should be done to make this world a better place.

Sprint ⟹

- *Enroll in a free online course in an area that interests you.* All schools have limited budgets, and if your school is not providing all you desire to quench your inquisitiveness, we challenge you to learn on your own. There are endless free resources online that allow you to explore and learn whatever is of interest.
- *Invent technology.* If you don't know how to already (many students do!), learn to code or design technology. Figure out a way to support a class you are taking with a new website, app, or other technological tool. Then see if you can get your app on an app store or your new gadget on the market!

Is Your School . . . ?		
TYPICAL HIGH	ASPIRE HIGH	ASPIRING HIGHER
Only teachers who are comfortable with technology use it as a tool.	Everyone is trained and supported in the use of technology for advancing learning.	Experienced teachers and skilled students do technology training internally.
Students take online courses only when a course is unavailable at their school.	Students regularly enroll in online courses to advance their aspirations.	Students and teachers cocreate and coteach online courses for other learners.
Connections with students in other countries is sporadic and has the feeling of a "field trip."	Using communication technology, purposeful connections are made with students from around the world.	Students are working on collaborative projects and products with students around the world.
Social media is banned for students and teachers in school.	Social media is used as a vehicle to share important information about the school to others.	Social media is used to express thoughts, opinions and ideas for school improvement to people around the world for feedback.
The school board sets technology policy (either banned or appropriate use). Administration enforces the policies. Teachers elect to support the policy or not.	Appropriate use of technology is self- and peer-monitored by students.	Students work with younger grades in their district or peers in other schools to help learn and teach appropriate-use policies.
The Internet is a glorified encyclopedia, used mainly for simple research purposes.	All learning units use technology to understand current events as they relate to what is being taught.	Students and staff make judgment calls on when learning can be enhanced through technology and use it accordingly.
Students help troubleshoot technology when teachers run into a problem.	Students regularly instruct teachers in the use of technology.	Students and teachers support technology learning in the local community.
Students use available and approved apps and websites. All other apps and sites are blocked.	Students are encouraged to create and design apps and other technological resources.	Students develop technology to benefit the local and global community.
Blended learning is used in some classes to fill in gaps.	Blended learning is expected and the norm in all learning units and projects.	Students help develop blended-learning modules to be used with the school and by other schools.
Adults oversee the IT department.	Students participate with adults in the IT department.	Students *are* the IT department.

(Continued)

(Continued)

Is Your School . . . ?		
TYPICAL HIGH	ASPIRE HIGH	ASPIRING HIGHER
The school website is developed by adults who are also responsible for regular updates.	Students and teachers design and maintain the school website in partnership.	Students and teachers work with local community organizations that need web support.
Student academic work and products are posted in the hallways and classrooms.	Student academic work and products are regularly demonstrated on the Internet (blogs, portfolios, movie clips, presentations, etc.).	Students connect with professionals to codesign and develop products along their career trajectory.
Students and teachers occasionally use technology to automate and hasten achievement of existing learning aims.	Students and teachers use technology as a tool to learn new things in new ways.	Students and teachers use technology to design and create new tools to have impact on their environment and learning.
Students use technology mainly to digitize traditional learning and curate work.	Students use technology to learn through exploration and discovery.	Students use technology to innovate, create, and learn.
Students and teachers use technology to aid rote learning. For example, they use digital flash cards instead of paper cards.	Students and teachers use technology to learn through the equivalent of working through electronic case studies.	Students and teachers use technology to increase authenticity in learning by using real data, interacting with real experts, addressing real challenges, and gaining feedback from readers and users of what students produce.
What's a MOOC (massive open online course)?	MOOCs are used as appropriate parts of the curriculum.	Students work with teachers to develop MOOCs that are offered free of charge.

8

Beyond Bricks and Mortar

What is life? It is the flash of a firefly in the night. It is the breath of a buffalo in the wintertime. It is the little shadow which runs across the grass and loses itself in the sunset.

—Crowfoot, Blackfoot warrior and orator

LISTEN

We return to Aspire High for the third and final day of our visit. As with our previous visits, we are greeted at the door by students. All guests are greeted by students who rotate to welcome, sign in, and escort guests—both expected and unexpected. The students who meet us today are our tour guides. They introduce themselves as Chris and D'Shonna. Although we followed Mr. Harper around for a while on our first day, it was not an actual tour of the physical plant. He decided to reserve that for our last day, once we had a sense of the school's mission, goals, curriculum, and approach. "Aspire High is not first and foremost a building," he said. "It's a way of being."

Unexpectedly, the students lead us back outside, and they start the tour in the flower garden. This turns out to be a small garden park just past an organic vegetable garden that students also manage. In the park, there are benches arranged in obvious discussion formations, as well as a small amphitheater.

"Looks like no one's out here right now," Chris says.

"I have a weather unit for my Statistical Patterns class out here this afternoon," D'Shonna adds. She notes that the class looks at all kinds of trends, from those on Twitter and other social media to those in nature and world history. "Peter—he's the Lead Learner in that class—he thinks that recognizing patterns is the best way to understand the world and even yourself. It's a cool class."

As we walk, D'Shonna goes on to note, "Students can have lunch out here, too, but to have a class out here, you have to have a real reason."

"Yeah," Chris adds. "We can't just come out because we want to be outside, though that's always a temptation." We agree. "So if you are leading a project or a lesson and you want to do it outside, you just have to work with the Lead Learner to explain why it works better outside. Then you can sign out one of these bench areas or the amphitheater."

"Then does Mr. Harper approve it?"

"Approve it? It doesn't get approved or anything. If you work out the reason, you just have to sign it out so there aren't conflicts."

We walk around the entire block that makes up the "campus" of Aspire High. We pass traditional athletic fields. There are good-sized trebuchets at one end of the football field, next to sleds. He explains that the fields are jointly owned with the town recreation department. The community and the school work together to raise funds and matching grants. As we turn the last corner, Chris points down the street away from the school. "About a block that way is where I did my internship last year. I was lucky—not all the internships are that close."

D'Shonna says, "I'm in this online class that's run through the community college. It's blended, so every other Monday, I start my day there. It's a little less than a mile. I don't mind the walk. Except when it rains."

We return to the building. For all the differences in its approach to education, Aspire High operates in a fairly traditional physical building. Classrooms off corridors, common spaces like a gym and cafeteria, and various meeting rooms are all part of the tour.

D'Shonna points out, "The Lead Learners all eat with us in the cafeteria or the Inspiration Café. They don't have a separate teachers' room like at my old school." D'Shonna is in her third year at Aspire High and was a first-year student in another state before her family moved. "At first, that was strange for me, but I got used to it."

We look in on the cafeteria, which is still serving breakfast fare. The adults we can see are sitting mixed in among the students, not together in a group apart.

As we move in and out of and sometimes through classes, we notice something we hadn't the day before. "Don't the teachers have desks?" we ask. Nearly every school we have been in has large teacher desks variously located in classrooms: some in the front, some in the back, some to the side. Regardless of its location, the teacher desk is typically a focal point for being unique in the room and anchoring a kind of open office space—some personalized to one degree or another. But these are missing at Aspire High.

"No," Chris says. "They just use the regular desks or stools like us."

D'Shonna adds, "They would be too hard to move anyway. We move the desks and tables around a lot in all our classes. It depends on what we are doing or working on. Sometimes we do a big circle, and sometimes little groups are doing their own thing. Sometimes you work by yourself. It all depends."

We notice that even though the overall shape of the building is traditional, the designers, or redesigners, have done a good job repurposing spaces. Some rooms are carpeted, others are not. Some rooms are filled with artwork (one even had a graffiti wall), and others have bare walls that seem to invite projection or other temporary displays. Many hallway intersections have a dead space that has been remodeled into a small, comfortable seating area. The corridors themselves are anything but sterile or simply utilitarian. Student artwork enlivens all common spaces. When we remark at how clean the school is, Chris says, "Mr. D, our head custodian, has this whole schedule for us. Every student has to pitch in at some point to help keep the building clean."

D'Shonna shares, "At my old school, kids had to do that as part of being punished. Here, it feels more like being part of a family."

Chris and D'Shonna bring us through the gym to what were obviously at one time two classrooms. The adjoining wall has been removed, and the larger space has been converted into a fitness room. A rubberized floor, a towel and water station, and a variety of weightlifting and fitness equipment are appropriately arranged around the room. A Lead Learner is instructing a group, which includes at least two adults, on the safe use of a weight machine.

Chris points out the window and says, "The building over there is a yoga studio. We can take class there if we want. Mr. Harper worked out some kind of deal. The schedule is on the wall here."

The other design feature we can't help but note is an abundance of natural light. Classes and corridors are bright. As we look up, we notice skylights and what look like various mirrored systems to channel light from outside into the building. Windows are large, and most shades (other than in rooms viewing a screen) are fully open. Stairways, too, are well lit. And even interior rooms, mostly conference rooms, are lit with what we guess is full spectrum light, as it has all the brightness of being outside.

During the tour, we learn that *students at Aspire High enjoy much more freedom of movement than we have come to expect in most high schools*. Students do not need to ask an adult's permission to use a bathroom. They can get up out of a desk and stand if they feel like they need to move, continuing to discuss or listen or focus on the task at hand. We learn from our guides that occasionally students will abuse this privilege and not be where they are supposed to be or spend a longer amount of time somewhere than they should. "Most of that is about someone wanting to see their boyfriend or girlfriend," D'Shonna rolls her eyes.

"What happens?" we ask.

"Well, they miss whatever they were supposed to be doing," Chris says. (Did we hear an implied "Duh!"?) "If it happens too much, someone usually calls them on it—another student or a Lead Learner. We all try to look out for each other. If you seem distracted in a way that is going to hurt your education, one of your friends lets you know."

At no time during our visit to Aspire High did we encounter chaos or what felt like overcrowding: not in a class, not during passing time, not in the cafeteria, and not in the hallways. To be sure, there is noise and movement. Most classrooms are clamorous, with multiple conversations going on at once. Occasionally, we heard a voice above the others ask, "Can we take it down a notch?" But for the most part, Aspire High's fêng shui is characterized by a kind of ordered flexibility. Classroom space and furnishings allow for movement, collaboration, hands-on learning, and blended learning. As we noted in Steve's classroom, there are tables and chairs but also stools and high-top tables and counters. Several classrooms had fitness balls for seats. While most rooms had technology, not all did. This was not due to a lack of resources, but rather a lack of purpose for technology, given the use of that particular space.

All spaces at Aspire High are fully exploited for learning purposes. Students in the culinary program work side by side with cafeteria employees to prepare food throughout the day. Students in premed intern at the nurse's area; students interested in accounting work with school leaders on budgets and fund-raising in their offices. Future police or military students work with the school security guard at the front door to understand what it means to ensure safety in a school. In order to accommodate the type of learning we have seen at Aspire High, the entire building has been redesigned as a Learning Center, where no space is off-limits to the learners.

There are several labs at Aspire High. In addition to the typical science, robotics, and computer labs, there is a video and audio production lab. There is a 3-D design lab. All of these are used in expected ways—for example, the video production lab is used to produce a daily student news show—but also as part of the integrated curriculum, as we saw with the World War II exhibition. There is also a news lab. This has several TVs and computers in it that are nearly always tuned to news stations. As we have seen, *much of Aspire High's curriculum is real-world relevant.* It is not unusual for students to be watching news programming on and off throughout the day or as part of a particular class or unit. Aspire High students are well informed about current events and mine the news for connections to classes, as well as connections to their aspirations and goals.

All at Aspire High recognize that learning cannot be restricted to a school building. We have already noted the use of field trips and internships as part of the curriculum. Community spaces are frequently visited to suit learning needs. A physics unit that studied hydraulics arranged time with the local fire department. An interdisciplinary environmental unit spent several Friday afternoons not only cleaning local parks but also studying litter patterns in those parks. They made an appointment to visit the director of parks and recreation to share their findings and suggest trash can placement, new signage, and revised maintenance schedules. Writers spend time at the offices of the local paper. The culinary students frequent bakeries and restaurants.

The overall effort of the way space is conceived and used at Aspire High conveys the clear message that learning is not something isolated to a school building or campus. We no longer live in a world in which everything is as clearly delineated or separated from each other. Our greatest learning resource—the Internet—is hyperlinked. The boundaries between the different domains are blurred. Collaboration and interaction are far more important than keeping the "walls"—both figurative and literal—that have been a part of traditional schooling. We must ask, "What story do we want our school buildings to tell?" (Scheeren, 2015).

In a sense, it would be a betrayal to say that students go to Aspire High to learn. *Aspire High students are learning all the time, at school and away from school, during the school day and long after the school day has ended.* Many of the tools and people that support and facilitate the learning show up at a particular place and a particular time together called Aspire High. That's because learning is a communal experience and requires a common space. But the learning is a function of the community, not the space in which it gathers.

LEARN

The physical space of Aspire High embodies the values and mission of the school. Students and Lead Learners have space to collaborate, build, design, and experience. The design of the building communicates the pedagogy of Aspire High—student-centered, student-driven learning. This includes all necessary accommodations for students with disabilities. As Getzels (1975) writes, "Our vision of human nature finds expression in the buildings we construct, and these constructions in turn do their silent yet irresistible work of telling us who we are and what we must do" (p. 12). The environment extends beyond the walls of Aspire High into both the local and global community. Students consider online learning experiences part of their "school," as technology is readily available and accessible.

In designing the space that is Aspire High, the school community took the time to understand the effects of natural light, outdoor space, the use of color, chair comfort, desk and table arrangement, and all the other physical elements that fit within a traditional school building—even the acoustics—because according to Fisher (2002), all of these aspects appear to have an impact on student behavior. The design of the circulation routes and the resulting air quality was also considered, as research indicates that the impact of excessive carbon monoxide levels negatively affects concentration and behavior and increases the chances of students falling asleep from exposure to stale air (Schneider, 2002).

Furthermore, students and designers consider the effects of sustainable products and resources in the building and maintaining of Aspire High. Global Green USA (2005) noted that the condition of school buildings has a direct impact on student performance. Edwards (2006) examined the impact of green-school designs in Hampshire and Essex in England. The quality of the classroom environment resulting from green-design principles reduced stress in teachers and led to lower rates of absenteeism or staff turnover, which in turn improved productivity. Edwards also found that teacher productivity improved 4% in green schools, that standardized test scores were 3% to 5% higher than at others, and that the staff and students felt their health and well-being were valued (Green Schools Initiative, 2005). Aspire High encourages students to take responsibility for improving their environment through recycling, conservation, and an overall awareness of the environment.

There are several distinct features of the physical environment of Aspire High, all of which have the effect of encouraging the principle that learning happens beyond the bricks and mortar of the physical space. By setting aside makerspaces, inviting the community into the school daily, having space in which students can move, and having internships off campus, Aspire High makes it clear that "school" is a set of learning experiences, not a building. In fact, they—the students and Lead Learners—are the school, not the building in which they happen to gather.

TEACHERS WITHOUT BORDERS

Julie Hellerstein, ninth-grade World History teacher, Mallard Creek High School in Charlotte, North Carolina

Julie is the coauthor of Student Voice: Turn Up the Volume, K–8 *and* Student Voice: Turn Up the Volume, 6–12 *(2015).*

Social media is an important learning tool in my ninth-grade World History course. My students are excited to showcase their learning on a platform that they are familiar with and that allows them to share their work with family and friends who are not in school. Students construct their own knowledge and can immediately share it with their network.

During the first week of school, my students had the task of creating an Instagram account for Çatalhöyük, a Neolithic settlement located in central Turkey. Students were excited to write witty hashtags for artifacts that are over 9,000 years old. Through researching artifacts and reading research articles from archaeologists, students were able to "dig up" insight on what it would be like to live in the New Stone Age.

In another assignment, students created a Snapchat story for one of the key contributors of the Scientific Revolution—for example, Sir Issac Netwon, Nicholas Copernicus, Galileo Galilei, or Francis Bacon. Each Snap was filled with historical content, emojis, text, drawings, and even geofilters. Students elaborated on the Snapchat by writing a thorough description. They were eager to share their stories with their peers inside and outside the classroom.

In a collaborative group exercise, students had to decide what images should be used to commemorate the dropping of the atomic bomb on Hiroshima and Nagasaki. Students were to select an image that would go on the United Nations website. Some of the group members represented the Japanese perspective and others the American perspective. Prior to the exercise, students had read a variety of primary and secondary sources (sheg.stanford.edu/atomic-bomb).

In another activity, students competed in a photo scavenger hunt using the Goosechase app. All of the missions were centered on the causes of World War I—militarism, alliances, imperialism, and nationalism. Students made interesting connections between nationalism and extreme school spirit, as well as alliances and high school friendship groups. While learning about the Renaissance, students went on a virtual field trip to St. Peter's Basillica and the Sistine Chapel. They explored the 3-D interactive tours and created their own faux travel blogs and screencasts.

My students certainly seemed to enjoy these learning experiences, as they were fun, creative, and relevant to their lives. Plus, they got them "virtually" out of school!

- Julie Hellerstein uses social media to "break down" the walls between the school and the rest of the world. How might you use social media in a similar way? What are the obstacles to that at your school?
- The Internet opens up the possibility of students interacting with the very organizations, entities, and even places they are studying (e.g., the United Nations, the Sistine Chapel, etc.). What interactions can you create for your students so that their learning is not confined to what happens in the school building itself?
- Gather a group of like-minded educators at your school and discuss ways you can "leave the building" with your students by way of the World Wide Web.

Makerspaces

Makerspaces at Aspire High have the primary purpose of encouraging students and Lead Learners to build, create, design, and tinker. The space is equipped with 3-D printers, microprocessors, robotics, and computer programming, all aimed at supporting creativity and design. West-Puckett (2013) describes how educators can design classrooms as makerspaces by focusing on student interest and by understanding learning as integrated and connected *through projects* rather than as an isolated set of skills. Makerspaces are also used by staff and students for the weekly "Genius Hour" that is built into Aspire High's schedule. Research has also demonstrated how the "making activities" result in participants learning principles of engineering, circuitry, design, and computer programming (e.g., Jacobs & Buechley, 2013; Kafai, Peppler, & Chapman, 2009; Sheridan, Clark, & Williams, 2013). "The real power of this revolution is its democratizing effects. Now, almost anyone can innovate. Now, almost anyone can make. Now, with the tools available at a makerspace, anyone can change the world" (Hatch, 2014, p. 10).

Additionally, *having space to build and create encourages students to self-direct and take control of their learning.* To achieve this flexibility, architects are designing classrooms, or "learning studios," with movable furniture and walls that can easily be reconfigured for different class sizes and subjects. In a sense, every classroom at Aspire High is a makerspace because every classroom can be remade to suit a learning purpose. The very decision to move desks so that the entire group can see one another is a statement about intended learning processes, goals, and outcomes. In that case, knowledge or a decision is what is "made."

Community Partnerships

Aspire High borrows many of the values and concepts of a community school. It is a place that people in the local community know they can receive support, services, and guidance. The community is also viewed and treated as a partner, not an adversary or mere funder. At times, people seek help with housing issues or voter registration, or they participate in a pick-up game of basketball or take an evening course taught by students. Being a community school requires different levels of security and personnel in the evenings. There is a small custodial crew that works overnight to prepare the grounds and building for the following day. The community school model promotes more efficient use of school buildings and, as a result, neighborhoods enjoy increased security, heightened community pride, and better rapport among students and residents (Blake, Melaville, & Shah, 2003). Joy Dryfoos (1994) collected the largest summary of evaluations of community schools. She found that 36 of 49 programs reported academic gains and that reading and math improvement were the most common results.

One major benefit of having robust community partnerships is the support they add to Aspire High's efforts in applied learning. Members of the community in various jobs, careers, and professions work alongside students, not in one-off career days or show-and-tell-type experiences. Rather, they participate as partners in *learning*. Volunteers from the community become students in their own field for a day or more. Motivated by issues that directly affect them and their work, they are happy to explore their thinking with the students at Aspire High (Beckwith & Lopez, 1997). For example, a lawyer may come in to wonder out loud about the implications of a recent Supreme Court decision to her practice. A pastry chef may come in to work through a new flavor profile she is unsure of with students. The key to this approach is that the community members are present to learn, not simply teach about their work. When the community members participating in this effort are parents, this has the added benefit of reducing negative outcomes and contributing to positive outcomes for students. Thirty years of research has consistently linked family involvement to higher student achievement, better attitudes toward school, lower dropout rates, and increased community support for education, as well as many other positive outcomes for students, families, and schools (Henderson & Mapp, 2002).

Students in the Community

As we have seen, *the bricks and mortar of Aspire High are permeable*. While the building and grounds are designed to support unique learning opportunities and diverse learners, the world beyond the walls of the building develops skills related to entrepreneurship, creativity, and innovation. The need to support entrepreneurship is well documented (Zhao, 2012). Throughout the world, there is growing interest in helping people develop and acquire entrepreneurial knowledge, skills, and attitudes (World Economic Forum, 2011). It is generally believed that entrepreneurs can produce innovation, contribute to economic development, and generate work for themselves and others (Kuratako, 2005). According to Zhao (2012), everyone needs to be entrepreneurial in the twenty-first century. This is why Cameron Herold makes a strong case in his TED Talk that schools need to be teaching young people to be entrepreneurs (2010).

> **Yong Zhao** currently serves as the Presidential Chair and Director of the Institute for Global and Online Education in the College of Education, University of Oregon, where he is also a professor in the Department of Educational Measurement, Policy, and Leadership. His works focus on the implications of globalization and technology on education.

During their years at Aspire High, students experience internships and various entrepreneurial opportunities that are integrated into the overall curriculum. Students and Lead Learners regularly collaborate with learners from around the world to tackle global problems. For example, some students enlist the community's help to design cleaner water filtration for towns with poor or no filtration systems, some students work with local farmers to develop drought-resistant strains of vegetables, and other students work with elementary teachers to develop learning apps that help ELL students with their sight words. All of these learning adventures occur outside of the physical building, as students must seek out experts, suppliers, and even space. "Great creative people are not accidents, but they are deliberately cultivated and supported" (Zhao, 2012, p. 152). This cultivation takes place in extended yearlong internships to learn a skill or profession at an in-depth level, while other students move from problem/solution to problem/solution. If students use their resources to solve a problem or add their input into another person's problem, then they simply move on to another challenge.

One of the closest approximations to Aspire High's approach to "bricks and mortar" we have seen is Health Sciences High and Middle College (HSHMC) in San Diego, California, led by Dr. Doug Fisher and Dr. Nancy Frey. The school's mission statement holds that

> HSHMC is a place where people want to learn about health and healthcare as part of a world-class education. HSHMC is a home away from home, an open door, a place of rigor and academia where students earn a diploma that matters.

Students work out of the building with health care professionals through job shadowing and internships to explore real-world applications of their school-based knowledge and skills as well as future career choices. HSHMC is a *vocational* school in the very sense of the word because they are preparing students for a vocation and an avocation—in fact, for their aspiration. In addition, each classroom at HSHMC is designed with the personality of its teachers and learners in mind. For example, an extremely sports-oriented teacher's classroom is carpeted in Astroturf, and the student seats are bleachers!

WORKING TO LEARN

Kinri Flanigan, high school senior

Through the Executive Internship Program [EIP], I have gained an abundance of knowledge, skills, and experience about life in college and the professional business world. EIP has helped me achieve college-level success in my course work and has helped me successfully engage within the professional environment of my internship site at Dunedin Elementary School. Moreover, this program has helped me develop management skills and refine my career preparation goals, as well as develop professional and effective leadership skills.

The orientation sessions of EIP facilitated me in achieving college-level success in my course work. The course work and assignments we received have and will greatly help in the near and destined future. Such work and assignments consisted of learning to write cover letters and résumés, developing interview skills, learning and developing a professional vocabulary, understanding how to use and navigate through available online resources, developing and understanding the specific career's professional code of ethics, and understanding the different career options available. My level of work has significantly improved for the greater.

Through EIP, I have become an effective self-directed learner. I have not only impressed my teachers, family, staff of Dunedin Elementary, and sponsor but also myself. The internship has given me the opportunity to be paired with a professional who models leadership skills in my career field interest. I have developed a more professional outlook and a better idea of what my career interest might be. My level of self-confidence has also significantly improved due to the amount of interaction required as a guidance counselor, or in my case as a child psychologist. Additionally, my use of vocabulary and the way I speak has changed to be more professional, and people view me as an adult rather than a high school student. Overall, the Executive Internship Program has been a defining life experience.

- Kinri Flanigan relates that being in the EIP helped her "achieve college-level success" in her course work. She clearly sees a connection between her work in the internship and her academic success. How would you describe this connection? Why do such "nonacademic" work programs help students perform better academically?
- The EIP also exposed Kinri to a career of interest. Why do you think this may or may not be helpful for a student in high school?
- Among the benefits cited is the opportunity to be paired with a professional in the student's field of interest. How might your reach out to local professionals to pair them with your students' career interests?

For Reflection

- ◊ How do you take learning—literally and figuratively—beyond the bricks and mortar of your building? What effect does this have on learning? On student engagement?
- ◊ Articulate how you take into consideration movement, light, space, and the needs of various pedagogical strategies when you create a learning space.

⬨ Gather a group of colleagues and discuss professional learning experiences you have outside of traditional conferences, books, and professional development (PD) settings.

⬨ Talk with friends not involved in education about how they engage in professional learning. Be sure to inquire about the space/ environment/circumstances of their learning.

LEAD

By now, it should be clear that *Aspire High is first and foremost a "way of being,"* not some specially designed building. Whether you are in rural America or downtown Hong Kong, you have all you need to create an amazing learning environment: students and staff. The key to building Aspire High is to move Student Aspirations and Voice away from being window dressing at your school to being the very bricks and mortar of the place. Self-Worth has to become the foundation. Engagement has to be the heating system. Purpose must be the very organizing structure. The real remodeling needs to take place in your mind.

Having said that, there is no doubt some facilities will foster the components of Aspire High more readily than others. As you consider or reconsider the physical spaces in which learning takes place—or if you have the fortunate opportunity to build a school from the ground up—we offer you two suggestions:

1. Make sure you design your physical space for learning with students. The key question to ask together is this: "What do we need in our physical structures that will enrich our learning and growth potential?"

2. Expect to make changes every year. Never forget the space is *about* and *for* the students you serve. Each year you have new students, so each year you need to rethink the physical space and how it is used.

Given the many and varied shapes, sizes, and configurations of school buildings, to say nothing of the often unconscionable differences in resources, it is unrealistic to offer challenges to principals, teachers, and students to Step, Stride, and Sprint toward school buildings and classroom spaces that may seem unattainable—or at least not within your control to bring to reality. For similar reasons, you will not find a chart to inspire you to Aspire High or Higher at the end of this chapter. Rather, we invite you— principals, teachers, and students—to get together and consider and discuss these five components as you think about recreating whatever physical spaces you must work with:

Flexibility—Is the structure/are the classrooms able to adapt to various learning situations? How can you make the spaces you learn in more flexible? What furniture, bookcases filled with outdated textbooks, oversized teacher desks, and old lab equipment might be removed so that the necessary furniture is more movable to suit various learning exercises? Minimalism is a great design principle. Simplify to flexify!

Freedom—Does the structure promote freedom of movement and freedom for the mind to expand? This is connected to the reduction of clutter we promote. Sitting in desks in neat rows all day is old school and gets old fast. Rethink spaces so that students and teachers can stand and keep learning. The brain works best when blood is circulating. Work in standing desks or on bouncy balls, and have plenty of room to move.

Innovation—How does the structure promote the ability to think differently, be creative, and be exploratory in nature? If you visit some of the best design firms or high-tech companies, their spaces, colors, use of natural light, artwork, plants, and so on just scream "Make something new!" Unfortunately, nothing says "Zzzzzzzz" like some of the classrooms we have been in. Wake the place up.

Growth—Your school is going to become the most popular kid on the block! Will the structure grow as the student body grows? How will it adjust to various numbers of students throughout the year? Start small, but think big. Plan to accommodate different demographic trends. Turn empty classrooms into useful spaces. Work with local business leaders to figure out how to expand. Trailers are not an option.

Security—What physical elements will be in place to ensure student safety? Consider that safety is both a physical and an emotional issue. For sure, work toward a school and community where metal detectors are unnecessary, but take whatever precautions are required at this crazy time. Do not neglect emotional safety as your redesign. Where are the safe spaces to cry? To have a break down? To shout for joy when you get into the college of your choice? Are there places to just chill? To grab a workout? Safety first (all kinds)!

9

The Challenges and Rewards of Being Bold!

Try not! Do! Or do not. There is no try.

—Yoda

LISTEN

As we walk away from Aspire High having said goodbye to Mr. Harper, Steve, and several other Lead Learners and students we met during our three-day visit, our tour guide Chris's words stay with us: "We all try to look out for each other." Although he was talking specifically about what happens when a student misses a class, it seems to apply to the entire approach taken at Aspire High: Everyone looks out for everyone else. Students are not competing against one another for grades or attention. Adults are not competing against one another for time or resources. Adults and students are not competing against one another for power or authority. Absent is the zero-sum game where if one person wins, another loses. There seems to be enough acceptance and respect and recognition and engagement and learning and trust and shared responsibility to go around.

To be sure, Aspire High is not idyllic, but *a cooperative spirit and willingness to listen, learn, and lead where people "look out for one another" is pervasive.* Lead Learners look out for their students, not wanting to manage or command and control them. Students look out for the educators they work with, realizing they are necessary supports for achieving their aspirations. Students look out for one another, seeing in one another allies, learning partners, and fellow aspirers. Lead Learners look out for their colleagues, fully knowing that successfully educating their students could never be about "autonomy" in the classroom, but rather teamwork of the highest order.

Upon reflection, we realize this climate of mutuality is more a result of Aspire High's mission than something they are trying directly to achieve. By focusing their school on the aspirations of each and every student—and not on grades or test scores or academic achievement however narrowly defined—each and every person (adult as well as student) is able to achieve a full measure of self-worth, engagement, and purpose in everything they do. No student's "value" lies in good grades or good behavior. No adult's value lies in the ability to single-handedly be super teacher. Each learner's value—and at Aspire High that means *everyone*—lies in his or her willingness to pursue today the dreams and hopes he or she has for tomorrow. And since no person can accomplish that task alone, every person at Aspire High looks out for each other.

LEARN

Components of Aspire High exist. Everything we have shared has its roots in something we have heard or seen or experienced in countless schools across the world over a combined 100 years as educators. Likely, you have encountered or may yourself use many of the teaching and learning ideas and techniques that make up Aspire High. Technology is more and more exploited for its engagement and learning capacities. Real-world relevance is called for by the most recent rubrics, teaching standards, and state mandates. A positive relationship between students and teachers continues to move closer to the center of education and is increasingly seen not as a replacement for rigor, but as its very foundation. Physical spaces are becoming more conducive to learning. And, at long last, Student and Teacher Voice are emerging as crucial and necessary components of school improvement efforts, hiring practices, and teacher feedback systems.

Yet Aspire High as a whole does not exist. While we really have seen all the pieces of Aspire High, we have not seen them all in one real place. Most of the components we have imaginatively assembled into Aspire High exist in isolation as often patched on, sometimes spreading, occasionally subversive elements in the inherited, industrial model of school. Students give presentations, but more for assessment purposes than actual teaching. Small pockets of meaningful professional development exist alongside more typical show-up-and-sign-in-so-we-can-check-a-box versions. Teachers from two different disciplines coteach, but they are not properly given the extra time needed this inevitably involves. Students participate in leadership, but they have little real decision-making influence or authority.

There are many examples of schools that achieve learning in new and creative ways. And while not every experiment in reimagining school is successful and not all the successful ones are scalable, still there is plenty of proof that we can do better. And if we can do better, we must do better. The challenge of many new approaches is that they require an entire reboot. Stop what you are doing and start over—that takes time. The fact of the matter is the rate of change inside our schools is already being quickly surpassed by the rate of change outside our schools. It is our responsibility, if not our moral obligation, to provide a rich learning environment that focuses more on where students are going and spends less time worrying about where they are from.

Aspire High can exist in all schools for all students. While the pockets of success being enjoyed here and there are inspiring, many are challenging to take to scale. The fact is that every day most students attend a school very similar to the one their parents attended, which was very similar to the one their parents attended. Subjects are taught discreetly to groups of students formed primarily by age, not ability. Learning stops and starts during the day, at the end of each day, at the end of terms, at the end of the year, and sadly, for many, at the end of it all. Curriculum is driven by high-stakes tests, not learning needs, to say nothing of students' aspirations. Rather than the trust and responsibility that are the hallmarks of genuine learning, the entire system is enslaved to schemes of testing and accountability.

It's time to set the learning free. We could set up a charter school as "Camp Aspiration" and build a learning fire that would kindle the aspirations of a few hundred students. But our aim is not to construct a fiefdom of success to benefit a few—we would rather light a fuse. Our goal is to inspire change from *within* the current system to affect *all* students. *You* are the key to the ensuing eruption of lifelong love for learning that schools can inspire—you, your students, your students' parents, your community. The fuel, the absolute transformative energy for this revolution, is your students' dreams and the relentless human desire and potential to bring dreams to reality. *When our schools refocus their intentions, efforts, and resources on the goal of helping each and every student dream and set goals for the future, and when they recalibrate or redesign policies, curriculum, and systems to inspire students in the present to reach those goals, then we will achieve tomorrow's school today.*

If you read *Aspire High*, put it on your shelf, and don't act, then we haven't done our job. Aspire High is not meant to be merely a learning experience or intellectual exercise. Nor is it about implementing these strategies in order to compete with Finland or South Korea. It's not a call to raise tests scores, improve your school's state letter grade, or advance our PISA (Program for International Student Assessment) ranking. If you are reading it for that purpose, indeed, put it on the shelf and walk away (again).

If you read *Aspire High* and the pages tatter, the binding breaks, and the covers fall off, *then* we have done our job! We challenge you to share, to revisit, to discuss, and—above all—to act. But make no mistake: *Tinkering with a few of our ideas won't be enough.* The information in *Aspire High* is designed to connect you with all the reasons why you became an educator. That passion to share a love of learning, a particular subject, a new insight. Those nervous butterflies you get every year you are about to meet your new and returning students. Those moments when you realize you have been entrusted with other people's most precious gift— their children. The sense of privilege that washes over you when you leave a meeting with amazing colleagues who have worked together to make a real, maybe even life-altering, difference for a school, a class, or even a single student.

We know you are out there. We have met you. We ourselves are privileged to work alongside you. To be frustrated with you. To be thrilled at the impact of some small change with you. To see Student Voice and Teacher Voice snowball into a transformative experience for you and your school and, most importantly, for your students. We challenge you to not simply put this book on a shelf and continue with school as usual. We challenge you to step up and LEAD.

Here is what we know: The status quo is not working for far too many students and teachers. Many students continue to drop out or sleep their way through school. Many work hard in school but don't see the point. Still others have their head in the clouds, imagining futures filled with NFL contracts and instant TV-type stardom. Equally alarming are statistics of the vast number of teachers who leave the profession or who make sure they take all their sick days or who find professional days meaningless and a waste of time. The inherited industrial model of school needs to be over. *Schools—starting today—must be models of Self-Worth, Engagement, and Purpose.*

You must fully commit to partner with students. To become their aspirations advocates and work with them in the present to guarantee their future, you must do these things:

- Let students teach.
- Be willing to learn from students.
- Commit to lead with students.
- Partner with students' parents and the community.
- Challenge irrelevant and meaningless inherited policies, and redesign school policy with your students.

- Be intentional about your pedagogical choices.
- Embrace the ever-emerging potential of technology.
- Think and learn beyond the walls of your classroom, school, and campus.
- Have a positive attitude—believe change can happen.
- Be and act bold for the good of everyone in your school!

The next step is yours—singular and plural—to take parts of *Aspire High* and put them together in your school.

Here's how you can start at a personal level:

- Circle your role: Principal   Teacher   Student

- Write a Step, Stride, or Sprint from each chapter into the "I commit to . . ." section of the chart (and list page numbers for easy reference by yourself and others).

Chapter	Pages	I Commit To . . .	Goal Date to Complete By
I. Students as Teachers			
Expected outcome:			
II. Teachers as Learners			
Expected outcome:			
III. School Leadership			
Expected outcome:			
IV. Involving Parents			
Expected outcome:			
V. Policies			
Expected outcome:			
VI. Pedagogy			
Expected outcome:			
VII. Technology			
Expected outcome:			

Share with a colleague and students. Repeat as necessary.

At a school level: Revisit one of the Lead charts at the end of each chapter. Discuss and determine where you are vis-à-vis the theme of that chapter and *commit as a school* to Aspire High or Aspiring Highest—the entire column! Use whatever process you are familiar with—SMART goals, school improvement plans, building leadership teams, and the like—to build Aspire High in your school. Set measurable outcomes. Learn from failure. Celebrate success. Repeat as necessary.

Aspire High is deliberately unfinished because you must write the next chapter. *But the next chapter must be written in action, not words.* Take something you read about, something you listened to, something you learned, something you feel inspired to lead, and make it happen. We challenge you to stop waiting for someone else to make a change. If you are a superintendent, stop waiting for your school board to change. If you are a principal, stop waiting for your superintendent to issue a mandate. If you are a teacher, stop waiting for your principal or your superintendent or your union to jump on board. Take something from this book you know would improve learning for your students, and put it into practice.

Raise your voice. Now is absolutely the time to Aspire High and be the change you want to see in yourself, your students, your school, and the future of education. Now is the time to . . .

LEAD!

[Let us know how the book ends @ CorwinPress #AspireHigh]

References

Anderson, S. A. (1994). *Synthesis of research on mastery learning.* (ERIC Document Reproduction Service No. ED 382 567)

Arredondo, D. E., & Block, J. H. (1990). Recognizing the connections between thinking skills and mastery learning. *Educational Leadership, 47*(5), 4–10.

Aschbacher, P. R. (1991). Humanitas: A thematic curriculum. *Educational Leadership, 49*(2), 16–19.

Atul, G. (2012, March). *Gawande Atul: How do we heal medicine?* (Video file). Retrieved from https://www.ted.com/talks/atul_gawande_how_do_we_heal_medicine

Baker, D. P., & LeTendre, G. K. (2005). *National differences, global similarities: World culture and the future of schooling.* Stanford, CA: Stanford University Press.

Balfanz, R., Byrnes, V., & Fox, J. (2013). *Sent home and put off-track: The antecedents, disproportionalities, and consequences of being suspended in the ninth grade.* Paper presented at the Closing the School Discipline Gap: Research to Practice conference, Washington, DC.

Barnes, M. (2014). *Teaching the iStudent: A quick guide to using mobile devise and social media in the K–12 classroom.* Thousand Oaks, CA: Corwin.

Barone, T. (1989). Ways of being at risk: The case of Billy Charles Barnett. *Phi Delta Kappan, 71*(2), 147–151.

Barth, R. (1990). *Improving schools from within: Teachers, parents and principals can make a difference.* San Francisco, CA: Jossey-Bass.

Barth, R. (2006). Improving relationships within the schoolhouse. *Educational Leadership, 63*(6).

Bateson, G. (1972). *Ecology of the mind.* New York, NY: Ballantine.

Beane, J. A. (1991). The middle school: The natural home of integrated curriculum. *Educational Leadership, 49*(2), 9–13.

Beckwith, D., & Lopez, C. (1997). *Community organizing: People power from the grass-roots.* Washington, DC: Center for Community Change.

Bill & Melinda Gates Foundation. (2010). *Learning about teaching: Initial findings from the measures of effective teaching (MET) project.* Seattle, WA: Gates Foundation.

Billig, S. (2010). Why service learning is such a good idea: Explanations from the research. *Colleagues, 5*(1), Article 6.

Black, P. J., & Wiliam, D. (1998). Inside the black box: Raising standards through classroom assessment. *Phi Delta Kappan, 80*(2), 139–148.

Blakemore, C. L. (1992). Comparison of students taught basketball skills using mastery and nonmastery learning methods. *Journal of Teaching in Physical Education, 11*(3), 235–247.

Blank, M., Melaville, A., & Shah, B. (2003). *Making the difference: Research and practice in community schools*. Washington, DC: Coalition for Community Schools, Institute for Educational Leadership.

Bloom, B. S. (1968). Learning for mastery. *Evaluation Comment, 1*(2), 1–12.

Bloom, B. S. (1971). Mastery learning. In J. H. Block (Ed.), *Mastery learning: Theory and practice* (pp. 47–63). New York, NY: Holt, Rinehart, & Winston.

Bloom, B. S. (1976). *Human characteristics and school learning*. New York, NY: McGraw-Hill.

Bloom, B. S. (1984). The search for methods of group instruction as effective as one-to-one tutoring. *Educational Leadership, 41*(8), 4–17.

Bonk, C., & Zhang, K. (2006). Introducing the R2D2 model: Online learning for the diverse learners of this world. *Distance Education, 27*(2), 249–264. doi:10.1080/01587910600789670

Booker, G. (1996). Instructional games in the teaching and learning of mathematics. In H. Forgasz, T. Jones, G. Leder, J. Lynch, K. Maguire, & C. Pearn (Eds.), *Mathematics: Making connections* (pp. 77–82). Melbourne, Australia: The Mathematical Association of Victoria.

Borko, H. (2004). Professional development and teacher learning: Mapping the terrain. *Educational Researcher, 33*(8), 3–15.

Borkowski, J., Carr, M., & Pressely, M. (1987). "Spontaneous" strategy use: Perspectives from metacognitive theory. *Intelligence, 11,* 61–75.

Boyer, E. L. (1991). Seeing the connectedness of things. *Educational Leadership, 39*(8), 582–584.

Bragg, L. Children's perspectives on mathematics and gaming. Retrieved March 7, 2016, from http://www.merga.net.au/documents/RR_bragg.pdf

Bransford, J. D., Brown, A. L., & Cocking, R. R. (1999). *How people learn: Brain, mind, experience, and school*. Washington, DC: National Academy Press.

Brown, A. L. (1987). Metacognition, executive control, self-regulation, and other more mysterious mechanisms. In F. E. Weinert & R. H. Kluwe (Eds.), *Metacognition, motivation, and understanding* (pp. 65–116). Hillsdale, New Jersey: Lawrence Erlbaum Associates.

Brunsma, D. L., & Rockquemore, K. A. (1998). Effects of student uniforms on attendance, behavior problems, substance use, and academic achievement. *Journal of Educational Research, 92,* 53–62.

Bryk, A., & Schneider, B. (2003). Trust in schools: A core resource for school reform. *Educational Leadership, 60*(6), 40–45.

Bryk, A., Gomez, L., & Grunow, A. (2015). *Learning to improve: How America's schools can get better at getting better*. Cambridge, MA: Harvard Education Press.

Bryk, A. S., & Schneider, B. L. (2002). *Trust in schools: A core resource for improvement*. New York, NY: Russell Sage.

Burns, R. C. (1995). Dissolving the boundaries: Planning for curriculum integration in middle and secondary schools. Appalachia Educational Laboratory, Charleston, WV. (ERIC Document Reproduction Service No. ED 384 455).

Caine, R., & Caine, G. (1991). *Making connections: Teaching and the human brain*. Alexandria, VA: Association for Supervision and Curriculum Development.

Carskadon, M. A. When Worlds Collide: Adolescent Need for Sleep Versus Societal Demands, *Phi Delta Kappan*, Vol. 80, No. 05, January 1999, pp. 348–353.

Catterall, J. S., Dumais, S. A., & Hampden-Thompson, G. (2012). The arts and achievement in at-risk youth: Findings from four longitudinal studies. Research report# 55. National Endowment for the Arts.

Child Trends Data Bank. (2015). *Home computer access and Internet use.* Retrieved from http://www.childtrends.org/?indicators=home-computer-access

Civil Rights Data Collection: Data Snapshot School Discipline. U.S. Department of Education Office for Civil Rights 23 Civil Rights Data Collection: Data Snapshot (School Discipline) March 21, 2014. http://blogs.edweek.org/edweek/rulesforengagement/CRDC%20School%20Discipline%20Snapshot.pdf

Clark, C. R., Guskey, T. R., & Benninga, J. S. (1983). The effectiveness of mastery learning strategies in undergraduate education courses. *Journal of Educational Research, 76*(4), 210–214.

Coalition for Community Schools. (n.d.).What is a community school? Retrieved December 7, 2015, from http://www.communityschools.org/aboutschools/what_is_a_community_school.aspx

Cook-Sather, A. (2002). Re(in)forming the conversations: Student position, power, and voice in teacher education. *Radical Teacher, 64,* 21–28.

Cook-Sather, A. (2006). Sound, presence, and power: "Student voice" in educational research and reform. *Curriculum Inquiry, 36,* 359–390.

Cooper, H. (1994). *The battle over homework: An administrator's guide to setting sound and effective policies.* Thousand Oaks, CA: Corwin.

Cooper, H. (2001). *The battle over homework: Common ground for administrators, teachers, and parents* (2nd ed.). Thousand Oaks, CA: Corwin.

Cooper, H. (2007). *The battle over homework: Common ground for administrators, teachers, and parents* (3rd ed.). Thousand Oaks, CA: Corwin.

Cooper, H., Robinson, J. C., & Patall, E. A. (2006). Does homework improve academic achievement? A synthesis of research, 1987–2003. *Review of Educational Research, 76*(1), 1–62.

Corso, M., Lucey, L., & Fox, K. (2012). Living the mission. *American School Board Journal,* 22.

Covington, M. V. (1998). *The will to learn: A guide for motivating young people.* New York, NY: Cambridge University Press.

Csikszentmihalyi, M. (1990). *Flow: The psychology of optimal experience.* New York, NY: Harper & Row.

Damon, W. (2009). *The path to purpose: How young people find their calling in life.* New York, NY: The Free Press.

Danish Ministry for Children, Education and Gender Equality. (2010, August 10). Use of Internet in exams is a success. Retrieved from http://eng.uvm.dk/News/~/UVM-EN/Content/News/Eng/2010/Okt/101008-Use-of-internet-in-exams-is-a-success

Darling-Hammond, L., LaPointe, M., Meyerson, D., Orr, M. T., & Cohen, C. (2007). *Preparing school leaders for a changing world: Lessons from exemplary leadership development programs.* Stanford, CA: Stanford University, Stanford Educational Leadership Institute.

Davenport, M. R., & Jaeger, M. (1995). Integrating curriculum. *The Reading Teacher, 49*(1), 60–62.

Davidson, C. (2012, February 21). Can badging be the zipcar of testing and assessment? Retrieved March 7, 2016, from http://dmlcentral.net/

Deci, E. L., & Ryan, R. M. (1985). *Intrinsic motivation and self-determination in human behavior.* New York, NY: Plenum.

Dewey, J. (1938). *Experience & education.* New York, NY: Kappa Delta Pi.

Diaz, L. A., & Entonado, F. B. (2009). Are the functions of teachers in e-learning and face-to-face learning environments really different? *Educational Technology & Society, 12*(4), 331–343. Retrieved from http://proxy1.ncu.edu/login ?url=http://search.ebscohost.com/login.aspx?direct=true&db=ehh&AN=44 785119&site=eds-live

Dryfoos, J. (1994). *Full-service schools: A revolution in health and social services for children, youth, and families.* San Francisco, CA: Jossey-Bass.

DuFour, R., & Marzano, R. (2011). *Leaders of learning: How district, school, and classroom leaders improve student achievement.* Bloomington, IN: Solution Tree.

Dwyer, B. M. (1995). Preparing for the 21st century: A paradigm for our times. *Innovations in Education and Training International, 32*(3), 269–277.

Dweck, C. S., & Leggett, E. L. (1988). A social-cognitive approach to motivation and personality. *Psychological Review, 95*, 256–273.

Dynarski, M., Agodini, R., Heaviside, S., Novak, T., Carey, N., Campuzano, L., . . . Sussex, W. (2007). *Effectiveness of reading and mathematics software products: Findings from the first student cohort.* Washington, DC: US Department of Education. Retrieved March 12, 2010, from http://ies.ed.gov/ncee/pubs/20074005

Eccles, J. S., & Barber, B. (1999, January). Student council, volunteering, basketball, or marching band: What kind of extracurricular involvement matters? *Journal of Adolescent Research, 14*(1), 10–43.

Ed.gov. (n.d.). *Ed data express: Data about elementary and secondary schools in the US.* Retrieved November 29, 2015, from http://eddataexpress.ed.gov/data -element-explorer.cfm/tab/data/deid/5353/sort/idown/

EdSource. (2008, January/February). Guiding the growth of California's school leaders. *Leadership*, 18–21.

Johnston, H. (2009). *Student dress codes and uniforms* [Research brief]. Retrieved from http://files.eric.ed.gov/fulltext/ED537953.pdf

Edwards, B. W. (2006). Environmental design and educational performance with particular reference to "green" schools in Hampshire and Essex. *Research in Education, 76*, 14–21, 23, 25–32.

Elmore, R. F. (2000). Building a new structure for school leadership. *The Albert Shanker Institute, 2.*

Er, E., Özden, M., & Arifoglu, A. (2009). A blended e-learning environment: A model proposition for integration of asynchronous and synchronous e-learning. *International Journal of Learning, 16*(2), 449–460.

Erikson, E. H. (1950) *Childhood and society.* New York: Norton.

Erickson, F., & Shultz, J. (1992). Students' experience of the curriculum. In P. W. Jackson (Ed.), *Handbook of research on curriculum* (pp. 465–485). New York, NY: Macmillan.

Everson, H. T., & Millsap, R. E. (2005). *Everyone gains: Extracurricular activities in high school and higher SAT scores—College Board Research Report 2005.* New York, NY: College Entrance Examination Board.

Fair test: The National Center for Fair and Open Testing (2012, October). Graduation test use declines; common core testing raises new issues. Retrieved October 15, 2015, from http://www.fairtest.org/graduation -test-use-declines-common-core-testing-r

Feierman, J., Levick, M., & Mody, A. (2009/2010). The school to prison pipeline . . . and back: Obstacles and remedies for the re-enrollment of adjudicated youth. *New York State Law Review,54*. Retrieved January 18, 2016, from http://www .nylslawreview.com/wp-content/uploads/sites/16/2013/11/54-4.Feierman -Levick-Mody.pdf

Fenning, P. A., Pulaski, S., Gomez, M., Morello, M., Maciel, L., Maroney, E., . . . Maltese, R. (2012). Call to action: A critical need for designing alternatives to suspension and expulsion. *Journal of School Violence, 11*(2), 105–117. doi:10.1080/ 15388220.2011.646643

Field, M., Lee, R., & Field, M. L. (1994). Assessing interdisciplinary learning. *New Directions in Teaching and Learning, 58*, 69–84.

Finholt, T. A., & Teasley, S. D. (1998). Psychology: The need for psychology in research on computer-supported cooperative work. *Social Science Computer Review, 16*, 40–52.

Finn, J. D. (1993). *School engagement and students at risk*. Washington, DC: National Center for Education Statistics.

Fischetti, M. (2014). *School starts too early. Scientific America*. Retrieved October 14, 2015, from http://www.scientificamerican.com/article/school-starts -too-early/

Fisher, K. (2002). *School issues digest: The impact of school infrastructure on student outcomes and behaviour*. Canberra: Department of Education, Employment and Workplace Relations. [online] Retrieved March 7, 2016, from http://eric .ed.gov/?id=ED455672

Flavell, J. H. (1976). Metacognitive aspects of problem solving. In L. B. Resnick (Ed.), *The nature of intelligence* (pp. 231–236). Hillsdale, NJ: Lawrence Erlbaum.

Flynn, E., O'Malley, C., & Wood, D. (2004). A longitudinal, microgenetic study of the emergence of false belief understanding and inhibition skills. *Developmental Science, 7*(1), 103–115.

Fox, K. M. (2011). *Veteran elementary teachers experiences with self-directed learning*. (Unpublished dissertation). Orono: University of Maine.

Freire, P. (1972). *Pedagogy of the oppressed*. Harmondsworth, England: Penguin.

French, M., Homer, J., Popovici, I., & Robins, P. (2015). What you do in high school matters: High school GPA, educational attainment, and labor market earnings as a young adult. *Eastern Economic Journal, 41*(3), 370–386.

Frodeman, R. (2010). Introduction. In R. Frodeman, J. Thompson-Klein, C. Mitcham, & J. B. Holbrook (Eds.), *The Oxford handbook of interdisciplinarity* (pp. 29–39). Oxford, England: Oxford University Press.

Fullan, M. (1991). *The new meaning of educational change*. New York, NY: Teachers College Press.

Fullan, M. (2001). *Leading in a culture of change*. San Francisco, CA: Jossey-Bass.

Fullan, M., & Hargreaves, A. (2012). *Professional capital: Transforming teaching in every school*. New York, NY: Teachers College.

Furco, A. (2010). The community as a resource for learning: An analysis of academic service-learning in primary and secondary education [abstract]. In H. Dumont, D. Istance, & F. Benavides (Eds.), *The nature of learning: Using research to inspire practice* (pp. 227– 249).

Galloway, M., Conner, J., & Pope, D. (2013). Nonacademic effects of homework in privileged, high-performing high schools. *Journal of Experimental Education, 81*(4), 490–510. doi:10.1080/00220973.2012.745469

Gantz, J., & Reinsel, D. (2011, June). Extracting value from chaos. *EMC Corporation*. Retrieved December 2015 from https://www.emc.com/collateral/analyst -reports/idc-extracting-value-from-chaos-ar.pdf

Garet, M. S., Porter, A. C., Desimone, L., Birman, B. F., & Yoon, K. S. (2001). What makes professional development effective? Results from a national sample of teachers. *American Educational Research Journal, 38*(4), 915–945.

Getzels, J. W. (1975). Problem finding and the inventiveness of solutions. *Journal of Creative Behavior, 9*(1), 12–33.

Ginsberg, M. (2007). Lessons at the kitchen table. *Educational Leadership, 64*(6), 56–61.

Giroux, H. A. (1981). *Ideology, culture and the process of schooling*. Philadelphia, PA: Temple University Press.

Global Green USA. (2005). *Do green schools improve students' academic performance?* Retrieved from http://www.ncef.org/rl/green_schools_learning_impacts.cfm

Goldsmith, T. E., & Johnson, P. J. (1990). *A structural assessment of classroom learning*. In R. W. Schvaneveldt (Ed.), *Pathfinder associative networks: Studies in knowledge organization* (pp. 241–254). Norwood, NJ: Ablex.

Goodlad, J. I., and R. H. Anderson. (1987). *The Nongraded Elementary School*. New York: Teachers College Press. Revised editions in 1959 and 1963 published by Harcourt Brace Jovanovich, New York.

Gourgey, A. F. (1998). Metacognition in basic skills instruction. *Instructional Science, 26*, 81–96.

Green School Initiative. (2005). *Thinking big about ecological sustainability, children's environmental health and K–12 education in the US*. Retrieved November 1, 2015, from http://www.greenschools.net/downloads/little%20green%20school house%20report.pdf

Grissom, J., Loeb, S., & Master, B. (2013). Effective instructional time use for school leaders: Longitudinal evidence from observations of principals. *Educational Researcher*, 433–444.

Guskey, T. R., & Pigott, T. D. (1988). Research on group-based mastery learning programs: A meta-analysis. *Journal of Educational Research, 81*, 197–216.

Harod, B. (2015). Why Ed Tech Is Not Transforming How Teachers Teach. Education. June 10 2015. http://www.edweek.org/ew/articles/2015/06/11/ why-ed-tech-is-not-transforming-how.html?r=1315854209&preview=1& user_acl=0 Retrieved June 20 2015.

Harris, J., Mishra, P., & Koehler, M. (2009). Teachers' technological pedagogical content knowledge and learning activity types: Curriculum-based technology integration reframed. *Journal of Research on Technology in Education, 41*(4), 393–416. Retrieved from http://files.eric.ed.gov/fulltext/EJ844273.pdf

Harter, P. D., & Gehrke, N. J. (1989). Integrative curriculum: Kaleidoscope of alter-natives. *Educational Horizons, 68*(1), 12–17.

Hastie, M., Hung, I. C., Chen, N. S., & Kinshuk. (2010). A blended synchronous learning model for educational international collaborations. *Educational Technology & Society, 10*(4), 281–294.

Hatch, M. (2014). *The maker movement manifesto*. New York, NY: McGraw-Hill.

Hattie, J. (2009). *Visible learning: A synthesis of over 800 meta-analysis relating to achievement*. New York, NY: Routledge.

Hattie, J. (2012). *Visible learning for teachers: Maximizing impact on learning*. New York, NY: Routledge.

Henderson, A., & Mapp, K. (2002). *The new wave of evidence: The impact of school, family and community connections on student achievement.* Southwest Educational Development Laboratory.

Henderson, A. T., & Berla, N. (Eds.). (1994). *A new generation of evidence: The family is critical to student achievement* (A report from the National Committee for Citizens in Education). Washington, DC: Center for Law and Education.

Henderson, A. T., & Mapp, K. L. (2002). *A new wave of evidence: The impact of school, family and community connections on student achievement.* Austin, TX: National Center for Family and Community Connections With Schools.

Herold, B. (2015, June). Why ed tech is not transforming how teachers teach. *Education Week.*

Herold, C. (2010, June). Cameron Herold: Let's raise kids to be entrepreneurs. [Video file]. Retrieved from https://www.ted.com/talks/cameron_herold_let_s_raise_kids_to_be_entrepreneurs?language=en

Higgins, S., Xiao, X., & Katsipataki, M. (2012). *The impact of digital technology on learning: A summary for the education endowment foundation.* Education Endowment Foundation. Retrieved from https://v1.educationendowment foundation.org.uk/uploads/pdf/The_Impact_of_Digital_Technology_on_Learning_-_Executive_Summary_(2012).pdf

Hill, N. E., & Tyson, D. F. (2009). Parental involvement in middle school: A meta-analytic assessment of the strategies that promote achievement. *Developmental Psychology, 49*(3), 740–763.

Hinton, C., Miyamoto, K., & Della-Chiesa, B. (2008). Brain research learning and emotions: Implications for education research, policy and practice. *European Journal of Education, 43*(1), 87–103. Retrieved July 5, 2016, from http://live.v1.udesa.edu.ar/files/programas/NEUROCIENCIAS/Brainresearch_learning_and_emotions_Hinton.pdf

Hiss, W. (2014). *Defining promise: Optional standardized testing policies in American college and university admissions.* NACAC.

Horng, E. L., Klasik, D., & Loeb, S. (2009). *Principal time-use and school effectiveness.* (School Leadership Research Report No. 09-3). Stanford, CA: Stanford University, Institute for Research on Education Policy & Practice.

Hughes, K. L., Bailey, T. R., & Karp, M. M. (2002). School-to-work: Making a difference in education [abstract]. *Phi Delta Kappan, 84*(4), 272–279.

Inan, F. A., & Lowther, D. L. (2010). Factors affecting technology integration in K–12 classrooms: A path model. *Education Technology Research and Development, 58,* 137–154.

International Society for Technology and Education. Retrieved from http://www.iste.org

Jacobs, H. H. (1989). *Interdisciplinary curriculum: Design and implementation.* Alexandria, VA: ASCD.

Jacobs, J., & Buechley, L. (2013, April 2). *Codeable objects: Computational design and digital fabrication for novice programmers.* Proceedings from the Association for Computing Machinery SIGCHI conference, Paris.

Jaleel, S., & Verghis, A. (2015). Knowledge creation in constructivist learning. *Universal Journal of Educational Research, 3*(1), 8–12. Retrieved December 22, 2015, from http://files.eric.ed.gov/fulltext/EJ1053918.pdf

Johnston, H. (2009). *Student dress codes and uniforms* [Research brief]. Retrieved from http://files.eric.ed.gov/fulltext/ED537953.pdf

Jonassen, D. H. (2000). *Computers as mindtools in schools: Engaging critical thinking.* Columbus, OH: Merrill/Prentice Hall.

Kafai, Y., Peppler, K., & Chapman, R. (2009). *The computer clubhouse: Constructionism and creativity in youth communities.* New York, NY: Teachers College Press.

Kavaloski, V. (1979). Interdisciplinary education and humanistic aspiration: A critical reflection. In J. Kockelmans (Ed.), *Interdisciplinarity and higher education* (pp. 224–244). University Park: The Pennsylvania State University Press.

Kegan, R., & Lahey, L. (2001). *How the way we talk can change the way we work: Seven languages for transformation.* San Francisco, CA: Jossey-Bass.

Kennedy, L. B., & Murphy, A. (2016). *Teachers College Record, 118*(1), 1–40. Retrieved January 26, 2016, from http://www.tcrecord.org

Knapp, M. S., Copland, M., Ford, B., Markholt, A., McLaughlin, M. W., Milliken, M., & Talbert, J. (2003). *Leading for learning sourcebook: Concepts and examples.* University of Washington: Center for the Study of Teaching and Policy.

Knowles, M. S. (1980). *The modern practice of adult education: From pedagogy to andragogy.* Englewood Cliffs, NJ: Prentice Hall/Cambridge.

Kohn, A. (2006). *The homework myth: Why our kids get too much of a bad thing.* Cambridge, MA: Da Capo Press.

Kozlovsky, J. D. (1990). Integrating thinking skills and mastery learning in Baltimore County. *Educational Leadership, 47*(5), 6.

Kozol, J. (1991). *Savage inequalities: Children in America's schools.* New York, NY: Crown.

Kulik, C. C., Kulik, J. A., & Bangert-Drowns, R. L. (1990). Effectiveness of mastery learning programs: A meta-analysis. *Review of Educational Research, 60,* 265–299.

Kulik, J. A., & Kulik, C. L. (1989). Affects of Ability Grouping on Student Achievement. *Equity and Excellence 23,* 1–2: 22–30.

Kulik, J. A. (2003). *Effects of using instructional technology in elementary and secondary schools: What controlled evaluation studies say.* Arlington, VA: SRI International. Retrieved March 12, 2016, from http://citeseerx.ist.psu.edu/viewdoc/down load?doi=10.1.1.207.3105&rep=rep1&type=pdf

Kuratako, D. F. (2005). The emergence of entrepreneurship education: Development, trends, and challenges. *Entrepreneurship Theory and Practice, 29*(5), 577–598.

Ladson-Billings, G. (1994). *The Dreamkeepers.* San Francisco, CA: Jossey-Bass.

Ladson-Billings, G. (1994). *The Dreamkeepers: Successful teaching for African American students.* San Francisco, CA: Jossey-Bass.

Lake, K. (1994). Integrated curriculum. In *School improvement research series* (Close-Up #16). Retrieved December 10, 2015 from http://education northwest.org/sites/default/files/IntegratedCurriculum.pdf

Lamborn, S. D., Brown, B. B., Mounts, N. S., & Steinberg, L. (1992). Putting school in perspective: The influence of family, peers, extracurricular participation, and part-time work on academic engagement. In F. Newmann (Ed.), *Student engagement and achievement in American secondary schools* (Chapter 6). New York, NY: Teachers College Press.

Leana, C. (2011, Fall). The missing link in school reform. *Stanford Social and Innovation Review,* 5–13.

Let them sleep: AAP recommends delaying start times of middle and high schools to combat teen sleep deprivation. Retrieved October 9, 2014, from https://www.aap.org/en-us/about-the-aap/aap-press-room/pages/let-them-sleep-aap-recommends-delaying-start-times-of-middle-and-high-schools-to-combat-teen-sleep-deprivation.aspx.

Levin, B. (2000). Putting students at the centre in education reform. *Journal of Educational Change, 1*(2), 155–172.

Livingstone, S. (2011). Critical reflections on the benefits of ICT in education. *Oxford Review of Education, 38*(1), 9–24.

Lopez, G. (2001). The value of hard work: Lessons on parent involvement from an immigrant household. *Harvard Educational Review, 71*(3), 416–437.

Lorenzo, G., & Ittelson, J. (2005). An overview of e-portfolios. *EDUCASE Learning Initiative*. Retrieved from http://www.case.edu/artsci/cosi/cspl/documents/eportfolio-Educausedocument.pdf

Lortie, D. (1975). *Schoolteacher: A sociological study.* Chicago, IL: University of Chicago Press.

Mancini, G. (1997, December). School uniforms: Dressing for success or conformity? Education Digest, *63*(4), 62.

Marsh, H., & Kleitman, S. (2002, Winter). Extracurricular school activities: The good, the bad and the nonlinear. *Harvard Education Review,* 464–514.

Martinello, M. L., & Cook, G. E. (1994). *Interdisciplinary inquiry in teaching and learning.* New York, NY: Macmillan College.

Martinez, T. (2013, November). Disproportionate discipline: Addressing implicit racial bias in suspensions [Webinar]. Retrieved from *Fix School Discipline Webinar Archive* at http://www.fixschooldiscipline.org/toolkit/webinar

Martinez-Caro, E. (2011). Factors affecting effectiveness in e-learning: An analysis in production management courses. *Computer Applications in Engineering Education, 19*(3), 572–581.

Maheady, L., Harper, G. F., & Mallette, B. (2001). Peer-mediated instruction and interventions and students with mild disabilities. *Remedial and Special Education, 22*(1), 4–14.

McDonald, B., & Boud, D. (2003). The impact of self-assessment on achievement: The effects of self-assessment training on performance in external examinations. *Assessment in Education: Principles, Policy and Practice, 10*(2), 209.

McKinsey & Co. (2014). *Global media report.* Retrieved March 7, 2016, from http://www.mckinsey.com/industries/media-and-entertainment/our-insights/global-media-report-2014

Meichenbaum, D. (1985). Teaching thinking: A cognitive-behavioral perspective. In S. F. Chipman, J. W. Segal, & R. Glaser (Eds.), *Thinking and learning skills, Vol. 2: Research and open questions* pp. 407–426. Hillsdale, NJ: Lawrence Erlbaum Associates.

Merriam-Webster Online. Retrieved December 10, 2015, from http://beta.merriam-webster.com/dictionary/pedagogy

Milyavskaya, M., Ianakieva, I., Foxen-Craft, E., Colantuoni, A., & Koestner, R. (2012). Inspired to get there: The effects of trait and goal inspiration on goal progress. *Personality and Individual Differences,* 56–60.

Mitra, D. L. (2009). Student voice and student roles in education policy and policy reform. In D. N. Plank, G. Sykes & B. Schneider (Eds.), *AERA Handbook on Education Policy Research* (pp. 819–830). London: Routledge.

Moll, L., Amanti, C., Neff, D., & González, N. (1992). Funds of knowledge for teaching: A qualitative approach to developing strategic connections between homes and classrooms. *Theory Into Practice, 31*(1), 132–141.

Montessori, M., & George, A. E. (1964). *The Montessori method*. New York, NY: Schocken.

Motamedi, V., & Sumrall, W. J. (2000). Mastery learning and contemporary issues in education. *Action in Teacher Education, 22*(1), 32–42.

NCTM and the National Standards for Mathematics Education https://www.nap .edu/read/5844/chapter/5 Retrieved January 8, 2016.

Newell, W. H. (1990). Interdisciplinary curriculum development. *Issues in Integrative Studies, 8*, 69–86.

Nielsen, M. E. (1989). Integrative learning for young children: A thematic approach. *Educational Horizons, 68*(1), 18–24.

Nietfeld, J. L., & Shraw, G. (2002). The effect of knowledge and strategy explanation on monitoring accuracy. *Journal of Educational Research, 95*, 131–142.

Noddings, N. (1999). Caring in education. *The encyclopedia of informal education*. Retrieved December 4, 2015, from http://www.infed.org/biblio/noddings_ caring_in_education.htm

Noddings, N. (2003). *Happiness and education*. Cambridge, United Kingdom: Cambridge University Press.

Noddings, N. (2009). The aims of education. In D. J. Flinders & S. J. Thornton (Eds.), *The curriculum studies reader* (pp. 425–439). New York, NY: Routledge.

Okonofua, J. A., & Eberhardt, J. L. Two Strikes Race and Disciplining of Young Students. Psychological Science May 2015 vol. 26 no. 5 617–624.

Organisation for Economic Co-operation and Development. (2004). Retrieved from http://www.centerforpubliceducation.org/Main-Menu/Instruction/ What-research-says-about-the-value-of-homework-At-a-glance/What -research-says-about-the-value-of-homework-Research-review.html#sthash .mguXoTKo.dpuf

Organisation for Economic Co-operation and Development. (2015). *Students, computers and learning: Making the connections*. PISA. Retrieved November 9, 2015, from http://www.oecd.org/publications/students-computers-and-learning -9789264239555-en.htm

Palmer, P. J. (1998). *The courage to teach: Exploring the inner landscape of a teacher's life*. San Francisco, CA: Jossey-Bass.

Parker, C. (2014, March 10). *Stanford research shows pitfalls of too much homework*. Stanford Report. Retrieved December 15, 2015, from http://news.stanford .edu/news/2014/march/too-much-homework-031014.html

Perrone, V. (1991). *A letter to teachers: Reflections on schooling and the art of teaching*. San Francisco, CA: Jossey-Bass.

Piaget, J. (1957). *Construction of reality in the child*. London, England: Routledge & Kegan Paul.

Pink, D. H. (2006). A whole new mind: Why right-brainers will rule the future. New York, N.Y.: Riverhead.

Prensky, M. (2010). *Teaching digital natives: Partnering for real learning*. Thousand Oaks, CA: Corwin.

Quaglia, R. (2016). *Principal voice* [In press]. Thousand Oaks, CA: Corwin.

Quaglia, R. J., & Corso, M. J. (2014). *Student voice: The instrument of change*. Thousand Oaks, CA: Corwin.

Rafaelle Mendez, L., & Knoff, H. M. (2003). Who gets suspended from school and why: A demographic analysis of schools and disciplinary infractions in a large school district. *Education & Treatment of Children, 26*(1), 30–52.

Ramdass, D., & Zimmerman, B. J. (2008). Effects of self-correction strategy training on middle school students' self-efficacy, self-evaluation, and mathematics division learning. *Journal of Advanced Academics, 20*(1), 18–41.

Reeve, J., & Jang, H. (2006). What teachers say and do to support students' autonomy during a learning activity. *Journal of Educational Psychology,* 209–218.

Repko, A. F. (2009). Assessing interdisciplinary learning outcomes [Working paper]. School of Urban and Public Affairs, University of Texas at Arlington.

Rheingold, H. (2015, May 7). EFF13 *Rethinking how we learn.*

Robinson, C., & Taylor, C. (2007). Theorizing student voice: Values and perspectives. *Improving Schools, 10*(1), 5–17.

Robinson, K. (2009). *The element: How finding your passion changes everything.* New York, NY: Viking.

Robinson, K., & Harris, A. (2014). *The broken compass: Parents' involvement with children's education.* Cambridge, MA: Presidential and Fellows of Harvard College.

Routman, R. (1996). *Literacy at the crossroads.* Portsmouth, NH: Heinemann.

Rowntree, D. (1982). *A dictionary of education.* Totowa, NJ: Barnes & Noble Books.

Rudduck, J., & Flutter, J. (2004). *How to improve your school: Giving pupils a voice.* London, England: Continuum.

Rudduck, J., & McIntyre, D. (2007). *Improving learning through consulting pupils.* London, England: Routledge.

Rutherford, B., Anderson, B., & Billig, S. (1997). *Studies of education reform: Parent and community involvement in education.* Final Technical Report: Volume I.

Sadler, D. R. (1989). Formative assessment and the design of instructional systems. *Instructional Science, 18,* 119–144.

Sandholz, J. H., Ringstaff, C., & Dwyer, D. (1997). *Teaching with technology: Creating student-centered classrooms.* New York, NY: Teachers College Press.

Schawbel, D. The High School Careers Study. http://millennialbranding.com/2014/high-school-careers-study/ Retrieved February 2, 2016.

Scheeren, O. (2015, September). *Ole Scheeren: Why great architecture should tell a story.* [Video file]. Retrieved from https://www.ted.com/talks/ole_scheeren_why_great_architecture_should_tell_a_story?language=en

Schneider, M. (2002). *Do school facilities affect academic outcomes?* Washington, DC: National Clearinghouse for Educational Facilities.

School starts too early. Retrieved October 16, 2015, from http://www.cdc.gov/features/school-start-times/

Schraw, G. (1998). Promoting general metacognitive awareness. *Instructional Science, 26,* 113–125.

Senge, P. M. (1990). The fifth discipline: The art and practice of the learning organization. New York: Doubleday/Currency.

Sheridan, K., Clark, K., & Williams, A. (2013). Designing games, designing roles: A study of youth agency in an urban informal education program. *Urban Education, 48*(3), 734–758.

Simonson, M., Smaldino, S., Albright, M., & Zvacek, S. (2012). *Teaching and learning at a distance: Foundations of distance education* (5th ed.). Boston, MA: Pearson.

Singleton, G. (2013). *More courageous conversations about race.* Thousand Oaks: Corwin.

Skiba, R. J., Horner, R. H., Chung, C., Rausch, M. K., May, S. L., & Tobin, T. (2011). Race is not neutral: A national investigation of African American and Latino disproportionality in school discipline. *School Psychology Review, 40*(1), 85–107.

Skiba, R. J., Simmons, A., Staudinger, L. P., Rausch, M. K., Dow, G., & Feggins, L. R. (2003). *Consistent removal: Contribution of school discipline in the school-prison pipeline.* Paper presented at the Harvard Civil Rights School-to-Prison Pipeline Conference, Cambridge, MA.

Slavin, R. E. (1995). *Cooperative learning: Theory, research, and practice* (2nd ed.). Needham Heights, MA: Allyn & Bacon.

Smith, B. L., & MacGregor, J. T. (1992). What is collaborative learning? In A. S. Goodsell, M. R. Maher, & V. Tinto (Eds.), *Collaborative learning: A sourcebook for higher education.* National Center on Postsecondary Teaching, Learning, and Assessment at Pennsylvania State University.

Sparks, D., & Loucks-Horsley, S. (1990). Models of staff development. In W. R. Hewson (Ed.), *Handbook of research on teacher education* pp. 234–250. New York, NY: Macmillan.

Spielberg, S., Rodat, R., Bryce, I., Gordon, M., Levinsohn, G., Hanks, T., & Burns, E. (1999). *Saving Private Ryan* [Motion picture]. USA: DreamWorks Home Entertainment.

Sprague, K., Manyika, J., Chappuis, B., Bughin, J., Grijpink, F., Moodley, L., & Pattabiraman, K. (n.d.). *Offline and falling behind: Barriers to Internet adoption* (pp. 1–128, Rep.).

Startup Business Failure Rate by Industry. http://www.statisticbrain.com/startup-failure-by-industry/. Retrieved March 15, 2016.

Startup business failure rate by industry—Statistic brain. (2016). Statistic Brain Research Institute, publishing as Statistic Brain. Retrieved January 24, 2016, from http://www.statisticbrain.com/startup-failure-by-industry

Sternberg, R. J. (1986). *Intelligence applied.* New York, NY: Harcourt Brace Jovanovich.

Stoll, L. (1999, January). *Realising our potential: Building capacity for lasting improvement.* Keynote presentation at Twelfth International Congress for School Effectiveness and Improvement, San Antonio, Texas.

Stoll, L., Mckay, J., Kember, D., Cochrane-Smith, M., & Lytle, S. Teachers as learners. http://www.educationalleaders.govt.nz/Pedagogy-and-assessment/Leading-professional-learning/Teachers-as-learners. Retrieved April 15, 2016.

Sykes, G. (1996). Reform of and as professional development. *Phi Delta Kappan, 77,* 465–467.

Talisha, L., Dewey, C., Gregory, A., & Xitao, F. (2011). High suspension schools and dropouts for black and white students. *Education and Treatment of Children, 34*(2).

The maker movement in education: Designing, creating, and learning across contexts. (2014). *Harvard Educational Review, 84*(4), 492–494.

Thiede, K. W., Anderson, M. C., & Therriault, D. (2003). Accuracy of metacognitive monitoring affects learning of texts. *Journal of Educational Psychology, 95,* 66–73.

Thrash, T., & Elliot, A. (2003). Inspiration as a psychological construct. *Journal of Personality and Social Psychology,* 871–889.

Tomlinson, C. (2003). *Fulfilling the promise of the differentiated classroom: Strategies and tools for responsive teaching.* Alexandria, VA: Association for Supervision and Curriculum Development.

Toshalis, E. & Nakkula, M. J. (2012). Motivation, engagement, and student voice. In the *Students at the center* series. Boston, MA: Jobs for the Future.

Truscott, D. M., & Truscott, S. D. (2004). A professional development model for the positive practice of school-based reading consultation. *Psychology in the Schools, 41*(1), 51–65. doi:10.1002/pits.10138

University of Minnesota. *Students grades and health improve with later school start.* Retrieved November 1, 2015, from https://twin-cities.umn.edu/news-events/students-grades-and-health-improve-later-high-school-start-times

U.S. Department of Education. (2012). *Office for Civil Rights data collection: Discipline.* Washington, DC: Author.

Vaill, P. B. (1996). *Learning as a way of being: Strategies for survival in a world of permanent white water.* San Francisco, CA: Jossey-Bass.

Voight, J. (2014, March 17). Which big brands are courting the maker movement, and why—from Levi's to Home Depot. *Ad Week.*

Vygotsky, L. S. (1978). *Mind in society: The development of higher psychological processes.* Cambridge, MA: Harvard University Press.

Wade, K. K., & Stafford, M. E. (2003). Public school uniforms: Effect on perceptions of gang presence, school climate, and student self-perception. *Education and Urban Society, 35,* 399–420.

Wagner, T. (2012, April). Calling all innovators. *Educational Leadership, 69*(7), 66–69.

Wang, M. T., & Sheikh-Khalil, S. (2014). Does parental involvement matter for student achievement and mental health in high school? *Child Development, 85*(2), 610–625.

Weimer, M. (2012). Deep Learning vs. Surface Learning: Getting Students to Understand the Difference. Faculty Focus. Higher Ed Teaching Strategies from Magna Publications. http://www.facultyfocus.com/articles/teaching-professor-blog/deep-learning-vs-surface-learning-getting-students-to-understand-the-difference/. Retrieved February 15, 2016.

Wenglinsky, H. (1998). *Does it compute? The relationship between educational technology and student achievement in mathematics* (pp. 1–40, Rep.). Princeton, NJ: Educational Testing Service.

Wenglinsky, H. (2006). Technology and achievement: The bottom line. *Educational Leadership, 63*(4), 29–32.

West-Puckett, S. (2013). ReMaking education: Designing classroom makerspaces for transformative learning. Retrieved March 8, 2016, from http://www.edutopia.org/blog/classroom-makerspaces-transformative-learning-stephanie-west-puckett

Weston, M. E., & Bain, A. (2010). The end of techno-critique: The naked truth about 1:1 laptop initiatives and educational change. *Journal of Technology, Learning, and Assessment, 9*(6), 5–10.

Whiting, B., Van Burgh, J. W., & Render, G. F. (1995). *Mastery learning in the classroom.* Paper presented at the annual meeting of the American Educational Research Association, San Francisco.

Wiggins, G., & McTighe, J. (2005). *Understanding by design* (expanded 2nd ed.). Upper Saddle River, NJ: Pearson Education/Association for Supervision & Curriculum Development.

Wiliam, D. (2011). What is assessment for learning? *Studies in Educational Evaluation, 37*(1), 2–14.

Wilson, J. I. (2002). A visit to the Springdale school system in 2012. In *Visions 2020: Transforming education and training through advanced technologies.* Washington, DC: US Department of Commerce. Retrieved from http://www.technology.gov/reports/TechPolicy/2020Visions.pdf

Workman, J. E., & Freeburg, B. W. (2006). Safety and security in a school environment: The role of dress code policies. *Journal of Family and Consumer Sciences, 98(2)*, 19–24.

World Economic Forum. (2011). *Unlocking entrepreneurial capabilities to meet the global challenges of the 21st century* (pp. 1–36, Rep.). Geneva, Switzerland: World Economic Forum.

Youth Employment Network. (2007). *Joining forces with young people: A practical guide to collaboration for youth employment.* Geneva, Switzerland: ILO.

Zhang, Z., & Richarde, R. S. (1999). Intellectual and metacognitive development of male college students: A repeated measure approach. *Journal of College Student Development, 40*, 721–738.

Zhao, Y. (2012). *World class learners: Educating creative and entrepreneurial students.* Thousand Oaks, CA: Corwin.

Zhao, Y., & Frank, K. A. (2003). Factors affecting technology uses in schools: An ecological perspective. *American Educational Research Journal, 40(4)*, 807–840.

Zickuhr, K., & Smith, A. (2012). *Digital differences.* Retrieved March 7, 2016, from http://www.pewinternet.org/2012/04/13/digital-differences/

Index